JOE JOSEPH

The Japanese

STRANGE BUT NOT
STRANGERS

VIKING

VIKING

Published by the Penguin Group
Penguin Books Ltd, 27 Wrights Lane, London W8 5TZ, England
Penguin Books USA Inc., 375 Hudson Street, New York, New York 10014, USA
Penguin Books Australia Ltd, Ringwood, Victoria, Australia
Penguin Books Canada Ltd, 10 Alcorn Avenue, Toronto, Ontario, Canada M4V 3B2
Penguin Books (NZ) Ltd, 182–190 Wairau Road, Auckland 10, New Zealand

Penguin Books Ltd, Registered Offices: Harmondsworth, Middlesex, England

First published 1993
1 3 5 7 9 10 8 6 4 2
First edition

Typeset by Datix International Limited, Bungay, Suffolk
Set in 12/14½pt Lasercomp Sabon
Printed in England by Clays Ltd, St Ives plc

A CIP catalogue record for this book is available from the British Library

ISBN 0–670–840831

For Jane and Thomas

Contents

Acknowledgements xi

1. Alarms and Diversions: Signposts for Absolute Beginners 1
Enigma variations – getting to know the Japanese – the problems of
communicating – the devil's language – misunderstanding the message
– a clash of cultures

2. The Corporate Warrior: a Dying Breed? 20
The work ethic – starting your working life – staying there – 'Can You
Work Twenty-four Hours a Day?' – dropping dead at the desk –
motivating the workforce – pay now, live later – letting off steam,
with a drink or a doll

*3. A Woman's Place (is in the Wrong): Making Tea with
Your PhD* 38
The second sex – love and marriage – sexual harassment – the pill and
abortion – making more babies for Japan – family life – 'Conjugal
Day' – washday – a woman of design and substance – office ladies

4. The Young, the Rich and the Lonely: a Gleesome Threesome 56
Keep young and beautiful if you want to have fun – finding a mate,
the old way and the new – spending it – gold fever – a Christmas
romance – hygiene mania – super-loos – the new art lovers – the
richest man in the world

Contents

5. Oh Why Do the Japanese Travel? A Time and No Motion Study 86
Moving with the crowds – the commuter crush – taxis to nowhere – flying, off the handle – the tourist boom – so why do the Japanese travel?

6. If the Media are the Message, the Wires Must be Crossed 104
Television – advertising – the world's most powerful advertising agency – keeping Japan under control – newspapers – adult comics – the rush for Hollywood

7. The Quality of Life: Pay Now, Live Later 127
A widening gap between rich and poor – nature by telephone – a noisy nuisance – sinking under garbage – pollution – the environmental record: a low-key tune – wailing about whaling – warning: earthquakes

8. One of Us: Unique Japanese and the Outsiders Looking In 146
Aliens – racism – the outsiders – the uniqueness of the Japanese – the hidden underclass – riots in Osaka

9. Japanese Bearing Gifts: It's Never the Thought That Counts 161
Present indicative – the debts of obligation – being Japanese means always having to say you're sorry – death by satellite – catholic beliefs, but not in Catholicism

10. A Modern Mikado: Now the Politicians Hold the Reins 180
Hirohito and after – wistful nationalists – from deities to democracy – the politicians who have taken over the reins – city of scandals – who will trust the Japanese?

Contents

11. Crime and Punishment: Everybody's Safe, Even the Gangsters 202
Yakuza – knocking on Tokyo's door – taking a share of shareholders' meetings – arrival of the drug dealers – policing the streets – who polices the police? – new mobsters on the beat

12. Education: Not as Sudden as a Massacre, but as Deadly in the Long Run? 215
School after school – never too young to start – examination hell – making the ideal Japanese – playing by the rules – no doubts about discipline – no Nobel – whitewashing history

13. This Sporting Life: More than a Game 230
Sumo, a national sport – baseball, a national craze – golf, a national obsession – pachinko, a national pastime

14. Where to Now? A Journey without Maps 246
The next few steps – the economic machine – the political future – the world's newest superpower? – war and peace – what does Japan think? – the Japanese influence in Britain: a template for the world?

Index 269

Acknowledgements

Without *The Times*, this book would not have been possible, which may not be that newspaper's biggest date with destiny, but it helped me a great deal. I would like to thank Charles Wilson, Simon Jenkins and Peter Stothard, my successive editors on the paper, for their encouragement and support, their regular cheques, and for allowing me to use here some material that made its debut in *The Times*.

There are very many Japanese friends, acquaintances, interviewees and passers-by who helped to give this book its flavour and whom I should like to thank. There were also quite a few who, frankly, were more of a hindrance. Many journalists at the *Asahi Shimbun* newspaper in Tokyo, where *The Times* has its office, gave handy tips, introductions and instruction on how to use the tricky coffee vending machines. Colleagues at the Tokyo bureau of *The New York Times*, which occupied a neighbouring berth at the *Asahi*, offered chirpy company and soaked up any belly-aching I might occasionally need to get off my chest. Steven Weisman of *The New York Times* probably suffered more of this than might have been his share, had listening duties been split on some strict rota system, so he may deserve special mention. We did, though, also share many laughs, sometimes about our lives in Japan, sometimes about fellow expatriates, sometimes about the strange things that came out of the *Asahi Shimbun*'s vending machines.

Tokyo's Foreign Correspondents Club was a haven of valued friends and lunching partners, who were always full of smart advice, snappy conversation and, if you were lucky, first-class

Acknowledgements

gossip. Several diplomatic friends at the British Embassy in Tokyo did a splendid job of hosting some of the most enjoyable parties in the capital.

My Japanese tutors at London's School of Oriental and African Studies, Yoshiko Jones and Hiroko Tayama, became firm friends. Suwako Endo, who kept my Japanese chit-chat in trim in Tokyo, was never daunted by the task.

Jane Winterbotham very kindly read the manuscript, so it seems only fair that she should share at least some of the blame for any sloppy bits.

1. Alarms and Diversions: Signposts for Absolute Beginners

Enigma variations – getting to know the Japanese – the problems of communicating – the devil's language – misunderstanding the message – a clash of cultures

Much as the Japanese are loath to remain unfathomable to the West, they are not bigoted about it.

'Hello. You American? You English? Can we talk?'

We are not in a backstreet bar in Bangkok, and this is not a beggar, or a young girl offering herself for dollars. This is a rattling commuter train in central Tokyo. It's mid-afternoon, so the carriage is crowded but not so crowded that you couldn't, if you really wanted to, look away, or shuffle a few steps along the compartment. You are new to the country, disoriented, and you are unsure what to make of this approach: the guidebooks said that Japanese were slow to come forward, reticent.

But you are anxious to explore any avenue that might help you understand what makes the Japanese tick. That's what lured you here. You don't want to know how to crack the Japanese market for brake linings or cane sugar. You won't lose sleep if Japan raises its interest rates next week. You want to know how the Japanese live, what they do, what they moan about, what they watch on televison, read in their newspapers, and what they make of it all. Are they religious? What do they think of the emperor, whom they once worshipped as a living god? What do they do with all that wealth? Do they really feel rich, what with their jam-packed trains, their compact homes, their long hours at the office and short holidays? How come there is so little street crime? And why will a Japanese never cross a street at traffic lights when the sign says 'Don't Cross', even if it is 4 a.m. and there is no car in sight?

So you look generously, though cautiously, at your pushy chatterer. He must be, what, forty? Forty-five? Well dressed in the anonymous Japanese uniform of blue suit and white shirt, company name-pin peeking loyally out of his lapel like a bonsai carnation. Probably a middle-ranking office worker riding on a slow escalator up a middle-ranking company. Actually, he looks a bit hot and harried, now that you inspect him more closely. Perhaps he has climbed the last couple of corporate flights by the stairs.

'Do you live in Japan? Do you speak English? Can I talk to you?'

'You are talking to me,' you say.

'Can I talk more, please?'

This is your first lesson in Japan and it has caught you off guard: you were expecting to learn, perhaps, how it is that the Japanese can drink themselves legless but avoid getting into the sort of fights that would accompany such behaviour in Britain, or why Japanese barbers always shave your forehead. Instead you fall upon something much more fundamental. You learn that all of a sudden, as the new millennium approaches, the Japanese are ruing their centuries of linguistic neglect. You realize that English is one of the few things, perhaps the only thing apart from Fortnum & Mason tea and Burberry raincoats, that the Japanese still want from the West. It remains the international language of business, diplomacy, academia and promotion. A Japanese who does not speak English has a more limited field of opportunity, whatever his field might be, except

2

perhaps mending roads or laying carpets. That makes it all the more curious that English is one of the few foreign ideas that the Japanese have not hijacked, taken apart in some secret laboratory, rebuilt and made better. Where they have dabbled they have left a trail of destruction, like a clumsy handyman who has decided to repair his own watch and discovers too late that he hasn't a clue how to put all the cogs and springs together again.

Japanese T-shirts scrawled with snappy English slogans like 'Hi baby', 'Mother Earth is crazy living', 'The time has come', 'Drink pitcher', 'Dandelion, let's catch a plane tomorrow forever sometime' might be useful if you are in dull company and can't be bothered to chat, even though the message offers little that is recognizably English. Maybe bashful Japanese English-speakers prefer to converse with your T-shirt than to converse directly with you.

This is your first setback. You have come face to face with the biggest difficulty in cracking the surface of the Japanese enigma. They speak the devil's language, and their attempts to ease the problem by incorporating bits of yours just make it more devilish.

There's not all that much that the Japanese and the Dutch have in common apart from their taste in odd wooden footwear and the fact that nobody else speaks their language, forcing both the Japanese and the Dutch to speak ours. The Dutch have managed this so impressively that many Dutch people speak far better English than the English. The Japanese have not been so diligent. Certainly not so successful. This is partly their own fault. They have been in Japan since at least 10,000 BC, possibly much earlier, but have been remarkably hostile to foreigners for almost the entire time. Chopping off heads was, for many years, regarded as a perfectly acceptable way to deal with foreign barbarians, though, to be fair, foreign barbarians were invited to mete out the same unfriendly welcome to fidgety Japanese who

3

landed on their own shores. It was when Commander Perry's black ships sailed into Yokohama Bay in 1853 that the Western powers and the Japanese realized that they hadn't a clue what the other was trying to say. As far as comprehension goes, little has changed since then. Worse still, the gulf in understanding may be getting wider and wider, threatening our hopes of ever fully reading the Japanese mind.

Newspaper stands on subway station platforms called 'Let's Kiosk' and bottled beers described as 'Super Dry Draft' are probably no worse than advertising jingles such as 'I Feel Coke', which sounds vaguely illegal. Best-selling Japanese drinks called Calpis and Pocari Sweat (a so-called 'sports drink') can be blamed on their producers' eagerness for a bit of English cachet, however unappetizing the brews might sound to English ears. Japanese market researchers do not seem to wonder why a drink like Pocari Sweat, sold and drunk on every Japanese street corner, has not taken London or Manhattan by storm. And as for a bottle of yellow-coloured Mucos, I've never had the courage to try it, even in the name of investigative duty.

Possibly the most baffling slice of the Japanese view of 'abroad' is a famous television, cinema and poster campaign for Lark cigarettes in which normally coherent actors like James Coburn and Roger Moore urge us all to 'Speak Lark'. They do not give away the secret of how to achieve this.

The Japanese listen to all this gibberish in much the way that the British listen to Sacha Distel crooning in French. Given that option you might well choose to 'Speak Lark'. For all we know, Sacha Distel *is* speaking Lark. What is far trickier for most foreigners in Japan to handle are the hundreds of English words that have been swallowed into the Japanese language, but only after some very brutal chewing. *Depato* is 'department store', *handubagu* is 'handbag', *waifu* is 'wife' and *raisu* is 'rice'; *aisu kureemu* is 'ice-cream', *gurasu* is 'glass', *kohi* is 'coffee', *hoteru* is 'hotel'; *pasocon* is 'personal computer' and *patocar*, somehow, is 'police car' (dammit, just when you thought you were getting the hang of the thing); 'cheese' becomes *cheesu* and 'nonsense' becomes – you've probably guessed it by now – *nonsensu*. Well that's fair enough. Every language borrows greedily from others. Half of the English words that the Japanese have filched were on loan from French and Latin anyway.

The trouble is that not only are the words 'hotel' or 'coffee', when pronounced the English way, more or less incomprehensible to the Japanese ear, their Japanese cousins – *hoteru* and *kohi* – are also likely to baffle residents of Tokyo and Osaka unless one uses the correct intonation, a subtle phrasing that both makes clear that the word is not Japanese but also sounds different enough from the original to sound like Flemish does to most Englishmen. Sidling up to this precarious pronunciation is as hopeless as trying to mount the kerb on a bicycle at an angle. It has to be done boldly, and head on, to stand any chance of success. It may mean nothing to you but it might mean everything to a Japanese.

One of the major benefits of acquainting yourself with the Japanese language and its 'Japlish' imports is that it tells you a lot about the Japanese character. Westerners often take the Japanese people's occasional blankness of expression as evidence of their famed inscrutability. But more often than not it merely shows that they haven't a clue what you are trying to say to them. There are so many ways of saying anything in Japan – counting one to ten is different for long, thin things like bottles, round things like apples and flat things like train tickets – that the swelling flood of new foreign imports is making normal communication a headache. Even more perplexing, the Japanese have recently taken a shine to the sound of Italian, which is used as background babble in television commercials, even though Italian speakers in Japan are rarer than miniskirts in the Vatican.

Looking on the bright side, the modern Japanese language, a magpie's trove of Chinese, Japanese and Japlish, has become so complex that almost anything you say means something to Japanese ears, even though it may not be what you intended. If you enter a Japanese restaurant and quote Chaucer in a Japanese accent, chances are you will get something to eat. Your first efforts may not be very palatable – maybe some fermented soyabeans, grilled squid and strawberry yoghurt, all on the same plate. The waitress will not query the request in advance because she will think that because you are a foreigner, you have strange tastes and probably eat such combinations all the time in your native land. Perhaps if you try a different bit of *The Canterbury Tales* next time you might strike lucky, although the chances of hitting on a hamburger (medium rare), chips and salad are, to be honest, probably remote.

Naturally, this twilight zone between what the English regard as English and what the Japanese regard as English creates something of a chasm in international understanding, a lot of pestering by eager students on commuter trains and some very good business for the English language schools in Tokyo that charge an 'armu' and a 'leggu' to drum grammar and vocab into middle-aged white-collar workers looking for promotion and rich young ladies looking for an even richer spouse. Why these language schools are thriving when all Japanese learn English in high school is a mystery, until one looks at how the English high-school teaching is done.

Most British people may not be able to recall much of their school French, but there is the memory of having once learned how to buy stamps and book a hotel room, and how to send the cold blue beefsteak back to the chef for a serious re-grilling. The Japanese, browbeaten all the way through an education system that prizes fact learning for exams above all else, can often quote Shakespeare but not ask for a cup of coffee, an order of priorities that breaks no ice with most English-speaking waitresses on Bond Street or Broadway. Somehow, a country whose cars and hi-fis carry romanized names like Toyota and Sony, a country which has probably the world's highest literacy rate, an élite corps of businessmen and diplomats who often speak English more gracefully than their British or American counterparts, and which has imported English wholesale into its vocabulary, is allowing its children to be brought up on English school textbooks that regard phrases such as 'My neck looked as if it were a piece of twisted bread', or 'He moved my head in such a way that it hung from the counter' as stepping-stones to fluency. One would not be surprised to hear from a T-shirt in Tokyo that said 'My neck looks as if it were a piece of twisted bread'. On a T-shirt this looks like a bit of displaced Martin Amis. In a school textbook it can scar for life.

The Japanese seem to regard a command of English as perhaps their last great battle with the West. They have mastered, well at least bought, *le style anglais*. They will happily pay £1,000 for a Dunhill blazer in Tokyo's smarter department stores. Anything with a Harrods label flies off the shelves. Japanese are rich enough no longer to bother asking the price. They know the value of it and that is enough. Now they are shelling out to learn English and round it all off. If they succeed in this task, they will be one giant step nearer to understanding us and we will be closer to understanding them. The signs, let's be frank, are not all that promising.

Most English-language students enrol in classes charging £20 and up an hour, where they are taught by a ragbag army of Japanese, qualified foreign teachers and backpacking Europeans, Americans and Australians paying their way around the Orient. Learning English has become a fashionable way to spend free time in Tokyo, a city where fashion is everything. For those too busy, too shy or too lazy to step outdoors, a telephone talkline

7

service offers conversation practice with native English speakers for around £4 for fifteen minutes. Marketing has become so intense that some language schools are now offering courses that combine English and aerobics, a novel marriage though not quite as novel as Tokyo's late-night 'English conversation bars', where the drudgery is taken out of declension by the in-house topless teachers.

'Can I buy you a coffee?' offers your cheery travelling companion and would-be friend. Yes, he's still there, hanging on to the train strap next to yours. 'We can talk.'

In New York, such a man would be regarded as a nutcase or a nuisance. In London he might provoke an embarrassed cough along the carriage. In Tokyo he is so earnest and eager that it would be insensitive to ignore him completely. Of course, it's hardly charitable, and as a way of improving understanding between nations it would probably rank rather low on a diplomat's list of strategies, but the most convenient response would be 'I'm afraid I'm rather busy just at the moment. Would you mind very much reading my T-shirt instead?'

Of course, there are always those who prefer to take the plunge, undaunted by hurdles. You may be one of them. So let us suppose that you have just got off a plane at Tokyo's Narita airport and you have pledged to do your best to understand. You hire an interpreter. You think it might help. Often it makes things worse. You immediately learn that almost every statement in Japan meets with the response, *'Ah, so desu ka?'* Literally, this means, 'Is that so?' But with you having just arrived after a twelve-hour flight and your interpreter-cum-new-friend eager to show compound interest in almost everything you say, you hit your first hidden reef. It seems to be an innocuous conversation but then it suddenly unravels into a testy confrontation. Were this taking place in New York, you might well be calling for handguns to settle the matter. And all because he is trying to be a pal.

JAPANESE: How was your flight?

YOU: Not bad, thanks, though I couldn't sleep.

JAPANESE: Is that so?

YOU: Yes. Still, I've got a week here before getting on another plane so I should recover.

JAPANESE: Is that so?

YOU: Yes. Although my wife isn't too pleased. I've been travelling a lot recently.

JAPANESE: Is that so? To where?

YOU: Oh, let's see, Boston, Delhi, Oslo.

JAPANESE: Is that so?

YOU: Yes, it is so, as a matter of fact.

JAPANESE: And do you have children?

YOU: Two sons and a daughter.

JAPANESE: Oh, really, is that so?

YOU: I suppose you know better than I do, do you?

JAPANESE: And where are you flying to next?

YOU: New York. Or don't you believe that either?

And this is before you have been exposed to the main skill of Japanese conversation, which is to appear to be talking without saying anything meaningful and to make sure to avoid confrontation whatever your interlocutor is saying. Whether someone says it's raining when the sun is beating down or whether they say they want to knock your head off, the thing to do is reply 'Is that so?' and you will get on just fine. If you should say anything that provokes a Japanese to answer 'That's very interesting', you may well be on the verge of a fist fight.

The problems of communication are distorted further by the dozens of breathtaking contrasts and paradoxes that give Japan its peculiar tang. They seem designed to trip up anyone looking for easy answers. Many probably were.

A Tokyo taxi-driver wears white gloves, always has a gleaming bonnet (on his cab, not his head) and would never dream of fiddling the change. But he also thinks it quite unremarkable to stop his car on a posh street corner and relieve himself. Tipping is thought rather odd, but without huge bribes Japan's money-oiled political machinery would shudder and croak. Many Japanese houses have high-tech computerized loos that offer an electronic wash-and-blow-dry alternative to loo paper and which look as daunting as a pilot's cockpit, but many houses in Tokyo are still not connected to mains sewers. Japan is the most heaving cauldron of capitalism, but you would search hard to find a more nannyish, conformist state, or another country where the maxim 'The nail that stands up must be beaten down' is thought such an obvious prescription for social harmony that most Japanese cannot see why it makes foreigners shiver.

What does make Japan tick? Even after living in Japan for several years, many foreigners find the question tricky to answer. More strangely, so do quite a few Japanese.

Many Japanese delight in spending an evening guiding foreigners through the essence of Japaneseness: they talk of tradition, of history, of the sensitivity, the creativeness, the diligence, of a passion for nature. After listening to all this you walk out into the Tokyo night to catch a taxi back to your hotel or apartment half expecting to step into a Japanese woodcut of willow trees and willowy women. Instead you enter a city that is brash, modern, tingling with neon, thin on parks, jangling to the noise of pinball arcades and thick with blue-suited businessmen, some more drunk than diligent. Confusingly, both sketches are accurate. Yet both distort reality. Together they magnify the enigma.

Part of the problem is that we have been taught to expect the Japanese to be inscrutable. They go a long way to match the cliché and few of us try very hard to melt our misconceptions. Most people in London or Paris or New York could recite the names of ten Japanese companies by scanning their living-rooms but would be hard-pressed to name three Japanese people. Even the Japanese prime minister. That sort of ignorance underlines the image of the Japanese as alien and unfathomable. But they are not a nation from outer space that has somehow broken loose and fallen to earth with the sole purpose of providing the rest of us with reliable cars and snappy stereos and of buying up Van Goghs and famous Hollywood film studios when louche Westerners can no longer afford to keep them.

Japan's ballooning wealth has done its bit to make its people a spectacle of fantasy, sometimes envy, for foreigners. There are few countries where a couple can pop out for the evening and spend £500 on dinner without really trying, where humdrum houses in humdrum Tokyo suburbs cost £500,000. One typical incident highlights just how rich and how different from you and me the Japanese have become. While people across Britain were rebelling against the unpopular poll tax brought in by Margaret Thatcher's government and when local councils in the UK were struggling to cut pennies and corners, at a time when the financial auditors in New York were warning the mayor that the city was on the brink of bankruptcy, Japanese ratepayers were working out how to squander billions of yen foisted on them as a keep-them-sweet gift by the country's Liberal Democratic government. The only proviso they were given was not to spend the cash too seriously. Forget new town halls or better sewers, they were told. Be imaginative. Japanese local government and village elders took the government at its word. One backwater in Yamanashi, central Japan, invited three thousand residents to view their village from a helicopter. Another in Miyagi, northern Japan, decided to build the country's biggest water-wheel. The world's largest gold bar was forged and an hourglass, holding one ton of sand, was ordered. Japan's biggest-ever wisteria trellis was lashed together. What kind of a country could afford such fripperies when the rest of the industrialized world was tightening its belts? And why would anyone want the world's biggest wisteria trellis?

Even taking a stroll through town is confusing. Japanese streets seem ramshackle and many modern buildings look as if they have been designed by someone wearing a blindfold. In fact most of Tokyo looks as if a schoolboy in the heavens has tipped out a box of Lego bricks, put a noodle shop on every other corner and left it at that. There is little sign of town planning and no apparent attempt at architectural harmony. All that most Japanese houses share with their neighbours is the same postman. But in the middle of this urban mess there actually are a few beautiful temples on winding backstreets and some old wooden houses tilting against time and against Japan's dizzy land prices. There are also starkly modern, glossy buildings. Many of the world's top architects say Tokyo is the last major capital that is rich enough, and haphazard enough, to allow them a decent canvas for their boldest ideas. The outrageous things that Philippe Starck does to kitchen chairs and lemon squeezers in Paris he does to office blocks in Tokyo. Now that Japan is rich enough to buy whatever it fancies, it has taken a fancy to foreign architects. Because Tokyo is so crowded, these architects are given plenty of money but not much room. As a result, the latest corporate headquarters in Tokyo designed by Sir Norman Foster might well stand next to a wooden shack with a family's futons and wet washing hung out of a window to dry. The last one did. For his next dramatic project Foster is looking for a roomier site, probably offshore in Tokyo Bay.

Equally confusing for anyone trying to make simple sense of Japan is why people who seem to care little about how their streets look will spend hours wrapping a present, or elegantly draping a strip of raw tuna on a sprig of cherry blossom so that their dinner guests can feast their eyes as well as their palates. The same Japanese who do not mind their city centres being marred by traffic-choked overhead expressways have become the world's most fashion-conscious race. Television sets and chic frocks are thrown out after a season to make room in cramped houses for the latest designs. Young Japanese are so style-conscious that Sony seems to bring out a new version of its Walkman pocket-size personal stereo machines every month to keep up with changing fashions.

And yes, most Japanese are workaholics. They work long hours. Some are dropping dead, literally, at their office desks through overwork. But can you imagine a British or American businessman spending a winter Sunday afternoon stripping in the icy open air and spending a few hours up to his neck in a sulphurous hot spring bath with a few dozen other naked men? The Japanese can think of nothing better. An open-air hot spring is a scene that always seems to jolt, and then enchant, foreigners who manage to squeeze in a visit to one during their holidays or during a break in their Tokyo business schedule.

Nobody could suggest that women are particularly liberated in Japan. Even working women with PhDs often spend their days bowing to their boss's visitors and making green tea. Those that wangle the same jobs as men get paid less for doing the same work. Women in politics are rare, women in boardrooms almost non-existent. On the other hand, women also run the households, make most of the decisions about where the family lives and how the children are brought up, and they expect their husbands to hand over their pay-packets. In return, the husbands get spending money to pay for their daily noodles at lunchtime and their evening drinking bouts.

Japanese are often prudish. Naked women in advertising posters have never really caught on, and not because of women's objections. The display of pubic hair in photographs or films is banned in Japan. Imported copies of *Playboy* come with hand-made scratch marks at the crotch. The more torrid love scenes in Western films come with those patchworks of multicoloured moving dots that keep private parts private. Yet sex is freely

13

available. Japan's so-called 'sports dailies' make Britain's brash *Sunday Sport* tabloid look tame. Alongside naked women in imaginative poses, they also carry telephone numbers and critics' reviews of 'Soaplands'. These are the massage parlours cum brothels that used to be known as Turkish baths until the Turkish government complained. It was Japan that invented the no-panty coffee bar, where the waitresses wore nothing under their short skirts and the floors were made of mirrors.

Japanese are courteous and polite. But ask the Chinese or South Koreans, who suffered at the hands of the Japanese Imperial Army, and they might well faint at such a suggestion. Japanese are eager to learn: children attend private evening school after finishing public day school and their fathers read business manuals for relaxation. But knowledge stops where nerve endings begin. History books are censored to smudge over the less glorious moments in Japan's recent past, such as the brutal Rape of Nanking or the colonization of south-east Asia by the emperor's soldiers. Japan's pacifism is enshrined in its postwar constitution, which bans it from having an army to wage wars abroad. Yet only America spends more on its military than Japan does on its meek-sounding Self-defence Forces.

The Japanese are hugely rich and powerful. It is difficult to believe that little more than a generation ago countries like the Philippines were wealthier than Japan, that less than half a century ago Tokyo was a pile of war-bombed rubble. Nobody can ignore the Japanese today. They want an international voice that matches their economic clout. Yet when it comes to speaking their mind on an issue that is convulsing the rest of the world, say turmoil in the Middle East, the Japanese are often tongue-tied.

They are international, yet also insular. They seem to know as little about us as we know about them. But an important difference is that they probably have a far greater influence on our lives now than we have on theirs. They make many of our cars, our video machines and our computer chips. They may provide the money that furnishes our house mortgages. They are funding swanky new galleries in our top museums and prestigious professorships at our universities. They have moved into Hollywood, although the new moguls have been careful to pledge not to interfere with the movie makers. But those who winced when Japan re-edited the film *The Last Emperor* to cut scenes depicting Japanese atrocities are not fully convinced. What underlies some foreigners' fears is not just that the president of a Japanese electronics company which now owns a film studio might try to stop a film being made, but that if he did there is little anyone could do about it. The difference between Japan and America, which also once had pots of money, is that the West feels it knows how America thinks. It still finds Japan a faraway enigma.

Many Japanese would themselves be baffled by such envy or anxiety. In Japan, it is often the Japanese who do the yearning. It is yet another paradox that although the Japanese have an acute sense of their own superiority and uniqueness, in Japan, West is also often best. European models advertise Japanese face-creams and cigarettes to Japanese consumers. Some young Japanese have plastic surgery to make their eyes look rounder. The Japanese find it curious that Japanese models are prized on Parisian catwalks, and that British high-street shops sell futons, the staple of the dowdiest Japanese bedroom, as the height of chic. Sushi has become fashionable in the West just at the time when young Japanese moan if their mothers do not produce hamburgers or pizzas for dinner. While their parents fumble with knives and forks, Japanese children fumble with chopsticks. The two cultures are mixing, but not always smoothly or elegantly.

Many might think it remarkable that the two cultures are

mixing at all, considering how little contact we have with each other. The name Japan crops up in newspapers, though many people still seem to know little more of the country than what they get from badly translated instruction manuals to their electric lawnmowers. Sometimes there is a chance for immersion in Japanese culture through visiting exhibitions at London or New York galleries and museums or through travelling drama troupes. The huge Japan Festival that brought everything from sumo wrestling and kabuki to archers on horseback and a Japanese version of *Jesus Christ Superstar* to Britain in the autumn of 1991 offered Britons a glimpse of a fascinating country without all the fuss of flying to Tokyo. But it is hardly a perfect introduction to Japanese culture. Coming out of an exhibition that tries to convey all the different flavours of modern Japan might leave you with a rather overcrowded idea of Japanese life: a bit like walking into an exhibition about New York to find three skyscrapers, a drugs deal, a bagel factory, a yellow cab and a violent mugging all in one small room. It might thrill you to bits. It might put you off for life.

Everything bombards the new arrival at once. Why do some people bow more deeply than others? Why is there a vending machine every fifty yards in Japan, even up Mount Fuji? Why does everyone, down to the hotel bellboy, seem to have a walletful of business cards to hand out every time he says hello to someone? Why does the driver on the subway train have to tell you at every single station not to fall asleep, not to miss your stop, to remember your belongings, to stand clear of the doors, to be careful as you leave the carriage? Why is every piece of fruit in the greengrocer's completely unblemished, and every strawberry identical to every other strawberry in shape and size? Why would anyone want to pay £50 for a musk melon? Why is it obligatory to slurp one's noodles in a restaurant but thought vulgar to blow one's nose in public? Why does everyone in Japan go to lunch at noon, precisely?

Why are there no towels in the washrooms of even the smartest office blocks? Why do women announcers in lifts and tourist buses think it sounds cute to talk in a sugary high-pitched squeak? Why do Japanese airlines ask your age when you book a seat? Why do Japanese agree to give it? Why do lampposts in Japan play music all day long? Why would anyone want a remote-control air-conditioner that tells you 'I am about to blow out some cool air softly' when you switch it on?

Why do you have to stop swimming every now and then for a compulsory rest period when you visit a public pool, even though you are not tired? How do they manage to make every single train run on time and to persuade drivers and guards to apologize to passengers should a high-speed bullet train be unfortunate enough to arrive even two minutes late after a five-hour journey?

There is a certain way of doing things in Japan. It is rarely the Western way. Sometimes the Japanese way is clearly superior. Sometimes the Japanese way drives you bonkers. I was fortunate to learn very early in my stay in Japan never to be dumbfounded by the course of a conversation with a Japanese person. Still recovering from jet lag in my hotel room, I received a telephone call from Mr Kato at the Tokyo branch of the international moving company I had hired telling me that my goods had arrived in Japan and to send them my 'unaccompanied baggage form' so that they could clear the shipment through customs.

'I'm afraid I don't think I have an unaccompanied baggage form. Where would I have got one?'

'They gave you one on the plane to fill in and sign. Please send that form to us.'

'I don't recall them giving me any forms on the plane.'

'Is that so?'

'Yes, I'm afraid it is. What should I do?'

'You know the unaccompanied baggage form they gave you on the plane, just fill it in and send it to us.'

17

'I have just explained that I haven't got one of those forms.'

'Is that so?'

'Yes.'

'Then what did you do with the unaccompanied baggage form they gave you on the plane?'

'Look, nobody gave me one. Is it a big problem?'

'It's very serious, I'm afraid. It's impossible to clear your shipment without that form.'

'Oh, come on, I can't be the first person ever to have landed here without his unaccompanied baggage form. There must be some way of getting the goods through customs.'

'Well, it's possible if we explain all the unfortunate circumstances to the customs office and apologize for our mistake.'

'Fine. I'll write a letter now and send it to you.'

'No. Don't do that. I have a draft letter which I will fax to your hotel. Just write it out in your own hand, fill in the flight details, return it to me and we'll see what can be done.'

A short while later the bellboy brought up a draft letter that had been faxed to the hotel by Mr Kato. It read:

SAMPLE

PLEASE PREPARE THIS FORM IN CASE UNACCOMPANIED
BAGGAGE FORM IS NOT AVAILABLE

To Yokohama Customs / Narita Customs,

I, the undersigned, arrived on board (Flight no.) at Narita Airport on (*arrival date*) from (*origin*) to take a new position in Japan.

Upon entry, due to my unfamiliarity with Japanese regulations, I did not declare my unaccompanied baggage consisting of my household goods.

I trust you will accept my sincere apologies for the above matter and take my situation into consideration for the importation of my belongings into Japan without delay.

If customs duties are imposed, I will take responsibility to pay for them.

18

Thanking you in advance for your kind consideration on this matter,
I remain,
Sincerely yours,

(*Signature*)

So, quite a drama, but not such a unique crisis after all. The shipment got through.

Now you can begin to understand the essential difference between recent arrivals in Japan and long-term foreign residents in the country: the recent arrivals look as if they've been in a state of bewilderment for the past two days. Long-term foreign residents have been bewildered for years.

2. The Corporate Warrior: a Dying Breed?

*The work ethic – starting your working life – staying there –
'Can You Work Twenty-four Hours a Day?' – dropping dead at
the desk – motivating the workforce – pay now, live later –
letting off steam, with a drink or a doll*

Imagine if you had just picked up a good degree from a top
university, landed a high-flier's job in a blue-chip bank and were
then told by your new boss to spend your first week on the job
ironing crumpled £5 notes, or standing outside in a slashing
downpour polishing the bank's brass nameplate. In Japan, where
each spring new graduates begin their working lives with bizarre
induction rituals, yours might rank as one of the more cushy
starts to life as a salaryman, one of the millions of corporate
warriors who spread like ants from subway exits every morning
towards desks in overcrowded offices. There, for maybe fifty
weeks a year, maybe more, they will fulfil their duties as guardians of the Japanese economic miracle.

It doesn't matter whether they come out of Tokyo University,
perhaps the best in Japan, these graduates still get down to
slopping out lavatories, polishing their bosses' shoes, running
marathons and doing SAS-style training courses. Of the million
or so new graduate recruits who join the workforce each year,
some have a less strenuous time of it. Meditating in temples,
perhaps. When it is all over, most will go on to sedate jobs
behind a desk.

Personnel managers looking to hire young men (mostly) who

20

will spend their lives with the firm are searching for what they like to call 'blank sheets of paper'. These rites of passage are designed to instil discipline, loyalty to the company and camaraderie with colleagues who are likely to stay colleagues for the next forty years or so. Since many new recruits also live in company dormitories and spend their evenings after work drinking together, this is also a time for learning the important Japanese art of building consensus and thinking as a group.

All new recruits to a company undergo the same treatment because all of them will be doing each other's jobs sooner or later. In Western companies people are hired as accountants or solicitors or marketing executives, but in Japanese firms it is common for employees to be shifted from one department to another every few years. The company you work for – and the company pin is there in your buttonhole for everyone to envy – is generally more important than what you do there. Ask a Westerner what he does for a living and he might answer, 'architect' or 'public relations'. Ask a Japanese and he will give you the name of his company. In Japan's subtly but strictly hierarchical society, the name of your employer says more about you than cash ever can. It can even secure you a better class of wife, or, at any rate, the swifter approval of the parents of the girl you fancy. (The reverse is not necessarily true in Japan, where men are still regarded as the natural hunter-cum-breadwinner, even if the bread they win is a stale mini-loaf.) Just how important it is to bag a job at the 'right' company is shown by the willingness of new recruits to stomach these unusual and testing training sessions even though a severe labour shortage in Japan has given prized graduates their pick of jobs.

Among the unluckier novices are those at Duskin, a big cleaning company which for the past thirty years has made its freshmen clean lavatories for a while. Duskin's managers say that it helps the newcomers to learn the pleasure of serving the public. At Mitsubishi Electric, young turks on the fast track have to run a twelve-and-a-half mile course to learn the importance of seeing a task through to the end. Mitsubishi Trust and Banking issues new entrants a Miss-Manners-style guide to corporate etiquette: the basic rules are to jump when a boss calls, don't scratch in front of a customer and never knock the company. At Ito-Yokado, a supermarket chain that runs Seven–Eleven convenience stores, trainees stay in the car park well after dark practising their bowing and learning the company song, 'Soaring into the Future' ('Hand in hand, my friends and I soar into the world with great hope . . . I-Y Group, tomorrow is dawning, I-Y Group, our pride'). Shocked by the declining standards of today's youth, the Japan Management Association puts out its own list of guidelines, covering everything from the horrors of being late for work to the correct angles when bowing (fifteen degrees to a colleague, forty-five degrees to boardroom bigwigs).

At least some managers are willing to join in the fun. At Columbus, a company which makes shoe polish, senior executives polish the shoes of the freshmen, then the freshmen repay the favour. A director of the company says: 'It is the best way to foster their love for our company and to communicate with each other.'

Once inducted by your new company and embraced by your new colleagues, life as a salaryman doesn't necessarily get any easier. For all its inventiveness in other fields, Japan has still not cracked the art of putting up its feet and enjoying its wealth. Working hours are long, holidays are short. You might have expected rejoicing and celebratory banzai chants all round to greet news that Japanese employers are nowadays allowing their workers about seven consecutive days off for their summer holidays. But in Japan, workers do not necessarily take all their allotted time off. This reluctance to take holidays reflects Japanese people's group mentality, their drive for consensus and

22

harmony, and their sense of obligation. Watanabe can't take a week off if his boss, Suzuki, is only taking a day or two. And even if Suzuki goes wild and takes his family to Tokyo Disneyland for seven days in a row – Tokyo Disneyland being the place Japanese most yearn to go whenever they have a spare moment – Watanabe might still think twice about copying his boss for fear of setting a bad example for his own subordinates. Also, few salarymen seem able to cope with the pressure of knowing that while they are enjoying themselves queueing up for two hours for a carnival ride in Disneyland their colleagues back at the office are having to share out their workload. It is so much easier if everyone turns up at the office every day and moans about the awful summer humidity.

Holidays also remain untaken because Japanese men spend such long hours away from home – there's all that commuting, the long days behind a cluttered desk, and, well, a few drinks after work with clients or workmates, purely professional – that many of them feel uncomfortable in the company of their own families. They say that their sons and their daughters barely seem to know them and that their wives are more interested in coaxing the children towards another exam success. A survey on leisure carried out by Japan's *Dime* magazine found that about half of those polled thought they had more than enough free time: asked what they would most like to do with their spouses, 34 per cent of husbands and 40 per cent of wives said they couldn't think of anything.

This uncomfortable social dislocation has given salarymen and their doctors something new to worry about in recent years. What with their work, their hours of travelling to the office, their evenings socializing and then travelling back late at night to fed-up wives, some office-workers have stopped going home at all. It is not adultery, it is a disease. It is called 'home-phobia', and the mostly middle-aged, male sufferers are turning more and more to neurologists to cure them of their depression. Doctors blame Japan's work habits for many of the cases. When the marital strains become too great, the men dissolve into depression.

Dr Toru Sekiya of the Sekiya Neurology Clinic in central Tokyo, which specializes in treating cases of home-phobia, says the disease is another by-product of Japan's rapid economic success: in the hectic 1960s, when Japan's economy really began to take off, fathers were even busier, but were still welcomed by their families. In those days, says Dr Sekiya, 'spouses waited even after midnight to welcome the breadwinners'. Nowadays, more self-confident wives complain that their husbands come home too late and see too little of their children. The marital tension breeds depression and insomnia. Foreigners telling them that they are among the richest people in the world probably only makes it worse. 'I attribute many of the cases to non-cooperative spouses,' says Dr Sekiya, 'but it is also true that many had been working too hard and lost the ability to adjust to the outside world, even, in many cases, their own family. Companies are partially responsible for this.'

There is an even worse affliction plaguing the salaryman. Nobody jokes about being dead-tired in Japan any longer because more and more apparently healthy young men are keeling over after spending years of doing overtime at their desks. The problem has become so dire that even the government, which for a long time averted its eyes and hoped the problem would go away, is now investigating whether just working in a Japanese office can kill you. One survey found that 40 per cent of Japan's white-collar workers fear they might drop dead through overwork. Nearly two thirds of the respondents said they take fewer than ten days' holiday a year, partly because they are worried about work piling up in their absence, partly because their bosses don't take long breaks, partly because they

24

fear falling behind colleagues in both paperwork and the boss's estimation.

It is difficult to prove a case of death from overwork, but doctors say the incidents run into hundreds, some say thousands. Middle managers, who spend their days bowing to bosses, their evenings listening to subordinates' frustrations and their weekends discreetly losing at golf with clients, are the worst hit. But taxi-drivers, teachers, salesmen and journalists have also been felled. 'Relax' has never been a word that trips easily off the Japanese tongue. But now the phenomenon of death from overwork has become so common that it has its own name, *karoshi*. Victims share a common pattern: fatal heart attacks or strokes after months, maybe years, of long days in overcrowded offices under heavy stress. In Tokyo, where a two-hour dangle from a train strap at the start and at the end of each day is common, stress builds up out of the office as well.

The Japanese press has blamed overwork for the death of several prominent business leaders over the past few years, men in their forties, including a senior publishing executive, the president of the Fanuc robotics company and the chairman of the huge Fujisankei media empire. Dr Kiyoyasu Arikawa, who runs a clinic in Tokyo where he tries to lure executives out of overdrive, says, 'It's not so much that they love to work, but they feel company loyalty demands that their whole life be work. Mental stress, business stress and private problems accumulate until the body just can't take any more.'

The government, at last acknowledging the problem, has agreed to finance a study into this sudden-death syndrome. But wary of the claims for labour insurance that might flood through its letterbox if it accepts the link between work and death, the government still refuses to let the word *karoshi* pass its lips. Instead, its investigation is titled 'Comprehensive Measures for Job-related Illness'. Officials already feel they are doing their best to help. The government has been running a campaign to improve the quality of life in Japan by persuading people to take longer holidays, to relax a little by leaving the office earlier, to spend more time with their families at weekends. Japanese on average work at least two hundred hours more a year than their European or American counterparts. The government wants to narrow the gap, but all its efforts have failed miserably. The Tokyo stock market and banks stopped doing business on Saturdays in 1989, under government orders. At the same time civil servants were given every other Saturday off, to set an example to the nation. Private companies were urged to move from a six-day to a five-day week. But employers have resisted. They say they can't afford to give more time off when there is such a labour shortage. Where the six-day working week has died it has often been translated into five longer days.

And still Japanese corporations are struggling to find new ways to improve productivity, to get a little more mileage out of their staff. So if one day soon you happen to walk into a Japanese office and the place smells of lemons, it will probably just be the boss's latest wheeze to try to get his staff to wake up, shape up and work a little harder. You see, Japanese researchers looking for ways to pep up further the performance of the country's workforce have seen the future and found that it's fragrant. Shiseido, a big Japanese cosmetics firm which is leading the research into the power of smells, thinks it has stumbled on to a new science of human behaviour. It is offering Japanese employers an aromatic timetable that it promises will deliver spectacular results.

Start the day with lemon to get the sleep out of everyone's eyes: lemon, like jasmine, apparently has a rejuvenating effect. At mid-morning, switch to a light floral scent to aid concentration. At lunchtime it's back to breathing fresh air for an hour. The afternoon begins with the refreshing aroma of a forest – much better for relieving stress than Muzak – then more lemon followed by flowers to dispel post-lunch drowsiness and then a final blast of lemon through the air-conditioning system to fortify the workers before their long commute home. Shiseido says its own experiments show that a changing flow of scents through the day increases productivity by 14 per cent. A light floral whiff led to 21 per cent fewer errors and faster work. Wood scents also did the trick, but generally with less dramatic results. More alarmingly, Shiseido reckons that apart from marketing its scents to offices and hotels, shopping centres might also become interested if it can develop a cocktail of smells that will make shoppers keener to open their wallets.

But Japanese employers aren't always satisfied with the softly-softly approach to higher efficiency. Most Westerners might think that the Japanese workforce is already so motivated that only electric-shock treatment could give it extra zip. But there are always laggards and slowpokes. In Japan, laggards and slowpokes get sent to 'Hell', a training camp where they learn the error of their ways and the path back to corporate respectability. Hell training is a curious mixture of Alcoholics Anonymous, an EST brainwashing seminar, *It's a Knockout*, *Candid Camera*, and a long, painful night with a vicious Miss Whiplash. The training can last up to a fortnight. It begins with an employee's pathetic admission of his faults and weaknesses, the burden he has been to his long-suffering colleagues and the shame he has brought on himself and his company. Then there is a busy programme of bowing, memorization, clear speaking, more bowing, exhausting exercise, icy showers, sleep deprivation, more bowing, learning respect, learning your place, weeping, a little more bowing, and, finally, the rendition before a perplexed public waiting on a crowded platform for a train or piling out of a supermarket, of some ballad or other, sometimes 'My Way' but more usually a tune that extols the virtues of hard work, respect, diligent salesmanship and bowing.

27

One foreigner who tried Hell training and thought that here was at least one thing the West could do better than the Japanese is Anthony Willoughby, an eccentric English adventurer who has trekked across jungles, run a leather-goods business and taken the world's skipping champion on promotional tours of Switzerland. He has lived in Japan since the mid-1970s. A few years ago he tried Japanese Hell training for himself and took against it. 'There is absolutely no self-development there whatsoever. It is purely repetition. You scream things like, "Take heed, there is no value in sympathy", or "To think you will be liked by your subordinates is wishful thinking. I say to you, throw down your shield and allow yourself to feel the arrows of criticism." All the time there is this ridiculous screaming. The aim is to degrade, to remove identity. It is very unpleasant. You watch people break down and cry. Most of it is about destroying individuality.'

Willoughby responded by setting up his own company to persuade Japanese bosses that a British Outward Bound-style course will make their employees more enthusiastic. Surprisingly, he is having some success. In the courses he holds in woods outside Tokyo, Willoughby tells participants that climbing rope-ladders, making rafts out of oil drums and singing 'Ging Gang Goolie' around a camp-fire will do them more good than traditional Japanese courses. His company is named after his philosophy – 'I Will Not Complain' – a motto born after someone on one of his trips through Papua New Guinea whined so much that he vowed to make all future travellers sign a document promising not to moan *en route*. Among the pledges are 'I will not complain if I get eaten or trodden on by animals' and 'If I have forgotten something I will not endlessly ask other people if they have got one.' Willoughby later showed these regulations to a Japanese businessman 'and he said, "Ah, that is the philosophy of life, the path to power." So although it started out as a bit of fun, I'm now going to companies and offering them the opportunity to develop this attitude within their firms.' At first he was taking bookings, up to eighty a month, from companies like Rover Japan, ICI, Cathay Pacific, Reuters and Chemical Bank. Then Japanese firms started signing up as well. And no need to pay any royalties to the composer of 'My Way'.

You might think that in the few hours which salarymen snatch away from the office they would take their minds off the job. Think again. Stroll around a Japanese bookshop and the thickest knots of blue-suited men are gathered round the latest business books – stock-market guides, economic predictions, industry analyses, company case histories, and so on – or the latest 'business novels'. If salarymen are not at their desks, they often like to read about how others are getting on at theirs. Since the 1960s, when the Japanese economy really started to take off, hundreds of these business novels have been published. Businessmen too impatient to wait for the latest titles to reach the bookshelves can often read the novels in instalments in magazines. Tamae Prindle, an assistant professor of East Asian languages at Colby College in Maine, has made a special study of these novels and was the first to translate several of them into English. She remarks that 'These novels alert us to severe economic reality, and suggest that we make the best of what little freedom we have.' Put more bluntly, the essential message of many of these businessmen's tales often turns out to be, 'Life is hard, and then you die.'

One of the first of the genre was *Made in Japan*, written by Saburo Shiroyama and published in 1957, a time when the words 'Made in Japan' on the underside of an electrical appliance still meant 'Cheap, tinny and liable to come apart within days'. The hero of this story is a hard-working manufacturer of top-notch thermometers who is struggling to sell his products in America. In the same year Takeshi Kaiko published the equally depressing novel *Giants and Toys*, in which an advertising executive for a confectionery company looks back on an exhausting summer spent trying to persuade little brats to buy more sweets, against stiff competition from rival confectionery manufacturers offering rival temptations, and wonders whether he wouldn't be better off dead. Questioning the fruits of all his hard work, the advertising man asks himself, 'Did we leave only an elusive shadow in the dim consciousness of children, and nothing else? . . . I smoked by the window, tasting an enormous amount of wasted effort.'

Not much cheer, either, in Taichi Sakaiya's 1984 novel *The Baby Boom Generation*, which bemoans the fate of Tomita, a loyal salaryman who always put his job and company first in his battle to get on in life and become a high-flier in his firm. Tomita had a tough time.

His performance had cost him his personal happiness and home life. He reported to the office early in the morning, and went home late at night. He was summoned to join golf matches – which he never enjoyed – on Sundays and special holidays. Frequently, he spent weekends and holidays drafting papers at the office. When his wife gave birth to her second child, he couldn't even take time off to visit her in the hospital. His absence had made a rubble of his home life.

As if this wasn't bad enough, the loyal Tomita is then blamed for some fiasco that had nothing to do with him and is banished from head office to live out his days as a corner-store shopkeeper, unable to get redress and unlikely to be able to get any other respectable Japanese employer to give him the time of day, let alone a job.

And still the Japanese salaryman pledges to dib, dib, dib and do his best. Indeed, most of them thrive on the challenge of being more workaholic than their colleagues. That became very obvious when a tonic drink called 'Regain' arrived on the market in 1988 with a marketing campaign targeted at the overworked, overstressed Japanese salaryman. Health tonics containing vitamins and supposed energy boosters have been around for a while in Japan. They generally come in small 50 ml brown bottles, and every chemist's and every station platform kiosk has a choice of dozens. Morning and evening, commuters slug them down on the way to the office and on the way home. A pick-me-up during that snoozy period at mid-afternoon also seems to be popular. Although the pricier brands contain ingredients like viper's blood and essence of ginkgo leaves, most deliver their pep through a shot of caffeine and maybe a tinge of nicotine.

Then Regain came along with its distinctive yellow and black label and its addictive television advertising campaign. It trumpeted the slogan 'Can You Fight Twenty-four Hours a Day?' and showed scenes of a businessman jetting around the world, bottle of Regain in hand, clinching heroic deals single-handed and swishing samurai swords through the air. At last, the salaryman had a tonic drink with which he could identify. Sales boomed. The Regain jingle, and its catchy, much-hummed, march-like theme song – 'Yellow and black are the sign of courage. Can you fight twenty-four hours? Businessman, business-man, Japanese businessman' – hit the pop charts. Nearly half of all new recruits to Japanese companies told pollsters that they wanted to model themselves on the man in the Regain com-mercials. Regain's commercials have developed the following of a soap opera, with millions of viewers waiting to see what happens to the 'Regain Man' in the next advertising campaign, a sort of businessman's novel on the box.

Some viewers say that the commercial sets out to make fun of the Japanese stereotype. But that was not the intention of Dentsu, the advertising agency behind the campaign, which was looking to create a new Japanese hero. Nor is that how millions of businessmen see it. The Regain jingle has become a party favourite of drunken businessmen, who sing it with the same I'll-

31

show-you-who's-boss bravado that some Americans affect when singing along with Frank Sinatra on 'New York, New York'. Japanese companies play the Regain theme song over office loudspeakers. Between ten and twenty people call Regain's manufacturer every day, seeking the words of the song. Some of the calls are from some of Japan's biggest corporations. The government's Economic Planning Agency and police stations have requested song sheets. The manufacturer even received a call from Tokyo's Labour Ministry, protesting that the advertising campaign was undermining government efforts to persuade the Japanese to relax a little and take life more easily.

Of course, even the most devoted salaryman can't fight twenty-four hours, day after day. And when he has made up his mind to relax, he does it with the same single-mindedness he directs to his office ledgers. He also usually does it on the company's tab. That is one of the perks of climbing the corporate ladder. Japanese businessmen spend nearly 6,000 billion yen, or around £25 billion, a year on wining, dining and teeing off with each other, according to figures compiled by Japan's tax authorities. This is more than Japan spends annually on defence, which is a feat, considering how lavishly Tokyo spends on tanks and troops.

It is hard for people who have never been entertained in Japan to fathom just how an army of businessmen can sign expense accounts that add up to more than the gross national product of many poorer countries. It has a lot to do with Japan's dizzy prices, even more to do with the pivotal role of entertaining in Japanese society. Just buying your round doesn't go very far in Japan, where dinner with an important client can run to £250 a head, with a really important client to £1,000 a head, including a few geisha who will chat, laugh at your jokes and tickle your ego for a fee. A prized round of golf, including a night at a local hotel to prepare for an early start at the first tee, perhaps even the hiring of a helicopter to fly over Tokyo's traffic, might set

32

the host back £2,000. But at the end of the day you have traded in a business contact for a life-long golfing buddy, a big advance in a country where few of the 15 million who claim to be golfers ever get the chance to take a swing on a real golf-course.

Obligation generally demands that whoever footed the bill this time will be the guest next time, guaranteeing steady business for the motherly *mama-sans* who preside over Tokyo's top restaurants and exclusive bars. Some of them are so exclusive that you need a recommendation to get in, because bills are sent directly to the salaryman's office and settled without a quibble, however large. Whether at the dinner table or the nineteenth hole, no business is discussed. It is an occasion for getting to know each other. Getting to know a businessman from a company with whom one may be dealing for generations – Japanese prefer to think long-term – is treated as a very serious affair.

When American Express, the credit-card people, published a report on this extravagance, it veered towards understatement. 'While a business lunch is a common form of entertainment in the United States and Europe,' it concluded, 'the cost of entertaining in Japan is extremely high and the management of such expenses is rather loose.' American Express reckons that Japanese companies spend three times as much on entertainment as their American counterparts and fifteen times as much as British companies. Belt-tightening is unlikely. Entertainment expenses are regarded as a socially accepted supplement to junior workers' modest pay-packets. Their bosses also prefer to spend company money securing corporate friendships than to cut back, only to hand the money to the government in higher corporate taxes.

Even so, and even here, a boss likes money spent on expenses to stay out of his competitors' pockets. As a result, you can be pretty certain that if a bar serves only Suntory brand beer, few of its patrons will be from, say, Mitsubishi, the giant trading firm, or from Sumitomo Bank. Mitsubishi employees go to bars that serve Kirin beer and Sumitomo salarymen gulp Asahi beer. The reason? Japanese workers are very loyal to firms which are linked to theirs by cross-shareholdings in a web of affiliated companies. These webs, known as *keiretsu*, drive foreign traders up the wall because Japanese companies prefer to do business within the web, even if the prices are higher. This loyalty is so powerful that one Japanese hotelier boasts, 'You can't call yourself a real hotel man unless you can tell what a guest's favourite brand of beer is simply from the company he works for.'

Does the Japanese salaryman enjoy his life? All of us fantasize, every now and then, about something. What do the salarymen fantasize about? When a nosy insurance firm wondered the same thing and asked them, it discovered that having love affairs with junior colleagues, changing jobs and seeking a divorce are the three most common secret dreams of male office-workers aged between twenty and fifty-nine. That's not exactly what they teach you about Japanese commercial thinking in business school, is it? Fukuoka Mutual Life Insurance Co found that 37 per cent of them fancy a sexual fling. More curiously, one in every four office-workers dreams of starting his own business, running away from home or beating someone up. Even the brief moments spent with their families are too much for many salarymen. One in five husbands asked revealed a secret desire to go on a trip by himself.

But some Japanese men have unusual ways of venting their frustrations. Just ask yourself this: are you the sort of man that dreams of waving goodbye each morning to an obedient, loving wife who yearns for nothing but your speedy return from the office? Are you looking for a female traffic warden who tears up your ticket and grovels for forgiveness, or a tame secretary who speaks only to say 'I'm so sorry' after you slap her across the face? If you have answered yes to these questions, why not try a customized talking doll. Thousands of Japanese men do. A big seller is the 'See You Later' doll. It is a favourite among lonely husbands who leave their wives behind when work leads them to a cramped bedsit and a spell in one of the company's provincial outposts for a year or two. Such separations are common in Japan, where employees go where they are told and their wives stay behind to avoid disruption to the children's education. Dressed in a kimono and kneeling demurely in the traditional Japanese manner, the doll responds to a gentle tap on the shoulder with 'See you later' and sometimes follows with 'Please hurry back', sometimes with 'It's a lucky day today' or 'Don't forget anything' or 'I'm really going to miss you'. Priced at £15, the 8½ inch high plastic surrogate is also popular with students who are living on their own for the first time, far away from home and the protective mother who has coddled them for years. Japanese mothers make Jewish mothers look negligent. The makers have sold more than 50,000 of the 'See You Later' dolls so far and sales are still swelling.

Much more fun for the knockabout salaryman, especially at the end of one of those frustrating days when the boss has warned him that his office suit is not a dark enough blue, or that he needs a wife by 1 January if his promotion is to go through, is an 'I Am Sorry' doll. Deeply apologetic and around twelve inches tall, the doll comes in three versions: a young police-woman, a middle-aged female employee and, for the sake of balance, a company president (invariably male in Japan). All three come to life when shouted at, but most owners prefer to get the dolls' microchips chattering with a sharp slap across the face. 'We designed it as a soft toy,' says its manufacturer, 'so that the doll could take a beating and still not destroy the mechanism inside. We picked these three particular characters because many people dislike the police, who watch out for parking violations, and policewomen are usually more beady-eyed about this than policemen. We brought out the office lady to help out those customers who like to let their frustration loose on women. And the president can stand in for your boss or your father.'

Car-owners have particularly taken to the policewoman, who turns from a harridan to a simpering wimp when roughed up a little. 'I am sorry for towing your car away. I'll waive your fine. Please forgive me, please forgive me.' After a slap or two the office lady also realizes her shortcomings. 'I am sorry,' she says. 'I won't make such a stupid mistake again.' The president is a little more dignified, but no less repentant at the hands of his owner: 'I am sorry. Forgive me, I'm such a fool.' There are probably worse ways to pass an evening. Certainly cheaper ones. The doll sells for £35.

For those who prefer to receive it rather than to dish it out, there is also an abusive policeman doll who will tell you whether you are drunk and then deal with you accordingly. Breathe into the doll's face and a sensor measures the alcohol level and barks one of three responses. The first two are cautions, along the lines of 'Take it easy, you're going a little over the top.' Those who have sunk too deep into the sake barrel are told sternly: 'Okay, you bloody old soak, you've really done it this time. You're under arrest.' There are bluer versions for those who really like it when a policeman talks dirty to them. A siren sounds to accentuate the drama of the arrest. 'We wanted to avoid making it too much like a Japanese policeman,' says the sales manager of Okada Corp, which makes the doll. 'That's why we gave it the face of a badger and put an American cop's hat on him. Most of the buyers are middle-aged men.' At the peak of the doll's popularity, there were five thousand tipplers a month in Japan apparently keen to court arrest by a badger-faced policeman.

Harried young Japanese men have also become some of the keenest and most unexpected buyers of a new range of quarter-life-size Barbie-type dolls. Some Japanese sociologists speculate that these office-workers, most of them in their twenties and thirties, may be finding it hard to cope with Japan's fast-changing society, in which more assertive young women are more reluctant to pour tea all day, to hold doors open for men and to giggle through gritted teeth when the boss pinches their bottom. The beautiful, though mute, dolls were designed for forty-year-old women who had played with Barbie-type dolls as children. But they seem to offer Japan's junior salarymen a convenient way to vent their frustrations. They also provide them with female company, sometimes hard to find at the end of a long working day.

The £70 doll, called 'LL' and pronounced '*Deux L*', is a one-quarter, to-scale model of what Japanese consider to be the perfectly proportioned woman. If blown up to life size she would measure 5 feet 7 inches, with a 34 inch bust, a 21 inch waist and 35 inch hips. Near her mouth is a mole, designed to set off her beauty. Most Japanese women have black hair, but LL's shoulder-length tresses come in blonde and chestnut brown too, for a continental look. Her wardrobe ranges from tight miniskirts to mink coats which sell for £400.

'We designed the doll to appeal to every girl's longing to look like a fashion model,' says Hachiro Watanabe, who dreamed up the doll for Japan's Takara toy company. Takara was as surprised as anyone when they found that one third of the stock was being bought by men in their twenties and thirties. Watanabe thinks that 'for many of these men, this pretty doll is an imaginary lover'. He reckons that only 1 per cent of male buyers are 'perverts'.

Watanabe gets fan mail for his creation. In one letter, a twenty-eight-year-old male office-worker writes, 'She has the most perfect eyes and facial features, no matter what angle she's viewed from. When I look at her from above, I am captivated by the beauty of her eyes and her seductive air.'

Just imagine if she could talk as well.

3. A Woman's Place (is in the Wrong): Making Tea with Your PhD

The second sex – love and marriage – sexual harassment – the pill and abortion – making more babies for Japan – family life – 'Conjugal Day' – washday –a woman of design and substance – office ladies

Japanese women are at the crossroads. But, like a lot of other things in Japan which always seem to be twitching on the brink of change, Japanese women have been at the crossroads for as long as anyone can remember. Given the longevity of most Japanese, as long as anyone can remember is an awfully long time.

It is true that Japanese women no longer have to walk three paces behind their husbands. But they are rarely with their long-working and late-drinking husbands anyway, so that was probably never all that much of a handicap. And General Douglas MacArthur, head of the American occupying forces, did manage to get Japanese women the vote in 1946 when the Yanks were running things after Japan's defeat in the war. But since then there have been only half a dozen token women in the Japanese cabinet. Among the world's developed nations, no country has a lower proportion of women members in their parliament than Japan.

A recent Japanese prime minister said his party would not be fielding women candidates in a forthcoming election because campaigning 'is too physically tough for women', which is probably why all those tiny sixty-year-old ladies have turned their backs on the rigours of politics and prefer bending over double in Japanese paddy-fields, up to their knees in water, planting rice. It is not hard to see why, in spite of the many advances they have made, many Japanese women still feel like third-class citizens. It is not that they are always maltreated, just that they are often regarded as a convenient feature of modern life, like fax machines and twenty-four-hour room service.

You might find it tricky to persuade the millions of Japanese wives who wake at dawn to cook boxed lunches of rice and several dainty somethings for their husbands, or the degree-laden office girls who spend their days making tea for the men, bowing to visitors and cleaning everyone's desk before going home, that the status of women is changing in Japan. It is, but often at the pace of a Japanese Noh drama. Old men with Zimmer frames move faster than a Japanese Noh drama.

Women do show their faces every now and then. The powerful Shinto deity Amaterasu Omikami, from whom Japanese emperors have traditionally received their divinity and who still makes a secret visit to new mikados on the night of their enthronement ceremony, is a goddess. And *The Tale of Genji*, widely regarded as perhaps the finest moment of Japanese literature, was penned by a woman, Murasaki Shikibu, a lady of the court. But that was in the early years of the eleventh century. Since then, Japanese women have been keeping their heads down.

Many hopeful Japanese women and millions of sketchily informed foreigners saw 1989 as a watershed for women in Japan. For the first time a Japanese prime minister, Sosuke Uno, was hounded into resigning because of his weakness for bar girls, or, at least, his failure to pick one who didn't talk. It seemed to close a chapter in which mistresses were regarded as one of the rewards of reaching the top in Japan, along with having a chauffeur and a £1 million membership of a top golf club. Japanese women, who are brought up to smile coyly, to laugh discreetly behind cupped hands and to speak a fluttering, feminine form of Japanese that institutionalizes their deferential role, have tended to make the best of being ideal wives and caring mothers and have taught themselves to tolerate their husbands' drinking and philandering as long as those husbands bring home a fat pay-packet every week: Japanese brides wear a cap during their wedding ceremony to cover their horns of jealousy, meekly signalling that they will not make a fuss when hubby comes home with lipstick on his collar.

The pressure on every Japanese person to know his or her place, to behave like their neighbours, not to shame their families and to avoid jolting social harmony means that many women slip easily into their prescribed roles. Every five years, NHK, Japan's television and radio equivalent of the BBC in Britain, carries out a wide-ranging survey of Japanese attitudes to various issues. In the latest polling of the people, NHK found that 24 per cent of all respondents agreed with the statement 'When a woman marries, she should devote herself to taking care of the family.' Another 39 per cent went along with the sentiment that 'Even when a woman marries, it is all right for her to have a job until she has children, but after that she should devote herself to looking after her family.' So 63 per cent of Japanese still feel that a woman's real place is cooking noodles and changing nappies. Even 59 per cent of women respondents held this view. The statistics are just as stark from a different angle: the average working wife spends $3\frac{1}{4}$ hours a day on housework. The average Japanese husband, whether his wife works or not, spends eight minutes.

Nevertheless, many Japanese women, particularly the younger ones, were galvanized by the foreign media coverage given to

Uno's hanky-panky. They started asking aloud why Japan, the world's newest superpower, was several decades behind its major Western allies in giving women equal rights and freedoms and in allowing women access to the top jobs. Many people, inside and outside Japan, thought a quiet revolution had begun. It was so quiet that little has been heard of it since.

Japanese men were far more disgusted with the disgraced Uno than were Japanese women. But the source of their outrage was different. Concubines have been one of Japan's subtle social institutions: it has always been a mark of a man's success and of his superior station in society to be able to afford two households, often with two thriving families. Japanese men scorned Uno not for his adultery but because it is only a pathetic man, without influence, who cannot buy a discreet silence from bar girls and hotel doormen. Japanese men, if they can afford it, still have nothing against spending the evening with a geisha who strokes their stomach and massages their vanity. Japan's geisha community is no longer what it was – there are fewer than 17,000 now, compared with 80,000 in the 1920s – and the shiny black rickshaws that deliver them to the back doors of Tokyo's posher restaurants certainly look out of place against the neon and concrete brashness of Tokyo. But they are still a common sight in the city's entertainment districts.

Just how little has changed was underlined only a few months after Uno handed over the reins of office. A senior editor at a small publishing company filed Japan's first-ever suit for sexual harassment, making many blue-suited businessmen blink with incomprehension. She was upset because for two years her boss had pestered her with lewd remarks and spread rumours around the office that she was promiscuous and an alcoholic. She filed suit after complaining formally to her company's management and being told not to bother turning up for work the next day. Lacking a phrase for this strange concept, Japanese linguists settled on *seku hara*, a hijacked Japanese version of the English phrase. But instead of becoming the subject of national soul-searching, *seku hara* became a subject for comedy routines about women who didn't realize that they should be flattered when office colleagues invented a stream of sexual innuendo about them. Magazine articles commenting on Japan's perplexed reaction to the novel lawsuit quoted men as saying that 'most office ladies work only because they are out to hook men' and that a man should be able to flirt with a female colleague without her getting upset. The most typical examples of sexual harassment are bottom-patting and teasing questions such as 'What colour panties are you wearing?' or 'Are you a virgin?'

A group of women lawyers in Tokyo who ran a one-day hotline to gauge how serious a problem all this was found they were flooded with callers, many of whom had been forced to have sex or who had been raped by a colleague, usually a superior. Often, when the women complained to senior managers they were told that the man's behaviour was normal. One woman said that during a job interview her prospective employer started to run his hands over her bust and hips. A freelance writer said editors expected her to go out with them in return for assignments. A female stockbroker was told by a client, 'If you sleep with me I'll make you a stock-market professional'; when she asked her boss how to handle the matter, he replied, 'Why don't you let him make you a professional?' It is not that such behaviour is unique to Japan, more that Japanese men find it unremarkable. Perhaps the mood of the moment was captured best by a Tokyo nightclub which chose 'Seku Hara' for its name. It hired young hostesses to sit at make-believe cluttered office desks while male customers paid to fondle them. In 1992, three years after filing Japan's first sexual harassment suit, the senior editor was awarded 1.65 million yen in compensation, or about £7,000, a modest bounty in Japanese terms at yen exchange rates.

A Woman's Place (is in the Wrong)

Directors of major Japanese corporations, who generally refuse to consider women for anything other than the most dead-end jobs even though Japan is suffering from an acute labour shortage, are privately bemused by American and European stockbroking firms which vacuum up talented Japanese women for responsible positions. In Japan, only one working woman in a hundred holds a managerial job at a corporation or government office, whereas roughly one in fourteen men do. There is an equal employment opportunity law in Japan, passed in 1985, but it doesn't even bark, let alone have teeth. There are no penalties for violators. Employers still pay women less than men for doing the same job. The average woman's wage in Japan is about half that of a man.

According to Mikiko Taga, a Japanese feminist author, some Japanese firms are so thrown by career-minded, strong-willed foreign women that they advise male employees who go abroad on business trips to keep their hands off American women. Taga says that, alongside advice to beware of pickpockets, one big Japanese corporation warns its staff to 'Please be careful of American women. Please don't touch them because they'll sue you.'

It's just the sort of advice that swells the flow of Japanese women who flee Japan for a life unburdened by the Confucianism that teaches women to serve their father, then their husband, then their eldest son. Men get served first at dinner, enter and leave the lift first, take precedence over their wives when there is only one seat left in the crowded train carriage. Now that you can get sushi almost anywhere in America, and can also buy Tiffany bangles more cheaply there by avoiding the overblown yen prices they charge in Tokyo, many young Japanese women pack their bags and go.

Single women who leave Japan also appreciate the fact that abroad they are not regarded as morally suspect if they live

43

alone rather than with their parents, that if they are still unmarried at the age of twenty-six they will not be referred to by male colleagues as 'Christmas cake' (both women and Christmas cake being too stale to be interesting after the twenty-fifth), that they can carry on working after getting married without being thought peculiar and can return to their offices after having a child without being regarded as hopelessly delinquent mothers. And they don't have to wear the prim company uniforms that most office girls have to put on every morning in Japan. Best of all, they don't have to make tea for everyone all day long. Few women in Japan escape this drudgery. Even the very few Japanese policewomen who get to go out on the beat and make arrests have to rush back to take their turn at the teapot, along with the rest of the girls hired as secretaries and photocopiers. Policemen, of course, are excused. To highlight just how few women escape this tea-making curse, I once bumped into a friend in Tokyo, a correspondent for the *Washington Post*, as she was returning from an interview with the head of one of Japan's leading makers of pornographic videos: during the interview, the company's star porn actress, who makes her fortune from writhing and fornicating in front of an inquisitive camera, unexpectedly arrived at the office. Within moments she returned with a tray of tea for her boss and his American visitor.

Even women who crack such male-dominated professions as journalism often find their path barred on the most unexpected occasions. Construction workers refused to allow a female reporter to cover the opening ceremony for a tunnel that was being built through a mountain because, the project supervisor said, 'the presence of women could anger the jealous goddess of the mountain'. The twenty-two-year-old reporter, Aki Omori, who was working for the *Yomiuri* newspaper, Japan's biggest selling broadsheet, was baffled that 'such an outdated practice based on an industry myth' should survive into the 1990s. But in

Japan such anomalies do survive. Japan's animistic tradition dictates that a jealous mountain goddess will cause landslides and other accidents if a woman enters a tunnel before it is completed. A few months before Omori nearly fell foul of the goddesses, Mayumi Moriyama, Japan's first woman chief cabinet secretary, was publicly humiliated when the Japan Sumo Association scotched her plan to present the Prime Minister's Cup to the winner of a sumo tournament. Sumo officials said that the sumo ring, a raised mound of clay, was sacred and no place for a woman, even a woman bearing gifts.

Women's fate has also been taken out of their hands in other ways. More than thirty years after the pill gave Western women a new sense of freedom and injected some extra swing into the sixties, Tokyo is still dithering over offering the same choice to women in Japan. Approval of the pill might end reliance on condoms and crossed fingers that results in half a million legal abortions a year. Add illegal abortions and the total more than doubles.

'Abortion,' says Yuriko Ashino of the Japan Family Planning Federation, 'has been one of the main methods of birth control in Japan, especially among young women.' Ashino says the government has blamed its foot-dragging on worries about the pill's side-effects, 'but behind the scenes there seem to be other reasons. The major source of income for obstetricians and gynaecologists in Japan is abortions. They have a strong political lobby and the pill obviously hurts their income.'

Condoms, freely available, are popular. A quarter of all condoms used in the world are used by Japanese. Condoms command nearly 80 per cent of the contraceptive market in Japan. In most countries the comparable figure is less than 10 per cent. Intrauterine devices are rare and diaphragms all but non-existent. Although hormone-based drugs similar to the pill have been available in Japan for a while for women with gynaecological problems, only about 1 per cent of Japanese women of child-bearing age use them. They are high in oestrogen and have a reputation for causing side-effects, although this is due to their composition and the side-effects would not occur with modern low-dose varieties. But sex education is sparse in Japan and patients follow the advice of their doctor, who is never expected to explain his diagnosis or his course of treatment. As a result, a trip to the abortion clinic has become almost as matter-of-fact in Japan as a visit to the dentist. The irony is that in spite of this reliance on abortion as more or less a primary form of contraception, abortion is technically illegal in all but extreme cases. There is a pragmatic confusion over the reading of the rulebooks. Abortions are allowed for 'economic reasons', the giant and ill-defined loophole through which more than 95 per cent of abortions in Japan are performed today.

One of the government's other big worries has been that mass availability of the pill will accelerate Japan's already falling birth rate, another area where Japanese women are in danger of forgetting their place and purpose in life. In the summer of 1990, when many Japanese officials got it into their heads that the Japanese race was about to become extinct, a senior cabinet minister blamed the country's falling birth rate on the rising number of Japanese women who are choosing brains over breeding. He raised few eyebrows among his all-male cabinet colleagues. The percentage of women school-leavers going on to college has more than doubled over the past two decades to about 37 per cent. The rise has skewed social patterns: coupled with the desire of young Japanese women to live a little before settling down to sterilizing teats and milk bottles, it has contributed to a trend towards slightly later marriages. Asked if the government was proposing a return to Japan's pre-war policy of encouraging women to 'give birth and multiply', Misoji Sakamoto, then Japan's chief cabinet secretary, replied wistfully, 'It isn't such an easy matter to get Japanese women to bear children for us.'

Nevertheless, the Japanese government has become increasingly frantic about women's failure to deliver more than 1.57 children each, the worst productivity rate in Japan's history. Having first tried, with winks and nudges, to persuade Japanese men to go home earlier and spend more time with their wives and families, the government moved on to a blunt appeal to patriotism. Apocalyptic officials have been warning that unless drastic action is taken soon, the Japanese race will be wiped out in a millennium. Nobody ever accused the Japanese of thinking short-term. A Health and Welfare Ministry advisory panel commissioned to investigate the crisis predicted disaster for the nation, concluding that fewer births would mean fewer taxpayers to meet the costs of caring for an already fast ageing society. The panel of experts warned that, 'Just as was the case in the last days of ancient Rome, the decrease in the number of children is a sign of a declining civilization.' Realizing that the threat of going the way of ancient Rome was not sending Japanese women diving dutifully on to their futons, the government now makes procreation financially more tempting by increasing child allowances and subsidies to nurseries.

Will Japanese women now do their duty? History is not on the government's side. For one thing, there is little to suggest that Japan's corporate warriors will change their habits and suddenly take their full two-week holiday allowance every year, or leave their offices earlier every evening, or cut short their after-hours drinking with workmates to get home before their wives are snoring on the sofa. Worse, the government has suffered abuse and ridicule over its suggestion of creating a new legal holiday to be called 'Conjugal Day', when husbands would take their wives out for a treat and enjoy the benefits of living in one of the world's richest countries (and, who knows, maybe even get up to some hanky-panky when they got home afterwards).

47

Many Japanese wives have grown used to seeing their husbands on Sundays only – and only then if they are not whacking balls at the local driving range. Because houses are small, Japanese tend not to entertain all that much at home. And because many Japanese live in suburbs that are a two-hour commute from the husband's office, and because business entertaining excludes wives, womenfolk stay at home, cooking dinner and making sure the children do their homework. When the children are at school, or have left home, wives will often go off, in large chattering packs, to while away the afternoon in cafés or at cinemas and kabuki theatres. As a result, many wives complained to the government that they had no business inventing things like Conjugal Day and that their husbands were a nuisance around the house. It is quite common for wives to refer to their husbands fondly as 'oversize garbage'. Rather less fondly, they call them 'wet leaves', because they get stuck to everything and are a headache to sweep up. One woman wrote to the bureaucrats behind the new Conjugal Day holiday (interestingly, this project was entrusted to the men from the Ministry of International Trade and Industry, which gives some idea of where the concept of leisure fits into the Japanese scheme of things) to tell them they were 'soft-headed', since 'conjugal relations do not improve because the husband is at home'. Japan's relatively high divorce rate for couples over retirement age seems to support this woman's view that, over the course of forty years of Japanese-style marriage and Japanese-style commuting, many husbands and wives grow out of the habit of spending much time together. On retirement, many of them find they are living with relative strangers.

In fact, many Japanese women seem to write their husbands out of their lives long before retirement comes around. One of the most curious manifestations of these let's-make-do-till-the-children-have-grown-up marriages was unveiled in a survey carried out by the *Sunday Mainichi*, a respectable Japanese weekly. The magazine discovered that what it thought might be an amusing aberration was, in fact, a widespread habit throughout the land: it found that 10 per cent of Japanese housewives wash their husbands' underwear separately from their own. Apparently many wives and children faint at the idea of daddy's boxer shorts swishing round the machine with their blouses and petticoats. Some women pick up their husbands' Y-fronts with chopsticks on washday. Others assign their husbands special towels, for their use only. Mikiko Yamanouchi, a lawyer, told the magazine, 'I sympathize fully. I somehow feel a man's smell will cling to other clothes if I wash them all together. Many of my relatives wash their husbands' pants separately, too.' Another manifestation of this trend is the 'Slim U', a slender urinal developed by Toto, Japan's largest manufacturer of baths and lavatories. Toto found that 70 per cent of women polled in a survey said they wanted their menfolk to use separate loos at home. Apparently Japanese women have taken to the Western-style lavatory, which has now replaced the old squat-style Japanese loo in 80 per cent of Japanese homes, but they have not taken to the possibility of tiny splashes created by men who lack proper marksmanship. Thus the demand for separate urinals in Japanese houses. And since Japanese houses are fairly small, the urinals have been shrunk to a width of under ten inches. But they do come in ten colours.

If the pace of change for Japanese women is slow, it is at least accelerating. Worried about the social effects of allowing more foreigners into the country for work, Japan is being forced to absorb more women into the workforce. These women, many of them young and still living at home, are earning salaries that may not go very far in Tokyo but which buy first-class hotel rooms and Hermes scarves in Paris. That purchasing power has caught the eye of manufacturers and advertisers and given women economic clout – far more persuasive with Japanese businessmen than bra-burning. Also, as Tokyo house prices stay uncomfortably high for one pay packet, more husbands are being forced to rely on a wife's second income to meet the mortgage payments. That has underpinned women's economic influence. At the same time, Japan's wealth has relieved the country's younger generation of the pressure their parents felt to rebuild Japan after its destruction in the war. Rich young men are less willing to devote all their spare time to the firm and rich young women – though not yet ready to flout convention completely – are more willing to postpone marriage for maybe a year or two and have fun in Hawaii before the first baby arrives.

Strong female role models might quicken the change, but there are only a handful around. Some of them are bolder than others. Few come more bold than Eiko Ishioka, who decided to gatecrash the male-dominated design world and then took it over with her innovative approach. Her wake-you-up poster designs, television commercials and stage sets have helped to sell everything from Issey Miyake frocks to London West End plays. In a country that thrives on being prim and predictable, Ishioka likes to shock. She plasters cities with naked bodies (some of them men, many of them black), with pictures of provocatively shaped peaches and with portraits of plainly beautiful African and Indian village women, in native dress, that gave an international tang to Japanese fashion advertisements long before Benetton knitted its first pastel green sweater.

Ishioka worked on designs for Paul Schrader's film *Mishima*, for David Hwang's play *M. Butterfly* and for the Phillip Glass opera *The Making of the Representative for Planet 8*. She landed a Grammy award for a Miles Davis album cover. Her bold advertising hoardings stare at you from Tokyo's grey buildings and graffiti-less subway walls. They turned the Parco department-store chain into *the* fashionable meeting place for Japan's young and have kept it trendy for more than twenty years, quite a feat in a country where teenage tastes change so fast that even the trendiest new outfit can be embarrassingly out of fashion before you have finished trying it on in the changing-room.

By the time Ishioka had done with it, an Issey Miyake fashion show had been turned into a cross between a Broadway musical and a one-act drama: they charged admission and played to packed houses for six performances.

Ishioka has a mane of black hair, striking looks and high spirits. She is so demanding that she can bring collaborators close to tears, but they work with her because the creative tension she generates glows in the end result of their work. She may produce unconventional images because she is unconventional herself. While other Japanese women might devote their lives to fathers, husbands and eldest sons, Ishioka is punchy, confident, unmarried and bows to nobody. While most Japanese women might allow themselves a shy giggle behind a cupped hand, Ishioka laughs out loud. This may sound normal to those who live in countries where women run everything from governments to street gangs, but it is still unusual in Japan, where women in positions of power and influence are rare, and women willing to flout convention rarer still.

'My father was a pioneer graphic designer. My mother wanted to be a professional woman, but she ended up being just a housewife. My grandmother told her that if she went to university she would never find a husband. So both my parents stressed that I should have an occupation. At the age of seven I realized that my father's job fascinated me and my mother's job bored me. I learned early on that I wanted to break through the social structure. So I went to Tokyo National University of Fine Arts to train as a designer. I studied architecture, graphic design, furniture design, everything. My father tried to deter me from opting for graphic design. He said it was bad enough for a man to

51

work in such a chauvinistic world, but for a woman it would be too hard to make it. That made me determined to be a graphic designer. My father accepted that going against the grain was part of my character, but that didn't mean he believed I would make it. That pattern has repeated itself through my life. I like challenges.

'When I started to become well known, male rivals used to say I was only famous because I was a woman, a novelty. I promised myself then that I would become so obviously special in my field that they'd have to shut their mouths.

'I like a strong woman. When I became a professional art director I worked for a cosmetics company called Shiseido. Until I came along all the advertising had been done by men. They portrayed women as dolls who never looked into the camera, and who walked three steps behind men. I wanted a woman who looked healthy, who could look a man in the eye, who had power, who had the confidence to live alone. When I left Shiseido and moved to Parco I wanted to continue using the sort of woman that didn't fit the traditional image of women as male mascots. People expect Japanese advertising to use Japanese motifs. But why can't I use black women or Faye Dunaway? But because I use women it doesn't mean I'm just talking about women. I use women to convey things about the human condition.'

She confesses that she pushes herself. 'Sometimes I feel that I'm involved in too many media, but most times I feel that my different interests give me new ideas and perspectives. They cross-fertilize. For example, when Paul Schrader asked me to work on *Mishima* I told him I didn't have the technical ability. But he said he was looking for someone who wasn't in the movie business, who would bring in fresh ideas. The technical support would be easier to get hold of. It was a fresh eye he wanted. It worked out very well. Also it helps me to develop a universal language, rather than a Japanese one.

'Ever since I studied design at university I have tried very hard not to exploit the fact that I'm Japanese, that I should not be limited to Japanese themes. Nowadays, the Japanese motif is changing and you can no longer really rely on cherry trees and geishas and things like that. But when I started it wasn't changing and I trained myself to look for new motifs. When I got my chance to collaborate with Europeans and Americans it came easily to me. I could work on international projects without first having to shed a Japanese skin. I don't know why other Japanese artists' work doesn't travel. Perhaps I want to work abroad more than they do. I would like to do more abroad. I want to direct a film. But commercials, films, posters, it's all the same to me. I don't see films as superior to posters.

'If you want to know who I really admire, it's Michelangelo. He is a big hero of mine. He always had a client, but he always managed to achieve his own spiritual statement, even on client work. I am in a much more humble position, but I would like to achieve the same with the work for my client.'

Ishioka used nudes in her advertisements as early as the 1970s, and some accuse her of trying to shock. But admirers envy her ability to make even a pile of bricks look erotic to people outside the building trade.

'There are three reasons I use nudes. First I like the human body, whether it's the bum or the tits or the shoulder, whether the body is a man's or a woman's. Secondly, 90 per cent of the people in this business use women, but the way the advertisements turned out bothered me. I was disgusted by the way male designers were treating women's bodies. They used nudes in a cheap, vulgar way. Sometimes it looked like pornography. My challenge was to subvert this way of treating naked bodies.

'Thirdly, during the 1970s I did a lot of advertisements, and to make a good advertisement you have to approach people's minds and bodies. Eroticism is a very important factor in

53

attracting people's souls, but it was not my intention to use naked bodies just to shock or to be eye-catching. After thrashing out an idea, after many twists and turns, the result turned out to be erotic. It just happened that way. If I were asked to make a TV commercial using just one stone, I suspect the end result would be something erotic. When I was twenty-five I won a prize in a Japanese poster-design competition. The poster was for a symposium. I used only geometric shapes. People said even that was erotic.'

Ishioka is hardly a common template of Japanese woman, but her brand of self-confidence, massaged by the new economic freedom, is filtering down to some of the meekest women in the country. Even the young office ladies, known in Japan as 'OLs', are rebelling quietly against the bosses who seem to think that they bow and make tea all day long because nothing could possibly fulfil them more. One observer compared these posses of decorative young girls – they are generally hired for their prettiness, and the sugary cuteness of a company's OLs is as much a sign of its social stature and its financial well-being as thick carpets and wood panelling in the boardroom – to the platoons of 'comfort women' that always accompanied Japan's Imperial Army into battle. Indeed, one of the OLs' common functions is to provide a convenient selection of marriageable women for junior executives who are too busy to find one in their spare time outside the office. Many OLs, providing they are still at the pre-Christmas cake stage, are more than keen to fulfil this function. It is pandering to the older, lecherous bosses that has sparked their rebellion. The sedition started in a column in a weekly magazine, where OLs spill the beans on such topics as 'Disgusting Sounds the Boss Makes' and 'Why the Boss is Totally Unsuitable as a Lover'. The anecdotes have become a resistance movement for OLs and required reading for their bosses, who are depicted as dim, disgusting, lecherous, loudmouthed, infantile and incompetent. Some OLs report how their bosses can't even grasp how to work the hold button on a telephone, or how they ask if a fax that has just been sent will arrive the same day. One OL hated making tea so much she squeezed a dish rag into the tea water. Another laced the teacup with soya sauce. Neither of their bosses noticed. Now it is the male bosses who are writing into magazines to complain about not being taken seriously.

But even pretty young things don't always find some handsome young accountant to sweep them off their feet. They take solace in various ways. They shop: preferably on Madison Avenue. They travel: everywhere from Sydney to San Francisco. They eat in Italian restaurants: they have made the Italian pudding *tiramisu* a requirement on every restaurateur's menu, even for those serving Japanese or French food. They play tennis: the current emperor, Akihito, met his commoner bride on a doubles court and young women have been practising their backhands ever since in the hope of duplicating this fairy-tale romance. They read magazines: the patronage of spend-happy OLs has made women's magazines a boom area of publishing, with new titles being launched almost monthly. Those who are still lonely and restless have taken up with reptiles. Many OLs have decided that small reptiles, like lizards and iguanas, are cute and the perfect pet for their compact apartments. They find the green faces welcoming after their late-night commutes to faraway suburbs. They have also become pally with pythons. OLs explain that reptiles are smaller than dogs, they don't need walks, they don't take up much room, they are fed on leftovers and they don't bark, which keeps landlords and neighbours happy. Because some reptiles are nocturnal they are still awake when their owners come home from a late night at the photocopier or the disco, looking for some cute and quiet company with their cocoa.

4. The Young, the Rich and the Lonely:
a Gleesome Threesome

Keep young and beautiful if you want to have fun – finding a mate, the old way and the new – spending it – gold fever – a Christmas romance – hygiene mania – super-loos – the new art lovers – the richest man in the world

If many Japanese men and women find the changes in their society confusing, the young and the rich seem the most at sea in their search for suitable jobs, suitable goals, suitable things to consume and suitable companions to consume them with.

Many young Japanese are in a tizz, torn between the freedom that recent wealth has brought them and the testing demands of a society which is still tradition-bound. Because the Japanese cannot see a problem without inventing at least twelve possible solutions (and putting seven of them into immediate mass production), this dilemma has spawned boom industries which cater to those who just want to have fun, those who just want to spend, those who are hunting desperately for a spouse and those who want to do all three at the same time. These businesses are finding it hard to keep pace with the needs of this new generation of young men and women who want to shake off their parents' puritanism and penny-pinching and enjoy life a little before the system and the children strap them in. Often, the more it all costs the better.

Having fun is not too difficult with a fat wallet. But one of the big headaches for the '*Nyuu Ritchi*' – confusingly, this is not the name of a 1950s Japanese rock 'n' roll star but the collective noun for Japan's new rich kids – is that while years of diligence and evening cram school have given them a job with a blue-chip company and enough loose change to buy a new Armani suit every month, they can't all find suitable marriage partners. And when they do come across them, they are often too shy to break the ice, or so clumsy they smash it completely. Fortunately for these shy young things, Japan's games manufacturers have come to the rescuc with inventive ways to bring bashful people together at parties. You could call it a way of breaking the ice, but some of the party games that young Japanese play could get you arrested in primmer countries.

Although marriage is still a high priority – it is extremely rare to come across an unmarried couple living together in Japan – more and more young Japanese want to find their own wife or husband rather than relying on the arranged marriages that bonded most of their parents. It is part of the freedom that comes with being able to afford pillar-box red sports cars and gold Ferragamo shoes, luxuries that their little-travelled parents barely knew existed, let alone coveted. But long working hours and short holidays are making it difficult for young adults to find the time to meet partners, for fun or marriage. What these people are willing to pay very big money for are good modern matchmakers, outrageous and expensive parties and the sort of party games you don't find in those manuals that suggest inventive ways of keeping children amused on rainy days. Sometimes it's a struggle.

Owners of many of the new introduction agencies that have sprung up across Japan say that many men haven't a clue how to talk to Japan's increasingly picky young women. One firm in Osaka, called Marriage Man Academy, is even running courses for rich but gauche young men in the basics of social behaviour, called 'How to Date Women'. The manager of Marriage Man Academy, Satoshi Noguchi, says he learnt the way into a woman's heart in his former job as a kimono salesman. He teaches his shy charges basic secrets such as: 'Always sit to the right of a woman. When she sits on your left, she hears everything you say through her right ear. Any words that are heard through the right ear go to the left side of the brain – the emotional side.' Gosh.

One would have assumed that even in their pre-Marriage Man Academy days, these suitors would have found themselves sitting on the right of the lady at least half of the time, by the law of averages, but Japanese are not always keen to take risks. A course of lessons at the academy, which includes everything from practising stand-up comedy routines in front of the school's female staff to having a long, hard think about that awfully dowdy hairstyle, are even videotaped for later analysis and constructive criticism. For all this advice and attention, the course seems cheap at 185,000 yen, about £800.

Run-of-the-mill dating agencies in Japan will charge anything between 150,000 yen and 350,000 yen for registration, plus around 10,000 yen a month for the chance to meet up to one potential partner a week. Realizing that many young people now have the will and enough money to buy their way out of the crowd, one very ritzy agency is charging ten million yen, or around £43,000, with no refunds. But it tries to ensure that none of its clients marries beneath his or her station, and its fee includes the cost of a marriage proposal in New York, a marriage service in the Japanese consulate in Manhattan and a seven-day honeymoon in the Caribbean. The potential newly-weds sleep in separate rooms until they are married. This agency carries around 165,000 men and women on its books, which says something about how rich its clients are (even though parents foot the bill for 70 per cent of the members) and how tricky these youngsters are finding it to mate in the unchaperoned jungle.

Those who prefer a less formal approach have taken to partying with the sort of vengeance that is also available only to those with very generous employers or very generous parents. As in London, Paris or New York, some young Japanese men and women find it difficult to enjoy themselves at a party unless it has cost them a lot of money to show up. Hence the fashion in Tokyo for extravagant costume parties. Less international, perhaps, is the requirement that there must be games to play and party favours to take home. We are talking about young adults here, remember, with serious blue-suited jobs to go to in the morning. One favourite game which has many young party-goers clutching their sides is called 'Say What You Want'. It is trumpeted as an educational game designed to help people overcome shyness in chatting about bodily functions: well that sounds reasonable enough as a mission, but why at a party? The first rule is that the game uses a life-size plastic faeces as a counter, which moves around a gameboard designed as a lavatory depending on how players answer questions about parts of the body and their functions. The rules get even less complicated after that.

Fashionable Tokyo discothèques are rented out regularly by young people who ask their guests to turn up in elaborate and expensive fancy-dress costumes specially made for the evening. Arabian Nights dress is particularly liked. Tokyo department stores have set up special party catering bureaux that offer everything from food to frilly frocks. Readers of the growing number of 'How to Party' guidebooks that fill the shelves of Japan's bookshops might prefer getting away from the capital for a sort of urban cowboy-style party, which offers horse-riding, barbecues and traditional American barn dances without all the inconvenience of trekking off to Kansas.

But there is still the problem of those who love to have fun, love to go to parties, love to play games, but are frozen with shyness when confronted with members of the opposite sex. For these people there are now many cures that help to break down inhibitions at even the most starchy parties. What about trying a game called 'Bodily Ruin', a kind of Pelmanism card game where, instead of just feeling jolly pleased with himself, a player who completes a matching pair can ask any other player to perform the task described on the card? A try-anything reporter for *East–West* magazine who has played it says that these tasks range from doing press-ups, which seems an unnecessarily tiring way to spend a social evening, to standing in a corner of the room with the card sticking out of your bottom, which must certainly deter other players from picking those same matching cards again, however sharp their memory. Another card in the pack allows players to stand on your crotch for ten seconds, 'with ten extra seconds if you scream out' – a card presumably designed for parties where standing room is scarce.

Compared with this, blowing up balloons that swell into untraditional shapes more usually encountered in teaching-hospital lecture rooms seems rather tame. So too is the game called 'Don't Take My Sailor Skirt Off', which consists of little Japanese schoolgirl dolls dressed in their traditional sailor-suit uniforms. When some of the dolls are picked up, their skirts fly into the air, disqualifying that player from continuing in the game. In 'Body Darts', a game young woman dons an apron depicting a bikini-clad girl and men aim phallic-shaped rubber darts at various, but fairly predictable, parts of her anatomy. By far the most intimate party-time contact seems to be offered by 'Clip', a game in which men and women are linked by a piece of string that is attached to a clip at each end. The spin of a wheel determines which part of a woman's clothes is attached to which part of the man's. Some of the lengths of string are fairly short, and a man might find his shirt collar, for example, clipped to the waistband of a young lady's skirt. It is tricky to tell how many marriage proposals have resulted from such playful evenings.

By contrast with these rich young things, the other main social group struggling to find spouses is Japan's farmers. Like farmers in many other countries, they have a decent income but they suffer from a lack of marriageable women because of the drift of population to the cities. Anyway, most Japanese women say they do not want to marry a farmer. Hard to know how many farmers have tried Japan's modern-day version of Pelmanism or Body Darts. If they have, it hasn't worked for them. In Kanagi, a town in the farming region of Aomori in northern Japan, the lonely farmers are so fed up that they have taken to importing their brides at two million yen a go from the Philippines.

So whatever happened to those ascetic Japanese who shunned anything gaudier than a florid turn of phrase at the end of a solemn haiku poem? The dash for fun and the spending frenzy have now spread to all sectors of Japanese society. Some Japanese are so eager to lighten their wallets that they buy mink covers for their loo seats and happily spend £20 for a loaf of bread flown in from Paris. This lust for luxuries by housewives who do their vacuuming in cashmere cardigans and whose children pay for their sweets after school from Louis Vuitton purses has become so dazzling that the *Weekly Yomiuri*, a respected Japanese magazine, asked its readers whether it is all just 'simply ridiculous, a healthy sign of the country's growing prosperity, or a manifestation of a growing ill in the nation's *nouveaux riches*?' Like those quizzes in *Cosmopolitan* that ask whether you like to spend your evenings 'in a theatre', 'indoors' or '*in flagrante delicto*', the *Weekly Yomiuri* made it pretty clear which answer carried top marks.

The Japanese have beaten Americans at making microchips and are now overtaking them in measuring a man by his bank balance. The accent may be Japanese, but money now talks very loudly in Japan. And for one reason or another more and more Japanese feel rich. Those who own land – it can be the size of a postage stamp, just as long as it bears a Tokyo postmark – have seen the value of their assets balloon over the past decade: they and their fashion-crazy children are willing to splash out a little. Notwithstanding the 1990s slump in Tokyo share prices, the boom in the Tokyo stock market over the course of the 1980s left shareholders in clover. Those who missed out on the land and stock price windfalls have decided that when even a tiny apartment in a drab Tokyo suburb costs £250,000, they will never be able to afford their own place unless they burden their grandchildren with a three-generation mortgage along with the family silver. They have decided they might as well stop saving and start having fun instead. Gold is always popular with those in the money, whichever country they come from, but the Japanese have turned their affection into something of an obsession.

The Japanese, like the French, have liked keeping their savings in gold, and away from the taxman, under the mattress. Officially the Japanese privately hold about 300 tons of gold. Unofficial hoards boost the figure to well over 1,000 tons. If Japan ever got into serious trouble it could probably swap its gold holdings for something warm and cosy, like Brazil.

But is that enough to explain the taste for sushi wrapped in gold? Or gold-flecked omelettes, golden noodles, gold ice-cream and bottles of sake that produce a drizzle of golden flakes when shaken, like some very high-class seaside souvenir? Even golden cheesecake has become run of the mill. Less run of the mill is the 50,000 yen cup of coffee, laced with gold, that has been dreamed up by the Sogo department store in Nara, a city which has traditionally been known for its discreet tranquillity and ancient Buddhist temples. Over £200 a cup, give or take a sip. Thirsty customers – only four at a time to eliminate distractions – get to stare at a Renoir while they sip their coffee in a room apparently modelled after the residences of British royalty.

For about £4,000 a Tokyo department store will sell you a 24-carat gold-plated refrigerator. In the same store, but on a different floor, you can hand over £5,000 for an 18-carat gold golf putter: one customer bought five the minute they arrived in the store. The Japanese arm of Reebok, the company that makes athletes' training shoes, has brought out a pair of gold-plated baby shoes priced at £100 a pair. There is gold lipstick, eyeshadow and nail varnish. And, of course, there is the gold massage, after which you leave the beauty parlour with a skin that has been rubbed with a few sheets of gold foil and a nose that has been rubbed in an itemized bill totalling £130. 'With its rich, bright shine, gold offers smoother skin than any massage cream,' purrs the beautician's ad. Well, maybe it does. Even so, would you feel truly confident about your ironmonger's mental well-being if he suggested that you use solid gold bars for your garden gate so that you could be certain of avoiding rust?

If you can't be bothered to go out and shop or to be toned up, stay at home with a £22,000 Panasonic television set. It has a 110-inch screen and you, unfortunately, have a compact Japanese apartment, so you may well have to watch TV from halfway down the road to avoid squinting. Make the best of it: rent a current video and charge the neighbours to watch too. Older shoppers have been the keenest customers for the mink lavatory whatnots that are on sale at the swanky Mitsukoshi department store in Tokyo: £1,000 for the seat cover, £1,650 for a mat and £400 for a door-knob cover. They come in white, black, grey or three shades of brown. Do the owners put them in cold storage during the summer? Would you want your mink stole spending the summer in a refrigerator hanging alongside a loo seat cover?

Some of the luckiest beneficiaries of all this spare cash are Japan's dogs. Japanese dogs got used long ago to dating services, to weddings at which they exchange collars, to pets-only hot spring resorts where they can soak away their aches, to take-away food, to bikinis, to yoga and even to nappies. But isn't serving egg noodles in chicken soup to a peckish Tokyo spaniel taking anthropomorphism a little too far?

The Japanese are not alone in treating their pooches as if they were human beings until an impish fairy turned them into dachshunds. Some dog-owners in England give their Labradors tea and biscuits at around 4 p.m. Lucky terriers in France are slipped *foie gras* and croissants now and then. Dogs play along by learning to bark in their owners' tongue. 'Bow wow' in English turns into *wan wan* in Japanese. Now the Japanese have decided that their dogs can no longer live without instant pot noodles, Japan's favourite home snack. A pot sells for about £1.20, for some reason triple the price of the made-for-humans version. For dogs who prefer something a little more sumptuous on Saturday night than noodles, there is the Sogo department store in Yokohama, which will rustle up a gourmet take-away tray of steak, ham, sausages, cheese and white chocolate for about £50.

If they're in need of a break there is the Kinugawa International Hotel in the chic spa resort of Kinugawa, north of Tokyo. It has a pets-only hot spring where overstressed dogs and cats can peel off their designer jumpsuits, have a soak, peck at a light supper of boiled chicken and then sleep it off on a pet-size futon. The only trouble with fashionable Kinugawa is that it can become a bit of a catwalk as dogs show off their latest outfits. A favourite shopping place is Adachiya, a pet fashion boutique in Tokyo that can provide everything from pet bikinis and kimonos to a £5,000 mink coat. For dogs who draw the line at wearing fur, the Mitsukoshi department store stocks fake Burberry raincoats. When the rainy season is in full swing, business is brisk. Prices go up to about £60, depending on size. Team it with a casual Snoopy T-shirt, also from Mitsukoshi. Only £20. But avoid weekends. The crush can be awful, especially when the new season's lines arrive.

Of course, everything has a price. All this fancy food is producing some fancy illnesses. Pampered dogs in Japan are suffering from gum disease because they no longer chew enough bones to clean their teeth. More and more owners are taking their pets to vets to have the plaque scraped off. In between visits to the surgery they brush Fido's teeth every day with one of a range of special dog toothbrushes that sell for about £4 each. Flab is also becoming a bit of a problem, but not so much of a problem now that the Japan Trimming School has arrived to provide jogging machines and yoga classes for Rovers who can't resist that extra after-dinner mint. Some pooches get so fat they pop the buttons on their tuxedos and can move no more. Pet funerals have also become big business. There are now eighty pet cemeteries in Japan. Some of them charge up to £5,000 for a one-square-yard grave. More convenient is the doorstep facility provided by the 'Pet Angel Service': a woman dressed in a pink jumpsuit pops your dead loved one in an incinerator in the back of her van, you place some flowers on a little pink altar, she plays a tape of a shrill woman's voice that says, 'Thank you for taking care of me until now,' and then whoosh. You get to keep the ashes.

If Japan's elegant young ladies are willing to spend this kind of money on their pets, you can imagine how much more they are willing to spend on themselves. You can tell things are getting out of hand when Japanese shopkeepers start mentioning figures that you regard as a down payment on a Jaguar as the price of a decent pair of stockings. Take Yasuhiko Hotta, for example. He is the president of a company which for more than twenty years has been importing expensive clothes into Japan, like Krizia of Milan or Jaeger of London (don't be fooled into thinking that European designers charge European prices or even sell European goods: at Dunhill, items like Vicuna overcoats are made especially for the Japanese). Hotta, speaking with the

I-told-you-so confidence of someone who has always known the earth is round and is not very surprised that everyone else is finally coming to their senses, confided to a reporter: 'Ten years ago, consumers raised their voices, asking "How come a sweater costs 700,000 yen (that's £3,000 remember)?" But now consumers understand high-quality products are expensive.' Well, of course they are.

Ask Japanese shoppers why they spend thousands on Rolex watches, on Maud Frizon shoes and on Louis Vuitton handbags and they will tell you that they want to look different from everyone else who strolls the streets of Tokyo. It's a tall order. Tokyo is now the biggest market for almost every expensive European and American designer label. Japanese shoppers buy around 40 per cent of everything Chanel makes, for example. The streets of Tokyo have become a fashion parade. If you really want to stand out in Tokyo, your best bet is to stock your wardrobe from Woolworth.

Money used to get you only so far. One thing that Westernized Japanese could not wangle was a Western face. Western models hog subway posters, magazine advertisements and television commercials in Japan. If Plain Janes feel they have a tough time living up to cover-girl stereotypes, imagine how much trickier it is for Japanese girls. They can become as thin as a chopstick but still there's the slope of those eyes. A problem no more. If the fate of the Greeks doesn't warn the Japanese against the dangers of over-contemplation of the human form, nothing will. Apparently nothing does. The latest in Japanese cosmetic surgery will alter the single oriental eyelid into a rounder, doubled eyelid. You won't be mistaken for Marilyn Monroe, but it's a start. The cost can easily top £2,000. Ambitious teen pop idols have the operation before starting their singing career.

But teen pop idols are not the only young men obsessed with their looks. Young people's wealth has led them into posh boutiques, and an obsession with how they look in the mirror has spilled over into a fetish for hygiene. Men who wear crisp white shirts and sober ties to the office and take work home at weekends are shaving their legs and chests. Young Japanese women wash their hair twice a day and wear anti-bacterial 'deodorant blouses' that kill the smell of sweat. More and more Japanese carry disinfectant sprays in their pockets so they can clean their hands after holding on to straps on public transport. Catering to this obsession is big business. Cleanliness may not be next to godliness, but it makes the cash registers sing. For those who have forgotten to carry their disinfectant sprays, some Japanese lavatories now automatically wrap a film of plastic around the seat when the flush is pulled. Even in Japan's 'love hotels', where rooms are rented by the hour, both by lovers and by parents seeking a bit of privacy away from the paper-thin walls that separate their bedroom at home from their children's, the luridly decorated suites are spotlessly clean and come supplied with shampoo, toothbrushes and condoms.

Odourlessness ranks high in young people's priorities. One poll found that 66 per cent of Japanese men and 80 per cent of Japanese women went out of their way to remove all traces of body odour. In another survey, carried out by Shiseido, Japan's biggest cosmetics firm, 80 per cent of male students said they thought they had no chance with young women unless they were spotlessly clean. Saburo Kawamoto, a popular social commentator in Japan, sees this phenomenon as another sad by-product of modernization, taking Japan one more step away from the rice fields that many romantic Japanese still like to feel represent their true spiritual home. 'Working used to mean getting soiled with dirt or oil, but now people think that working and getting dirty are two different things.' Kawamoto is not the only one with a furrowed brow. 'If the love for cleanliness progresses further,' Yukio Suzuki, a marketing specialist at the Mitsubishi Research Institute, warns darkly, 'tolerance for uncleanliness will be lost.' Suzuki foresees possible discrimination against students and workers from Japan's Asian neighbours, 'countries with poor sanitation and less stringent social standards'. But society has already moved faster than Suzuki. Many Japanese take it for granted that other Asians, particularly those with darker skin, are slapdash when it comes to keeping themselves clean and fragrant, and that rubbing shoulders with them may not just be unpleasant but insanitary as well. When a Japanese friend once called the health ministry in Tokyo on my behalf to inquire whether any vaccinations were needed or recommended to visit a nearby Asian country, she was told that as long as I was travelling on a Japanese airline, say JAL or All Nippon Airways, then I would be fine, but if I was flying on another Asian national carrier, then it would do no harm and – between you and me – would be advisable to have a few injections, just to be on the safe side.

But what is a poor boy to do if girls want hairless scent bottles to take them out on Saturday nights? The peacock male is hardly confined to Japan, but the sort of young Japanese who have taken to removing all their facial and body hair by electrolysis are not necessarily the sort who stare moodily out of fashion magazines. 'Esthe Up', a beauty salon chain, set up special men-only shops when it found that about half its customers were men. Three quarters of its male clients come in for depilation, mostly for face, but also chest, legs and arms. Their average age is twenty-three and most of them are corporate warriors or students about to start their careers. The reasons for choosing body baldness vary. Some hate their hairy bodies, others say they need to get rid of the hair for work or because they are looking for a job. A small percentage admit to being sent there by their girlfriends. Many Japanese women turn their noses up at hairy men. 'It may be hard for non-Japanese to understand,' says one Tokyo beauty parlour manager, 'but it's not flattering to be hairy in Japan these days.'

Hygiene and hairlessness are so important nowadays that they represent two of the trump cards that young Japanese men play when they are trying to win over the girl of their dreams at Christmas. With so few Christians in the country, Christmas is not a religious affair in Japan, although there are Christmas presents, £120 Christmas trees and unconventional season's greetings (the one outside Nissan's Tokyo head office, for example, wishes passers-by 'Merry Christmas Hello Safety'). In Japan Christmas is a time when young men's minds turn to luring on to a futon the girl they have fancied for the past twelve months. Christmas Eve is the moment, a posh French restaurant and a two-hour slot in a 'love hotel' are the places, and a Tiffany necklace costing up to £1,000 is the inducement. Even cheapskates do well to escape with spending less than a month's pay for this night on the town. At these prices, for a once-a-year crack at the bullseye, you leave nothing to chance. You certainly don't wander around with excess hair or any trace of body odour. Even the magazines say so. *Hot Dog*, one of the most widely read of the young men's journals in Japan, counsels its insecure readers about everything to do with the big night, from when and how to pop the question, which restaurant and hotel to pick, and how to dress for sexual success. But there it is again, in *Hot Dog*'s 'Seven-day Grooming Technique to Succeed with Your Date on Christmas Eve':

Six days before: check body odour and clean your body. Five days before: wash and massage your face. Four days before: wash your hair, rinse it very well. Three days before: get rid of plaque in your mouth to prevent bad breath. Two days before: shave. One day before: set your hair with styling mousse. On the day: put on cologne. Extra tips: put on hand cream to make your hands smooth (to hold your girlfriend's hand). Clean your ears. If your feet smell, spray them. Use lip cream to smooth your lips (to kiss your girlfriend).

On the morning of the twenty-fifth you wake up and go to work. In Japan, Christmas is just another day.

So is all this just 'simply ridiculous, a healthy sign of the country's growing prosperity, or a manifestation of a growing ill in the nation's *nouveaux riches*'? Consider the Yokoyama family of Tokyo.

You and I might think of only 472 things we would rather spend £8 million on than a largish four-bedroom house in a humdrum part of Tokyo. Not the Yokoyama family. The Yokoyamas, more attuned to how far your yen goes at a Tokyo estate agent (not very), had their dream £8 million brown-brick home built for them in the summer of 1990. Another £120,000 went on importing furiously stuffed and gilded Italian sofas and tables made in the style of Louis-something-else. Huge reproduction Monets and Renoirs break up the walls without breaking the bank. The house is cordoned off behind black metal and gilt-tipped pikestaff railings. They blend into the backstreet scenery as quietly as a ferris wheel. But what makes the Yokoyamas' home really stand out from its small wooden neighbours is that it is one of few houses in the world that is 'fully automatic'. The Yokoyamas have installed a 128-button computer console in the kitchen that allows them to control every light switch in the house, start the bath running at precisely the temperature they choose (42°C, as it happens), lock all doors and programme air-conditioners to come on and switch themselves off at pre-set times. The console and the wiring cost over £20,000 alone. The appliances are extra. They have twenty-six air-conditioners connected to the system. Either they like to keep the air very chilled or they are worried about the atmosphere getting split ends. The air-conditioners cost nearly £1,000 each. The price soon adds up. But can you afford to be without it?

'Home automation' is the wave of the future. The Japanese lead the field. The *nouveaux riches* Japanese lead the order

books. You can, if you wish, telephone your computer on your
way home from work and tell it to start running your bath so
that it is ready by the time you open the front door. Or you can
telephone it to suck a certain amount of rice from a storage
chest into the automatic rice cooker and start preparing dinner.
You can call up and check that you locked all the doors. The
system's data base can handle the family housekeeping. By the
turn of the century, house automation is expected to be a
£4 billion-a-year business in Japan, a country where houses and
flats are so petite that you can usually cross from one end of
them to the other in less time than it takes to sneeze.

You might expect someone who felt drawn to such high-tech
gadgets, and who had £8 million to spare on a house, to have
created something snappily modern, architecturally clever. It is
hard to recall having entered a pricier home that wasn't half
supported by the National Trust. Harder still to recall having
entered so expensive a home that camouflages its price tag so
well. Partly, of course, this is a reflection of Tokyo's crazy land
prices. When the patch of land that houses the Imperial Palace in
central Tokyo is theoretically worth more than the whole of
California, then £8 million on a house is not bad going.

The interior was designed mostly by Mr Yokoyama, the
director of a machinery company owned and run by his father.
Mr Yokoyama wanted something in the spirit of the glittery
state guest-house in Tokyo, where bigwig foreign guests are put
up by the government. The Yokoyamas' house might pass for a
state guest-house only if the state were Disneyland. The main
doors in the downstairs living area are made of fancily etched
glass. They slide open and shut automatically when your passing
thighs trigger a sensor. If you pad about while talking on the
telephone near the door that leads from the kitchen to the
dining-room, the glass door swings open and shut like a frantic
metronome. The place has the feel of a chilly hotel lobby.

Miyoko Yokoyama, the lady of the house, says home automation is a boon. She stands in front of her 128-button console in the kitchen punching buttons like a check-out girl at Tesco's. 'If you press this button, the bath starts filling. We set the level of the water and the temperature. We set our shower to 40°C. There are forty lights connected to this console and twenty-six air-conditioners. You can also lock the front door, the front gate and the garage with these buttons here. Since I go to bed last among my family, I always check the console to make sure that everything has been turned off. We are using all the 128 buttons on our console, so we don't have room for any more gadgets. It has changed our lives. We don't have to waste our energy. The more rooms you have, the more convenient it is.'

But doesn't it make you lazy?

'I think it's convenient. That's a bit different to being lazy. Even with home automation you can't do everything lying down.'

Past Monet's *Water Lilies* in the dining-room ('The original is in the Museum of Fine Arts Boston' says the brass plate on the frame), past Renoir's *Dance at Bougival* ('ditto') in the chandeliered drawing-room, and up the staircase to the hotel-style bedroom. 'This is the good-morning button,' says Mrs Yokoyama at her bedside. 'You programme it so that when you wake up, whichever lights you want to come on, come on. This is the goodnight button. It turns them all off at night.'

The most daunting room in the house is the lavatory. The Yokoyamas have turned their backs on loo paper in favour of a space-age 'spray' toilet, a sort of sanitary equivalent of a wash and blow dry at the barber's that comes with the maker's promise that 'Your bottom will like it after three tries. Don't let people say behind your back that you have a dirty bottom.'

These new computerized super-loos are made by Toto, Japan's leading toilet maker and a company fired by a mission to turn

Tokyo into what it calls a 'Bottom Heaven'. They would be a dramatic innovation anywhere. But they are an especially dizzy advance for a country where, until fairly recently, a family's sanitary comfort depended on the direction of the wind and on whether the night-soil collector arrived on time. Many houses in Japan still lack indoor plumbing and you can sniff raw sewage in the drains of Ginza, Tokyo's swankiest shopping district. Already one in eight Japanese households has forsaken the old squatting toilets for these computer-controlled thrones. The Yokoyamas' 'spray' or 'shower' toilet is flanked by two consoles, each studded with knobs to heat the seat, to adjust the aim of the rinsing nozzle, to blast jets of warm air and to spray deodorant. It is a perfect marriage between Japan's obsessions with hygiene and high-tech. Many foreigners are too scared of being electrocuted by the sanitary circuitry to relax and feel pampered, or even go to the loo at all.

The Yokoyamas' model comes with a wireless remote control to turn on the front and rear sprinklers, presumably for those Japanese who have grown so used to remote-controlled televisions, telephone-answering machines and microwave ovens that they now distrust anything that comes without a keypad to fiddle with. Mrs Yokoyama says she hasn't a clue why their loo comes with a remote control. 'Ask Toto,' she says. Toto is too busy working on the next generation of super-loos, an 'intelligent toilet' which has built-in sensors that will monitor your heart rate, weight, temperature and blood pressure. Another sensor will perform a chemical analysis of your urine and tell you if anything is wrong. Also in the pipeline is a system to transmit all this information to a computer in a medical centre for further analysis. No mention yet of a surgery or prescription service, but it makes relying on an apple a day sound a bit old-fashioned.

Sociologists see more than convenience in the rise of these new super-loos. They say that the shower toilets, which sell for an average of £750, are also another way of burning up spare cash in rich Japanese pockets after the new Mercedes is in the garage with a set of gold-plated golf clubs tucked in the boot. Actually, the Yokoyamas have a Jaguar *and* a Mercedes in the garage. Also at Tokyo land prices, the space taken up by the Yokoyamas' loo is worth almost as much as a weekend estate in Wiltshire. It may deserve to be made a fuss of.

Toto has also tailored its products to meet the insecurities of Japan's coy female loo users. Modern, sophisticated Japanese women apparently feel shy about carrying loo paper back home from the supermarket. This has given rise to firms that specialize in delivering toilet rolls. It has also helped to promote these new paperless shower toilets. A trickier problem for Toto was noise. Japanese women flush several times – 2.5 times a visit on average, according to research – to camouflage possibly offensive noises. Toto has come up with a way to save water and cope with women's embarrassment by building a lavatory bowl that plays a recording of flushing water at the touch of a button. Simple, really. It didn't seem polite to ask Mrs Yokoyama if hers had this facility.

As advanced as the Yokoyamas' home is, it may soon look clumsy. Ken Sakamura, a scientist at Tokyo University, is working on a house that is governed by a thousand computers, sensors and electronic switches. Dr Sakamura's dream house is so smart that it opens and closes windows by itself, depending on the weather outside. Curtains close automatically and lights come on when the room gets dark. If you decide to practise the bongo drums late at night, the central computer will automatically close all doors and windows to avoid disturbing the neighbours.

Mrs Yokoyama, still punching away at the check-out till, is not itching for more gadgets just yet. Instead, this poor little rich girl dreams of a trip abroad. But she is held back by the strictures and obligations of Old Japan. 'We never travel abroad. I'd love to make a trip to Europe or America. But my father-in-law is too scared about having any member of his family go abroad. Unless my father-in-law allows us to go, my husband won't take me. My husband says he will take me abroad sometime, it's just that he doesn't want to upset his parents.'

What would the Yokoyamas make of Versailles?

They might well want to buy it. In fact, buying top European art has also fallen into the price bracket of a surprising number of Japanese. When Ryoei Saito, the wealthy head of Japan's second biggest paper manufacturer but not a noted art collector, coughed up over $160 million in less than a week in 1990 for Van Gogh's haunting *Portrait of Dr Gachet* and Renoir's *Au Moulin de la Galette*, the world's art dealers gasped. When he later confessed that he would have been willing to fork out $200 million for the two canvases, they fainted. When the buyer's identity became known, Miss Tomoko Inukai, a Japanese television commentator on social issues, said, 'Following these purchases, Japan's image as a *nouveau riche* nation has been aggravated.'

Saito must have felt hurt by the carping. He was hardly breaking new ground. More and more Japanese own masterpieces that the rest of us enjoy only on laminated table mats. Art experts reckon that in the boom years of the 1980s, four out of every ten top-quality paintings sold at the world's better auction houses found their way to Japan, neatly reversing the pattern of a century ago when priceless Eastern treasures filtered out to the West. In 1990, at the peak of the buying craze, Japan imported paintings worth $3.4 billion. But anonymous purchases, and the flow of some pictures through several dealers before they reach the final buyer, makes it hard to know exactly how much Western art is in Japanese hands.

Many of Japan's new art collectors, perhaps unable to squeeze a large gilded frame into a small Japanese front room, are opening little museums to show off their acquisitions. According to one estimate, five hundred new museums have opened up across Japan over the past decade, many of them in unlikely locations. One Japanese pinball-arcade millionaire houses his Picassos, Chagalls and Renoirs in a museum he built by the side of a billowing volcano in a remote part of southern Japan. Art lovers wanting to gaze at Picasso's *Les Noces de Pierrette*, which became the most expensive Picasso ever sold when it was knocked down to a Japanese car-parts company in 1989 for 300 million French francs, will have to trek down to a museum that the painting's new owners have built next to their race track in southern Japan. Michimasa Marauchi, who became rich by selling a few well-located rice paddies to hungry property developers, runs a furniture shop in a so-so Tokyo suburb in which he displays his spectacular collection from the Barbizon School, including ten Courbets and as many Corots. Masahiro Takano, who runs the Green Cab taxi company, has built the world's biggest collection of paintings by the French artist Marie Laurencin, very popular with the Japanese: the works are on show at an out-of-the-way hilltop resort.

So have the Japanese really become too rich for their own good? Do they have more money than they know what to do with? Amehiko Aoki, a well-known Japanese columnist, is one of many local commentators who despair at the glitz. 'It's a flash-in-the-pan extravagance that comes from living in rabbit hutches,' he says. 'I think it's sad.' Some foreign observers say the danger is that a society already obsessed with television and now worried far more about the cut of the latest outfits from Chanel than about life after *détente* or deforestation will contribute less and less to international culture. 'It's perfectly clear that Japan is a less attractive subject today than it was thirty or forty years ago,' says Edward Seidensticker, the author and award-winning translator of the novels of Yukio Mishima, among others. 'Too much money and too much television have had a bad effect on the arts. When Paris had money, it had great art. When New York had money it bloomed artistically. That hasn't happened here [in Japan]. Any country that has as much money as Japan and doesn't know what to do with it is dangerous.'

By Seidensticker's yardstick, Japan must be getting deeply dangerous. Just how much money Japan now has would surprise most foreigners. We know that many Japanese are very rich, that they go on the sort of four-carrier-bags-in-each-hand shopping sprees down Bond Street and Avenue Montaigne that once only movie stars, New York financiers and Third World dictators could afford. But what about serious, go-to-hell money? Yes, they have that too.

The inability of most Europeans or Americans to name more than a dozen really prominent Japanese men or women, dead or living, is one of those blind spots that has survived Japan's rise to wealth and glory. Even Japanese who are very big in Japan, and whose financial or political influence spreads abroad, have somehow stayed out of the paparazzi's flashlights. But in today's lists of the world's hugely rich you would search in vain for the names of Getty and Rockefeller. You would do much better to look, instead, for a brash, illegitimate Japanese tycoon called Yoshiaki Tsutsumi, a man who once proudly posed for a newspaper photo holding up one of his tattered shoes, patched together with black sticky tape. He likes taking snaps himself. Every year he makes a calendar of his landscape photographs which he sends to four thousand or so friends and acquaintances instead of the whisky bottles and £50 melons that usually change hands at New Year in Japan. But he seems to find it a nerve-racking hobby. 'My problem is the film,' he says, as if still pained by memories of past profligacies in the darkroom. 'If I have three or four shots left, I agonize over whether to get the roll developed as it is or use it up.'

In spite of this careful housekeeping, Tsutsumi has managed to fritter away several billion dollars in recent years, according to Forbes magazine, which is an awful lot of sticky tape and 35 mm camera film. But even when the chips are down and business has been tough, Forbes reckons that Tsutsumi still has over $10 billion left to play with. That buys a decent living even at Tokyo prices and has put Tsutsumi at the top of the list of the world's richest people for several years running. Forbes excludes the world's royalty from its sums on the grounds that they haven't really earned their money or their Monets.

Tsutsumi is unmoved by all the fuss, probably because most people in Tokyo think that Forbes has just scratched the surface of his real wealth. They value Tsutsumi's railways, property and hotels empire at nearer $400 billion, most of it privately and secretively owned. Shareholders of even public companies are kept in the dark about wheeling and dealing in their company's boardroom: to seek to know more than the little they are told would seem ungrateful, even vulgar, and might imply that shareholders suspected the board members of being untrustworthy. The financial affairs of privately owned firms are so tricky to fathom that Japan makes even Liechtenstein look indiscreetly unbuttoned.

However he does it, everything Tsutsumi touches seems to flourish. In 1978 he bought a run-down Japanese baseball team for peanuts. He renamed it the Seibu Lions, pumped cash into it and turned it into one of the best and most consistent championship winners in the professional league. Since in Japan personal obligations count, the team's fan club has swelled somewhat since it joined the Tsutsumi portfolio: many of Tsutsumi's faithful employees, even many of the strap-hanging commuters who squeeze into his company's railway carriages each morning, have switched their loyalties to the Lions. Tsutsumi owns two ice hockey teams, too. Even so, little is known about him. He gives fewer interviews than the Pope, shuns parties and is so unchatty that even a long-time friend confessed that he doesn't know whether Tsutsumi's three children are sons or daughters. Few people outside Japan have even heard of the reclusive billionaire, though his name is as familiar as sushi to most Japanese. This is not all that exceptional for someone who is probably richer than King David, who is widely hailed among his rivals as a genius in business, or who plays golf on one of his thirty-one golf courses with prime ministers and then entertains them elegantly in one of his sixty-five plush hotels, and who, some say, might even be prime minister himself one day.

As if this were not enough to keep him in the headlines in Japan, Yoshiaki also maintains a sizzling sibling rivalry with his elder half-brother Seiji, who is the legitimate son of their powerful and promiscuous father, the head of an empire almost as grand as Yoshiaki's even though he was all but written out of their father's will, a one-time student Communist and a part-time but critically successful poet and novelist. Understandably, the two billionaires' unsheathed hatred for each other is manna to Tokyo gossip columnists. It also has become a curious spectator sport in Japan, even though the breadth of the feuding and the twists of the intrigue would baffle all but Hollywood's most imaginative scriptwriters. Weaving racy tales of money, power, adultery and corporate conflict into a backcloth of fraternal rivalry, the history of the Tsutsumi family would have been hard to swallow even for Sam Goldwyn, the legendary Hollywood mogul whose idea of a good plot was one that began with a catastrophic earthquake and built up to a stunning climax from there.

An illegitimate but favoured son of one of Yasujiro Tsutsumi's mistresses, Yoshiaki Tsutsumi owes everything to his father, a sharp wheeler-dealer who made his money in property, his name in politics as an MP for thirty years, rising to become speaker of the house, and his reputation as a thrice-married man who kept pretty mistresses on the side. Yasujiro's buccaneering business style earned him the nickname 'Pistol'. His biggest coup was vacuuming up some of the best real estate in central Tokyo at bargain prices at the end of the Second World War from ruined members of the imperial family and associated aristocrats who could not rustle up the cash to pay their inheritance taxes. Typical of Yasujiro's cheek, he called the hotel chain that he built on this blue-blooded land 'Prince'. The Takanawa Prince, for example, was once the Tokyo mansion of Prince Takeda. The Tokyo Prince Hotel was built on the former cemetery of the Tokugawas, the shoguns who ruled Japan for two and a half centuries before the Meiji Restoration began in 1868.

Yoshiaki spent his schooldays accompanying his father on tours of building sites and property deals. He has tried to run the business he inherited in his father's autocratic style. 'Work three times harder than your employees do,' his father told him, 'and they will follow you.' But they have to move jolly fast to keep up. With the help of his helicopter, Yoshiaki manages to have his say, and his way, on almost everything in almost every part of his scattered empire. Best not to take too literally Tsutsumi's management philosophy that 'I like capitalism and liberalism and I hate control; that is why I entrust almost everything to my employees. It is important for their education that they are given some authority.' It is one of the privileges of being rich that nitpickers don't quibble when you say one thing and do another. No detail is too trivial for this tycoon. He chooses the colour of the sofas in his Prince hotels and the shape of the glasses in the restaurants. An expert skier who would put many professionals to shame, Tsutsumi prefers to slalom down mountains and uncharted forests and design his company's ski runs himself. He owns thirty-four ski resorts.

Famously rude and brutish, he barks orders to employees – 'I don't need employees with a fancy college education,' he once said, 'I want people who can do what I tell them' – and makes sure everyone is as frugal as he is. Towels in all the Prince chain of hotels are used for an extra year, after which they are used as rags in Yoshiaki's office. 'Customers won't come to stay at my hotels if the carpets are ageing or old-fashioned,' he said. 'But if carpets have to be changed, I tell my employees to cut up the old ones and use them in their offices.'

Then again, when Tsutsumi had an impetuous hunch one day that there was too much sugar in the little sachets that his hotel guests were receiving with their coffee, he demanded smaller ones. Within a day all his terrified employees in every corner of his empire had refilled the sugar bowls with sachets that better suited the boss's new sweetness scale. Tsutsumi says his stinginess was walloped into him by his father, who would 'beat me if I left any soya sauce on the side of my plate at dinner when I was little. He would say, "Why did you pour out so much soya sauce? Can't you work out something as simple as how much soya sauce you are going to need?"' It makes you wonder how the cuddly Yasujiro treated his less-favoured sons.

It certainly left its mark on Yoshiaki. 'Even now,' he says, 'I can't use a brand new memo pad because I feel sort of guilty about wasting paper. But I think it's important to feel that way. I own more than seventy companies and I have over 30,000 employees. I firmly believe that when they go to the toilet none of them would think of using more water or more paper towels than was absolutely necessary. If I were to come across someone on my staff who didn't put less food on his plate when he had no appetite and, as a result, left uneaten food without feeling guilty about it, I would sack them.'

Not surprisingly, nobody has much of an appetite for crossing Tsutsumi, especially if they are on his payroll. He commands the sort of awe from his staff that Emperor Hirohito used to command from the Japanese in his heyday, according to those who have witnessed Tsutsumi landing like an unexpected tornado at one of his hotels or ski resorts. An unalert employee was once caught smoking in front of him. Being a shrewd executive, Tsutsumi demoted not the employee, but the employee's boss, a far more effective punishment. 'The workers are terrified,' Taro Tawa, a journalist and long-time friend of Tsutsumi's, told a reporter. 'If his orders aren't carried out as soon as possible, thunder breaks out.' Tsutsumi passes off his gruff contrariness as a corporate asset. Kazunari Kobayashi, who wrote a book about him, notes, 'He often says things that are the complete opposite of what he is thinking. Questioned about his inscrutable face, he replied, "There's no president who would answer when he is asked where he would place his nuclear missiles. I never talk about my strategy."'

But Tsutsumi's life is not all battle plans and boardrooms. Like his father, he has a reputation as a ladies' man. An affair with a secretary hit the headlines of the scandal sheets. Sport is also a passion. In between making sure that his business is blooming, he also finds time to josh with influential politicians the way that his father did. Perhaps it is more accurate to say that influential politicians find time to josh with him. Although he loathes donating to anyone or anything, Tsutsumi is generous when it comes to his political friends. And Tsutsumi's 38,000 employees, their wives, husbands, sons and daughters comprise a useful army of voters at election time. In Japan employees usually set great store by what the boss thinks would be a healthy electoral outcome, for the company and the nation. When Yoshiaki's mother, Tsuneko Ishizaka, died in 1984, three former prime ministers, as well as the then prime minister

Yasuhiro Nakasone, attended the funeral. Tsutsumi's employees also bend to Yoshiaki's devotion to his father, who died in 1964 and is still rated by Yoshiaki as 'the greatest entrepreneur I've ever met'. Every New Year's Day, at five o'clock in the morning, while their families sleep, five hundred senior executives from various parts of the Tsutsumi empire gather at a cemetery in Kamakura, one and a half hours' journey outside Tokyo, to pay their respects to Yasujiro Tsutsumi's grave.

With all this to chew on, it is hardly surprising that Japan's gossip columnists feel themselves to be twice blessed that Yoshiaki Tsutsumi carries on a feud with his half-brother Seiji that makes Cain and Abel look chummy. Both brothers shun publicity, both are seen as quiet kingmakers behind the scenes in Japanese politics – although they naturally back different candidates – and both are tipped for even grander things ahead. Nobody would be surprised if one of them followed their father into front-of-house politics as well. But beyond that, the two are as similar as *Coronation Street* and *King Lear*. Seiji is as cultured and cool as Yoshiaki is gruff and fiery. Seiji is the son of Misao Tsutsumi, a noted poet. He wins literary prizes for his own poems, published under the pen-name of Takashi Tsuji; after working on his business affairs until 10 p.m. he retreats to his study to write until dawn. He gives generously to the arts, building museums and theatres, and to young artists. He donated £200,000 to keep Britain's National Poetry Library in funds. Yoshiaki was, until recently, head of the Japan Olympic Committee, but he is not very much interested in buying paintings or tasting culture.

Seiji inherited the right to the Tsutsumi name but almost nothing else when his father died. Perhaps the young Seiji was even more slapdash with the soya sauce than the sloppy Yoshiaki. But his seething sense of injustice quietly fired Seiji. He turned the obscure department stores he was bequeathed into the Saison

Group, now one of Japan's biggest and most dynamic retailing, hotel and credit empires. The centrepiece has been his chain of Seibu department stores, up-market, one-stop convenience emporia where customers can book a holiday, borrow the money to pay for it and buy everything, from clothes to a suitcase, that they might need for the trip. Many Seibu stores have top-notch art galleries. The service is so chic (and pricey) that even a packet of noodles in Seibu often comes gift-wrapped. Seiji's empire is not as big as his kid brother's, but it is grand enough to put Yoshiaki's nose out of joint.

The sibling rivalry is played out at arm's length, like chess-by-post. For example, Yoshiaki's hotels and resorts refuse to accept the Saison credit card, even though they accept almost all others. And, sensitive as he is, Seiji is not one to forget a grudge. In the middle of the funeral for Yoshiaki's mother at Tokyo's Zozo-ji temple, an advertising blimp scudded across the sky promoting the opening of a new store in Seiji's Seibu chain. Apparently, Seiji had still not forgiven the younger, illegitimate Yoshiaki for presiding over their father's funeral as chief mourner twenty years earlier.

Ironically, the fraternal jealousy oils the two brothers' business rivalry, spurring both Yoshiaki and Seiji to build larger empires than they might have done, were each less keen to drive the other into the ground. Yasujiro probably knew his sons well enough to realize that the surest way of expanding his legacy was to set one son against the other. Their rivalry has ensured that the Tsutsumi name flourishes in several diverse fields. Both brothers' business empires thrive. In a poll, eight hundred top Japanese executives, politicians, analysts and economists rated as 'opinion leaders' picked the Tsutsumi brothers as Japan's two most influential businessmen for this decade.

Having virtually carved up Japan between them, both are now looking to flex their muscles abroad, mostly in the hotels and leisure business. Seiji's move away from department stores and into Yoshiaki's domain of hotels has added a tang to the sibling battle. Seiji entered the hotel business by opening a discreet and exclusive hotel in Tokyo's fashionable Ginza district. Then in 1987 he teamed up with Club Med to open a ski resort in Japan, within snowball-throwing distance of one of Yoshiaki's ski resorts. A year later Seiji bought the one-hundred-strong Inter-Continental luxury-hotel chain. Japanese shoppers who have learned to rely on the quality of his Seibu department stores know they can trust the service in the hotels. Also they can settle their bills with the same Saison credit card that they use at their local store in Japan. As the wealthy Japanese get used to taking longer holidays, there will be fat profits for hoteliers who can make them feel at home from home: that is why more and more hotels in places visited by Japanese, like Korea and America, have bedrooms with futons and *tatami* mats on the floor and have tuna and octopus sushi on the room-service menu. Yoshiaki is not about to allow his brother to swim too far upstream. He too is buying up hotels overseas, in places like Hawaii, Alaska and Singapore, and he is pushing into areas like cable television. The rivalry is likely to get spikier as the battlefield expands overseas.

The brothers appear to be relishing the challenge of playing out their battle on a larger map than Japan. This might finally introduce the name of Tsutsumi to an audience that usually catches such adventures only on the more far-fetched television mini-series.

5. Oh Why Do the Japanese Travel?
A Time and No Motion Study

Moving with the crowds – the commuter crush – taxis to nowhere – flying, off the handle – the tourist boom – so why do the Japanese travel?

People who rarely travel much beyond their local video shop have a habit of saying snappy things like 'It's better to travel than to arrive.' But try it out on most Japanese and they just blink in amazement. For most Japanese, travelling is about as little fun as you can have.

Roads in and into Tokyo are so choked with traffic that taxi rides are best suited to people who want to catch up on their sleep, write long letters home, or learn all of Shakespeare's sonnets off by heart. Airline seats must be booked months in advance. The chances of walking into an empty train carriage in Japan are thinner than rice paper. There are no off-peak train tickets because there are no off-peak trains.

Like cramped houses and five-a-side tennis, travelling cheek to cheek is one of the prices 123 million Japanese pay for living in a country built for maybe half that number. Japan is so crowded that even a ramble on a remote hillside usually turns out to be as tranquil as Twickenham during the Calcutta Cup. The quarter of Japan's population that lives in greater Tokyo suffers the worst. Few suffer more than the commuters who bend and fold and buckle themselves into the morning commuter trains. Opening up a newspaper is a pipedream. Breathing is the challenge.

Shinjuku, far and away the world's biggest railway station, sits on the western edge of central Tokyo. It gives and takes most of the commuter beating. You can find out more about the horrors and pleasures of modern Japanese life by spending ten gawping minutes in Shinjuku station than by reading a dozen industry textbooks. More than three million people file through Shinjuku station every day. Twenty railway lines send three thousand trains criss-crossing through the station daily. The metal hand punches that the ticket collectors use to clip tickets at Shinjuku wear out after three days. If you are looking for frenzy, this is it.

Taking a stroll through Shinjuku station is as ludicrous an idea as taking a stroll through Pamplona when the bulls are running. People move through Shinjuku faster than most cars move in second gear. Somehow, they cope. Even more remarkably, the station copes. On the busiest lines, trains arrive every ninety seconds and never run late. You could set your watch by them, though, all in all, it's probably easier to set it by the platform clocks, which also keep perfect time.

Let's take a typical morning at Shinjuku. It is sunny, it is spring, and it is shortly after eight o'clock. We are on the platform of the Yamanote circle-line train, the world's busiest railway line. We have reached the platform after queueing for a while on the steps approaching the platform. We will have to queue a while more before we get close enough to stand a chance of fighting our way on to a train. We can pass a few minutes by looking about us.

Shinjuku station is within spitting distance, in one direction, of a busy web of shopping streets; in another of the former imperial gardens, where Emperor Hirohito's funeral took place before a huge collection of world leaders in 1989; in another of the nest of 'love hotels', where parents who have no privacy in their tiny homes rent luridly decorated rooms by the hour next door to courting couples and shadier pairings; and of Kabukicho in another, Tokyo's gangster-run red-light district. When people say 'spitting distance' in Tokyo, they often mean it. Japan may frown on the practice of blowing noses in public, but it isn't bothered about spitting. Usually only men indulge. Spitters can complicate life on a crowded train platform, though not as much as blue-suited office workers who urinate where they must after a few evening beers. Happily, it is morning.

We have missed the next train too. Somehow, hundreds of people got off the train and hundreds more got on without bumping into each other or creating any measurable cracks in the human wall before us. Certainly the platform seems no emptier or airier. Most of those who have got off head for another platform, for another train, maybe one of the two underground lines that pass through Shinjuku. *En route* they have some morning rituals. First of all, many of them dump their newspaper in the bin, which serves as a sort of informal media swap shop. They might pick out another to tide them over the next lap of their journey. This is something of an odd habit because the main Japanese papers, unlike British or American ones, are very nearly identical. You could start an editorial in the *Yomiuri* newspaper, move on to the *Asahi* and end with the *Mainichi* – Japan's three biggest selling dailies – and not detect the join. This makes the degree of conformity in Japan less baffling. Each day millions of Japanese read almost the same stories and editorials, even though they take different newspapers. They digest the same facts and opinions. This goes some way towards explaining why tea-break squabbles at the office are rare and why the same political party has been in power in Japan for four decades.

Passing the platform kiosk some will stop for a magazine, some for a tonic or vitamin drink. Some of these pricey pick-me-ups contain viper's blood, which is apparently an aphrodisiac. These lines sell better in the evening. The kiosk also sells handkerchiefs, ties and white shirts. All Japanese carry handkerchiefs to dry their hands because of the rarity of towels or hand-drying machines in even the poshest office washrooms. For some reason, you can buy a tie almost anywhere in Japan. Souvenir shops sell them. Some religious shrines even sell them. If you're the sort of man who gets anxious if he can't pick up a tie in a hurry should the need suddenly arise, then Japan is the place for you. Now, the white shirts. I have never actually seen anyone buy a white shirt from a station kiosk, but presumably they would not stock them if they did not sell. It is hard to imagine that any man, however absent-minded, would forget to put on a shirt before leaving home. I assume customers either come dishevelled from the 'love hotels' or bedraggled from the nearby capsule hotels and need a clean change of shirt in a hurry. Capsule hotels specialize in small, coffin-sized bedrooms. Cheaper than normal hotels, they are an affordable way for drunk office workers who have missed the last train back to a distant dormitory town to avoid a £200 taxi fare home.

The circle-line platform is still thick with people. A fresh batch has arrived and somehow mingled into the crowd. Many of these people began their journeys two hours earlier, travelling to Shinjuku on one of the six private railway lines that decant commuters into the basements of the many department stores built on top of the station. This tidy set-up is cleverly Japanese. The department stores built the railway lines in the first place, to deliver customers from the suburbs into their shop. Often they built the suburb as well. The geographic arrangement is now convenient only for those who make a habit of doing some department-store shopping on their way to work. For the rest of the millions who commute into the capital, the detour just adds to the miles of corridors and shopping arcades they have to cover to get from one railway line to another inside the Shinjuku jungle. Anyone who regularly changes trains at Shinjuku and takes other exercise as well is usually a keep-fit fanatic.

Another train pulls in and this time we have a chance. We are standing right in front of the yellow dots on the edge of the platform that signal where the train doors will stop. They always stop in front of the dots. Various guards, flag-wavers, megaphone announcers and white-gloved body-pushers are guarding, waving, announcing and getting ready to push. A Moses-like path opens up for those leaving the train and we swivel into the carriage. The sensation is similar to walking into a wardrobe chock full of thick winter coats and randomly folded duvets. When the carriage is full, the body-pushers ignore nature and compassion and squeeze a dozen or two more on board. One assumes they must work on piece rate.

All in all, this is not an attractive sight. Fortunately, few morning commuters have a habit of taking snaps for the photo album. Whether you make this journey in a position that allows you to breathe occasionally is down to luck. You may well find yourself giving your unintended but undivided attention to a middle-aged man's scalp problems. We could, if we wanted, let go of our briefcase without fear of it falling to the ground: the bodies are too tightly pressed together. Sometimes it is safest to let go. As bodies get on and off the train you find your arm, still clutching the case, wrapped around some lady's midriff. This seems rude if you have not had a chance to introduce yourself first. It can also be misinterpreted. Gropers are not uncommon. Some men read a book, held with both hands at head height. Of course, it is impossible to read in this position on a busy train. The men are merely signalling that any straying hands in the carriage are not theirs. This is our stop. All things considered, it is an advance on arriving by horse and cart, but only just.

The Japanese are masters of making the best of things, including a shortage of habitable land, a lack of natural resources and prices that make Westerners faint. They have grown so used to crowds that an empty beach makes them suspicious and uncomfortable. Their trains are crowded, but they are also clean, graffiti-less, safe and highly reliable. It is difficult to recall that a couple of decades ago Japan's railways were plagued by disruptions from striking workers. Timetables went haywire. Nowadays, if one of the country's famous Shinkansen bullet trains is delayed by a couple of minutes, there is a stream of apologies over the intercom system. If it is more than fifteen minutes late, it usually makes the main evening news bulletins. Japanese trains are clean. Station chiefs are not caught off guard every time it rains or when leaves fall on the track. The food is fresh, usually topped up or changed at every big station, it is generally appetizing and it is trundled frequently through the carriages. On the bullet train, the trolley pushers and most of the ticket collectors will bow deeply to passengers on entering and leaving the compartment. Foreign visitors who are spared the rush-hour madness go home envious. The Japanese are not only unbowed by the hardships, they remain dauntingly eager. One rail line into Shinjuku runs English conversation classes for the crushed but self-improving commuters.

It is difficult to accept that the sleek bullet trains, which were launched in 1964 in time for the Tokyo Olympic Games, still offer such a superior service to most of their Western rivals. France's Train à Grande Vitesse, the TGV, can better the bullet train's top speed of 160 m.p.h., but the bullet train's record for punctuality and safety (apart from a few suicides, there have been no fatal accidents in the train's history) is hard to fault. The bullet train is no longer something special in Japan: twenty-two Shinkansen trains run between Tokyo and Osaka every hour. They are on routine, everyday service, carrying 1,340 people per train, each train about 400 yards long. In all, they have carried more than three billion passengers. Given the reliability of Japanese trains and the awful traffic jams on Japanese roads – six-hour tailbacks are routine on Sunday evening road traffic back into Tokyo and bank-holiday jams are notorious – it is surprising that railways have been losing out in recent years. The boom in Japanese car production in the 1960s made Toyotas and Nissans affordable. Whereas in 1970, railways and cars carried about half each of the nation's passengers, nowadays about one in three goes by train and about 60 per cent of passengers prefer to drive. And if they are not driving their cars, they're usually washing and waxing them.

Japanese cars are always spotlessly clean, usually white, and rarely more than four years old. (Unlike foreign manufacturers, who happily stick to one design for anything from seven to fifteen years, Japan's car-makers revamp their models every four years. Most customers, loyal to one make throughout their life, like to keep pace with the latest version of their Toyota or Honda.) The chauffeurs of the black limousines that purr patiently outside the top restaurants in Tokyo's Ginza or Akasaka entertainment districts spend their evenings brushing imaginary dust off their car bonnets with huge feather dusters. When it is raining, they use a sort of large windscreen wiper blade to wipe away the unsightly raindrops that are marring the mirror sheen of the bodywork. Naturally, this thankless toing and froing with the wiper-blade contraption lasts as long as the rain does, but the chauffeurs seem to regard the task as being as natural as bringing in the washing from the line when the heavens open.

A ludicrous sort of MOT car-inspection system called the *shaken* also plays a part in Japan's thirst for new cars. After three years on the road every car in Japan has to undergo a biannual check-up to make sure it is roadworthy. In England, an MOT test costs a few pounds plus the charge for any repairs needed to bring the car up to scratch, although with a three-year-old car, given the reliability of most car marques today, repairs should be minimal. In Japan, where manufacturers are so confident of their automobiles that their warranties often last three years anyway, the *shaken* sets you back at least £700. It is a bit of a racket that has been engineered by the Japanese garage industry, but car-makers are just as pleased to see it continue because many car owners prefer to plough the £700 into a new model from the showroom.

The result is that Japan has more second-hand cars than it knows what to do with. In recent years it has found a ready market for these used cars in not-so-well-off countries, like Russia, and places like New Zealand, which has no native car industry. New Zealand has been importing more than 80,000 of these cars a year. Ireland and some of Japan's Asian neighbours have also been eager customers for Tokyo's cast-offs.

Another reason why Japanese prefer to drive themselves is that the alternative is a taxi. Japan's taxi-drivers are not the country's best-loved feature. The Japanese and Western visitors both have their complaints.

Many young boys wonder what it might be like to be the Invisible Man. Many adult Westerners looking for a cab after a night out in Tokyo find out. What they discover is that to most Japanese taxi-drivers they do not exist. There are many reasons for this, some intriguing, some cultural, but none quite consoling enough to put you in a forgiving mood. About one fifth of the formal complaints lodged every year in Tokyo by Japanese passengers concern a taxi-driver's refusal to take a passenger where he wanted to go. But at least these would-be passengers got to talk to the cabbie before being spurned. Being ignored altogether is a different matter. You could, of course, start signalling wildly, but you run the risk of being run over by drivers who are bemused by the sight of this foreigner waving both arms like a frantic groundsman on an airport runway.

93

Naturally, the competition for taxis in Tokyo is fierce. As the hostesses from the bars and restaurants of Tokyo's main night-time haunts in Ginza and Akasaka (where the businessmen and politicians go) and in Roppongi (the young people's fashionable catwalk) bow their customers out on to the pavements, battle begins for a taxi home. Naturally the bigwigs slide off in their chauffeur-driven sedans, company flags flapping on the bonnet. Elderly men in dark suits and high spirits are escorted out of executive, £500-a-head dining clubs by young geishas in silky pink kimonos. Sometimes the silky pink kimonos accompany their charges into the back seat of their limousines, presumably to make sure they make it to their front doors, in case the chauffeur has forgotten the address. The rest of us take our chances on the pavement.

In a country in which form is only slightly less important than breathing – in some more extreme cases, more important – the technique for hailing a taxi is important. Shouting or waving is vulgar and, anyway, Japanese ears attuned to '*Takushi*' do not easily recognize the similar, but European, 'Taxi'. Instead, stand face on to the traffic. Extending your arm horizontally, gently paddle your fingers to and fro, as if testing the water temperature in an imaginary bath installed at shoulder height. Now watch the late-night street cabaret.

Spotting a Westerner, the driver of the first available taxi (watch out for their first clever trick: vacant taxis in Japan show a red light in the window, occupied cabs a green one) will look fixedly at the traffic lights ahead, even though there are none. The second will temporarily have averted his eyes to adjust the radio. The third, who sighted the Westerner a fraction too late to look convincingly distracted elsewhere, simply swerves danger-ously into the middle of the road, as if he were steering a bumper car at a funfair. All three cabs will screech to a halt to pick up a Japanese fare just five yards further up the road. You

can, of course, try to stop cab drivers from realizing that you are
not Japanese. By wearing a balaclava mask, for example. One
often successful trick is to hide your features behind a large,
black umbrella, though carrying a large, black umbrella on a hot
summer's night is a bore and hiding behind its canopy just seems
to invite unwelcome stares.

What really confuses Westerners in Tokyo is that in the
world's less scrupulous capitals, foreigners are sought out by
taxi-drivers the way snake-oil salesmen in the Wild West used to
seek out gullible old fools. But Tokyo's always well-dressed and
white-gloved taxi-drivers are, on the whole, fairly honest. If you
leave your wallet on the back seat, they will try to track you
down. If they do not know an address – which happens
frequently in a city that has few street names and in which a
dinner invitation without a detailed accompanying map is a
useless dinner invitation – most Tokyo cabbies will try to look it
up before flicking on the meter.

This is a pleasant courtesy, since the flag falls at more than £2
and proceeds to jump more swiftly and more regularly than a
hurdler doing the 400 metres. But sadly, the fact is that more
often than not this modest map-reading makes no difference
whatsoever. It is generally safest to allow a Tokyo taxi-driver
twenty minutes to pinpoint his target once he is within, say, fifty
yards of your destination. It is said that the anonymous maze of
streets in Tokyo was devised to confuse any enemies who might
land in the capital, but it has all backfired terribly: when first
visiting an unfamiliar house or office, even Tokyo natives like to
be met by their hosts at the nearest landmark, like a subway
station, and escorted from there, like a child.

Just as confusing, Japan seems to have only one template for
its town centres, which seems a sign of remarkable laziness in a
country which is so feverishly inventive in other spheres: stand
with your back to any suburban train station and you would be

hard pressed to guess where in Japan you are since the urban landscape is identical. There is always a pachinko pinball parlour more or less opposite, a middle-market department store to one side and a knot of bars and restaurants to the other. Even Japanese find it difficult to locate distinguishing marks.

If getting around Tokyo streets baffles Japanese, it baffles foreigners even more. Taxi-drivers must know that most foreign passengers would not realize if they were being taken for an extra-long ride. Also most foreigners, unused to a country where tipping is unknown, would probably pay a percentage over the meter reading. Yet Tokyo taxi-drivers refuse all blandishments and return all tips. Unfortunately, they also often refuse Western passengers as well. What is the problem? Well, in fairness, there isn't *always* a problem. Some Tokyo taxi-drivers are charming and friendly. Some like to practise their English. Some like to tell you what they think of the prime minister. One, trying kindly to while away the hours in a traffic jam, twiddled his radio until he found an English-speaking station that he thought might keep me amused. It was clear he could not understand what was being said. It was a Japanese station broadcasting an English lesson – useful in case I had forgotten how to buy stamps in a post office, but otherwise not all that educational or entertaining. But it was a nice thought.

A more usual journey starts like this. You somehow hail and get into a cab before the driver realizes who you are. Once you are inside, it is tricky for him to throw you out because passenger doors in Japanese taxis are swung open automatically by a button next to the driver, so he can hardly accuse you of barging into his car. Next, you tell him where you want to go. The chances are that this will be met by a bellowing noise that starts deep in the stomach and sounds like the end-of-day klaxon at a factory. It is the Japanese equivalent of 'You what?'

He might pretend that he doesn't understand your Japanese.

You must be firm. If you have a map to hand over, you have him on the run, even though he might turn it this way and that, as if he was trying to work out which way up to hang a Jackson Pollock canvas. More likely than not he will realize he is beaten and start the meter. To teach you a lesson, and to make sure you do not do such a cheeky thing again, he will give you a ride second only to a fairground helter-skelter. If you play along and say 'faster, faster', he will usually slow down. Then he might repeat your destination slowly, over and over again, as if it were somewhere only wild beasts would go. Often it is as mysterious as Oxford Street might be to a London cabbie or the Empire State Building might be to a New York cabman, so this constant murmuring of 'Oxford Street . . . that's a tricky one . . . Oxford Street, you say . . . Oxford Street, eh . . .' tends to grate after a while. Best to tell him that you are doing him a favour by leading him to one of the city's busiest thoroughfares. This sometimes elicits the klaxon-like bellow, which is then followed by silence.

What most taxi-drivers feel too uncomfortable to tell you to your face is that they do not like to pick up Westerners because Westerners tend not to live a two-hour drive into the suburbs and Westerners often cannot speak enough Japanese to guide the driver through those final, crucial fifty yards of backstreets. Unless you know where you are going you can be standing outside a house and not know that it is the house you were meant to be inside, three quarters of an hour ago. If you see a Westerner in a Tokyo side-street with a bottle of wine in his hand calling out someone's name, he is not drunk, he is merely trying to locate his host. The ones calling out names, but without a bottle in their hand, are hosts trying to locate their guests.

Unlike taxi-drivers in many other countries, Japanese cabbies hate taking passengers on short journeys. Although £2 for a three-hundred-yard cab ride (a common mistake made by new visitors who have yet to pinpoint their hotel on the city street map) may seem a lot to you, it will just about buy your taxi-driver a coffee in Japan. The journey from Tokyo's Narita airport into the centre of town costs about £100 if there is no traffic, at least twice as much if there is. Corporate expense-account entertainers will be given chits by their offices to hand to taxi-drivers to cover their £100 taxi rides home to suburbs late at night. The streets of Ginza are carpeted at night with pre-booked taxis, their meters running up huge sums while they wait for executives to leave their favourite hostess bars after one last burst of 'My Way' or of a Japanese love ballad on the karaoke machine. Persuading Tokyo's taxi-drivers to give up all this for a £2 ride is like trying to tempt mating pandas out of their cages in the zoo with the offer of a currant bun – only less successful.

Japanese taxi-drivers can obviously tell Westerners at a glance, but what criteria do they use to decide how to discriminate against Japanese would-be customers? Well, when things get busy, cabbies have ways of distinguishing passengers who will run up a large fare on the meter. Late at night, women and teenagers tend not to be travelling as far as men, so they are left stranded on the kerbside along with the foreigners. Drivers say that any woman living far away from Tokyo would catch the last train home, so those flagging taxis must be locals. Men over fifty also tend to be ignored on the grounds that they are old enough to have bought their houses before Tokyo property prices went through the roof, and so probably live in or very near town. Drunken businessmen are also unappealing because they fall asleep before directing the driver to their address, so that wipes out another large slice of late-night business. Carrying a large briefcase helps: taxi-drivers think it means that you live far enough from the city to work on the train into town. Also, if you are carrying an umbrella on a fine day, cabbies assume that you have travelled in from somewhere far enough away for it to have different weather from Tokyo, so you may well be lucky. It's a trying way to get home at the end of a hard day. But if everyone attempting to get from one place to another gave up at the first sign of adversity, the nation would probably never get out of bed in the morning.

Even fleeing the big cities for the countryside, or escaping from Japan altogether for a holiday, is no guarantee of trouble-free travelling. Especially if you are planning to leave or re-enter Japan by aeroplane. Many transport economists and government officials believe there is some kind of link between a country's transport infrastructure and its economic development. When British ministers get into a flap about, say, France's plan to expand Charles de Gaulle airport in Paris it is because they fear that Heathrow will fall behind, European business will flow to France and economic growth in Britain will suffer. It might calm them all down to fly to Tokyo and see just how vibrant an economy you can have in spite of relying on an airport that would make many Third World nations blush with shame.

You can spot the tell-tale look of a foreign businessman arriving for the first time at the chaos that is Tokyo's Narita airport. The look says: 'If this is the best that Japanese enterprise can muster, surely the West can't have too much to worry about.' By his second visit he is as angry as everyone else who has to jostle through the crowds and the squalor. This clogged funnel into Japan has become a test of a businessman's commitment. If he is really serious about doing a deal with the Japanese, he will not mind spending over two hours in the immigration hall, paying the £100 or more for the two-hour taxi ride into Tokyo, or wasting most of a day doing the same thing on his way out of the country. Does he need to change his schedule in a hurry? Sorry, most flights have been booked up for months. There is only one runway at Narita, compared with three at

Heathrow and five at New York's Kennedy airport. This helps to limit the number of flights to and from Tokyo and to inflate the price of air tickets to a point where it generally costs twice as much to fly from Tokyo to anywhere as it does from anywhere to Tokyo. Would the visiting business traveller like to catch a flight to Hong Kong or Bangkok at the end of a day's meeting? Sorry, most flights to Asian destinations stop at around 6 p.m. A few long-haul flights leave later, but there is a curfew after 11 p.m., which makes the daytime congestion that much worse. Everyone realizes that Narita ranks as a business-school case study of mis-planning and mismanagement.

Built to handle 7.5 million passengers a year, it is already handling nearly three times that number, with more than thirty million passengers expected by the end of the century. A second runway is being delayed because farmers owning 2 per cent of the planned building site have kicked up a fuss. The need for consensus in Japan forbids heavy-handedness in forcing them to sell. Occasional protests by radicals who held up the opening of Narita until 1978 have added to the headaches: increasingly, passengers miss flights because of the traffic that builds up outside the airport, which is ringed by barbed wire and patrolled by long-faced policemen in full riot gear. An International Air Transport Association (IATA) report has concluded that Japan's airport capacity problems are 'the most critical' in the Asia–Pacific region, a region for which Japan has become the economic hub. The airlines that have slots are frustrated, but not as frustrated as the forty carriers still waiting for landing rights.

Not surprisingly, compliments about Narita airport are rarer than an upgrade from economy to first. It makes travelling through Heathrow feel like lunching at the Savoy. Bear in mind that business travellers are generally far better catered for than tourists, and you get some idea of how much fun the Japanese have when they pack their bags for Hawaii and Hong Kong. But still they do, knowing very well that the most expensive hotel in Hong Kong is cheaper than the sleaziest bed-and-breakfast in Japan and dinner in Bangkok costs less than a packet of Kleenex in Tokyo.

More than ten million Japanese travel abroad each year, about 85 per cent of them tourists heading for America, South Korea, Hong Kong, Taiwan, Singapore, France, Germany and Thailand, in that order. These tourists spend more than $30 million a year. Japanese spend more when they are abroad than any other nation's tourists, and they bring back twice as much luggage as they take with them. It is customary for Japanese to bring back souvenirs for everyone from their mothers to their dry-cleaners when they go on a trip, even if it's only a weekend in the country. That is why you always see Japanese buying tins of Fortnum & Mason teas and Chanel handbags as if they were in a cash and carry supermarket. Many short-break holidays to places like Hong Kong or New York are specifically designed as shopping trips so that Japanese can take advantage of buying things like Japanese-made personal stereos at cheaper prices than they would find in Tokyo. Young office girls sometimes fund one of their circle to fly off by herself with a communal shopping list: these are the girls who walk into Tiffany on Fifth Avenue and order fifteen silver open-heart necklaces, a bauble that no self-respecting Japanese girl's jewellery box can be without.

Nevertheless, the Japanese generally prefer travelling in packs. They even try to travel at the same time. During the week-long clot of national holidays that fall in early May and which have come to be known as 'Golden Week' to the leisure-starved Japanese, everyone throws himself into a vacation. Naturally when all 123 million Japanese decide to go on holiday at the same time, fun flies out of the window. Golden Week turns into a crazy carnival of fifty-mile traffic jams, day-long waits at airports and standing-room-only trains. Anyone at all serious about travelling by plane or train will have booked their seats by the previous winter at the very latest.

Naturally, because they travel in such numbers, because they sometimes think that everywhere is as safe as Japan and because most Japanese still wander round with fat wads of cash in their back pockets rather than with a concertina of credit cards in their wallets, they have become easy prey for foreign bandits. At Narita airport you could leave your suitcase unattended for a couple of hours and it would still be there when you returned. At some foreign airports, suitcases are stolen when they are passing through the customs hall X-ray machine. This inexperience is one of the reasons why Japanese roam Venice and London in posses of fifty, following a Japanese-speaking tour guide waving a yellow flag. The group offers them safety. If they stray from the group they fear that they will be raped, robbed and nobody in the Gucci boutique will be able to explain the prices clearly.

Still, the Japanese abroad are easy and easily identifiable targets. The government has got worried enough about the problem to issue warning pamphlets to Japanese travellers, with suggestions such as 'Do not trust people who appear to be sympathetic, who mumble a few words of Japanese or pretend an interest in Japan, especially if you meet them at airports or tourist spots . . . Do not eat what they offer you and never invite them to your hotel room.' Other dangers, the pamphlet says, include sleeping powders in soft drinks in Russia, Turkey and Hong Kong, gambling in Malaysia and drugs in India and Nepal. The Philippines is dangerous, full stop. A *Self-defence Handbook* published by the Japanese Overseas Enterprises Association urges travellers not to decorate their luggage with Japanese flags and to avoid attaching labels showing their names in Japanese. It recommends, instead, identifying suitcases with names like 'T. Smith' and 'J. Williams'. So the next time you are waiting to pick out your holdalls at some airport carousel and fifty-three suitcases belonging to someone called 'T. Smith' trundle down the chute, do not automatically jump to the conclusion that an extravagant fellow passenger has just run up a huge bill for excess baggage. The chances are that it's only another Japanese tour group about to hit town.

6. If the Media are the Message, the Wires Must be Crossed

Television – advertising – the world's most powerful advertising agency – keeping Japan under control – newspapers – adult comics – the rush for Hollywood

If a country gets the media it deserves, you would have to wonder what Japan had done that was so unforgivable. It is no quirk of fate or language that Japan has not matched exports of its highly regarded television sets with sales to Europe and America of its highly derided television programmes. No one lost money underestimating the Japanese public's taste for schmaltzy TV dramas and silly quiz shows, both often spiced with a pinch of violence, voyeurism or mild pornography that contrasts uneasily with Japan's popular image as a nation that is largely law-abiding, hard-working, discreet and politely prim.

Often you catch yourself staring at Japanese television with the grim fascination of someone watching an old episode of *Crossroads*, wondering how much worse it could possibly get. But the Japanese, at whom it is, after all, aimed, devour it. Although Japanese houses are small, few have only one television set. Many have four, one of which might well be in the loo. Watching television is more popular than almost anything else. You can watch telly in taxis. A Japanese electronics company has produced a slim television that snaps into a Filofax. Can 123 million Japanese all be wrong?

NHK, Japan's public broadcasting network born to live up to and match the ideals of the BBC, runs two television channels that aim for sobriety and quality – they roughly mirror the BBC1/BBC2 split – and a clutch of radio stations, including a world service. NHK is the face that Japan would like to show to the outside world. Nothing too ritzy, too garish, too controversial, too trendy, just neatly dressed presenters who bow to the unseen audience at the beginning of every broadcast. Its radio presenters probably also bow before reading the news into the recording studio's microphone. NHK is funded by a licence fee, not advertising. It has also scored something of a success beaming two satellite channels into Japanese homes, broadening the general diet to include films, sport and foreign news broadcasts, including snatches of BBC and CBS news, albeit at rather disorienting hours because of the time difference between Tokyo and London. The remainder of Japan's airwaves are thrown over to five independent national networks that fight viciously for audiences and advertising in an age when remote-control technology enables us all to graze through the channels in every commercial break. The television stations, which have few restrictions on what they can transmit, delight in coming up with ever more bizarre ways to keep their viewers loyal.

Like all modern television stations anywhere, Japanese broadcasters pad their schedules with chat shows and quiz games. Some of them are of the vaguely disturbing 'Endurance' type, popularized in Britain by Clive James, in which contestants are forced to do things like sleep in a coffin full of rats, or swim naked in an icy sea, or find out how long they can hold a flame to their skin without squealing in pain, or maybe fill their underpants with a swarm of live wasps. Many of the programmes are of a more ordinary nature that demand the endurance of the viewer more than of the participants. Late at night some of these chat shows and quiz programmes will find almost any excuse to invite young girls to take their clothes off, sometimes in fantasy sex scenes, sometimes by sending them off to 'report' on a hot spring resort that requires them to send back their appraisal while standing stark naked in the middle of a shallow pool of water. In case any viewers are not concentrating properly, the television camera traces every intimate curve and crevice of these teenage bodies with the loving attention that Jacques Cousteau's cameraman devotes to a rare breed of manatee.

This kind of camerawork would bring shrieks of protest in London. In Tokyo this location report might well hand back to a young giggling anchorwoman in the studio. She, in turn, might then ask some T-shirt-clad girls standing under specially erected bathroom showers a number of quiz questions. Wrong answers trigger a dousing and dousing, sooner or later, turns into an ersatz wet T-shirt competition. In Japan, it seems, you have to get wet to have fun. Again, in case some of the audience at home have missed the point of it all, a studio host might decide to tweak and fondle the girls' breasts so that their nipples catch the glint of the studio lights. Japanese women, because of their traditional subservience in society and their tolerance of their husbands' philandering and organized sex tours to Bangkok and Manila, are steering their lives on different coordinates. But it still surprises Westerners to see female Japanese TV presenters colluding in this soft-core pornography without a murmur. And on a regular national network.

One show that draws heavy flak from foreigners, but not from the Japanese, is a variety entertainment that its producers call *Super People of the World* and its critics call a tasteless freak show. Parading a gallery of dwarfs, obese men, abnormally hairy boys, huge-breasted women, even a hermaphrodite, this is probably the most controversial programme in Japan. Its producers boast that it is also the most popular.

In a typical scene from one of the shows, an Indian had his

long, twisted fingernails cut for the first time in twenty-five years, for an undisclosed fee. As the last fingernail was clipped, he broke down and wept. Curiously, no Japanese are brought on to the show to flaunt any unusual physical characteristic or skill or abnormality. Ken Haga, the show's associate producer, who scours the world for suitably startling turns, told a reporter, 'The Japanese enjoy this kind of entertainment, it's very unusual. We laugh at the people because they are too big or too small. Some people say it's a fake or a freak show, but many people like to come to Japan to get money from us.' Foreigners do not even have to be deformed to reduce the Japanese to side-clutching laughter. Being foreign is usually enough. Non-Japanese-speaking foreigners called to appear on Japanese chat shows are usually used as unwitting straight men, forced to adopt a vacuous studio grin while the show's compere babbles on in Japanese to the viewers, making fun of his unsuspecting guest. Every now and then, another question might be tossed to the interviewee: sometimes it will be about their film/music/writing career, more likely it will be about whether they have ever eaten raw fish and whether they can use chopsticks. No? What a scream. The guests on *Super People of the World* get up to $10,000 for coming along to parade. Haga explains that no Japanese appear on the show because Japan does not have any 'special people'.

Other peculiarly Japanese shows include one that descended on the rich and famous from Cannes to California. There is little new in this formula of blending nosiness with drop-jawed envy. What is new is the Japanese television programme's twist of visiting an eighteenth-century *palazzo* in Tuscany or a mansion in the Hollywood hills, interviewing their owners, then taking telephone bids from Tokyo to buy the places or their contents. To add insult to injury, every time the owner of a palace or a yacht names a price, the male interviewer's female sidekick (a standard, decorative ego-support to many Japanese anchormen

107

and news readers) squawks 'Cheap!' or 'Bargain!' with the incredulity that comes naturally only to those paid in yen.

Even in more routine drama or sit-coms Japanese networks struggle to give their shows a Japanese tang. For example, in one serial based on the ups and downs of a newly-wed couple, the hour-long episodes were interwoven with sets of statistics, a Japanese obsession. In the opening episode, in which the couple got married, the drama gave way to a table of statistics showing that a typical honeymoon for Japanese lasts about six days and costs around 460,000 yen, or about £2,000, if taken in Japan and 1.1 million yen if taken abroad. Hawaii is the top destination. Where do couples first meet? About one in five meets at the office, and so on. It may not be Shakespeare, but it's certainly novel. Viewers apparently find it educational.

But traditional samurai dramas are making a comeback on television after a thirty-year absence. Most follow the classic pattern of justice-beats-evil and are grabbing ratings of between 10 and 20 per cent. Yoshio Shirai, a film critic, reckons that this renewed popularity reflects 'a kind of catharsis'. He says the Japanese have no problem materially but feel frustrated by the 'shadowy' aspects of their society, such as the wide-ranging bribery scandal that brought down a prime minister and several senior politicians at the end of the 1980s. 'The samurai dramas, in which heroes best evil-doers, help alleviate that frustration,' according to Shirai. But costumes apart, the texture of the drama is pretty much the same as the rest.

In Japanese television drama there is an awful lot of indignant and meaningful face-slapping, a good deal of coy matchmaking through intermediaries, several tales of love thwarted by the pressures of family or society (marrying into the right family is so important in Japan that even today the family background of a future son- or daughter-in-law will be checked thoroughly in Japan's equivalent of Somerset House and parish records before consent is given) and quite a few men forcing themselves on unwilling but eventually submissive women. No one seems to have much fun, even though the Japanese are, on the whole, pretty cheery people. Even less convincing are the unlikely murders in unlikely places that leave corpses with neat red blots of blood on their lapels that do not mar the line of their designer clothes. It is true that any drama of the *Miami Vice* kind starts with a handicap when set in Tokyo, a city where crime is comparatively scarce, policemen patrol on bicycles if at all, and people are too scared to jaywalk, let alone have a shoot-out in the high street. A small-time hold-up at a corner grocery store will make the news headlines on a slow day.

Every country's television adapts to the tastes of its public and we should all be wary of casting the first stone. Japanese viewers turn their noses up at foreign programmes. Maybe they can only take so much of foreigners on the box. Even *Dallas* failed in Japan. Yet French TV often baffles British viewers as much as Japanese television would. The best British drama has conquered the world, but what on earth do foreigners make of Bob Monkhouse?

Even so, it would be hard to argue that Japan produces shows that travel well. Only a couple of dozen Japanese programmes have transferred to other countries, seven of them from NHK. The NHK programmes are largely documentaries, while the commercial output is heavy on pro wrestling and sumo. But perhaps some Westerners are not giving Japanese programmes a fair watching. In Iran, for example, a Japanese soap opera about a young girl called Oshin growing up amid great suffering in postwar Japan became such a hit that traffic stopped on Saturday nights when the programme was aired. When the heroine's father died, an Iranian newspaper published a full-page obituary. The drama was picked by Iranian officials to serve as a role model for Iranians during the country's long war with Iraq, when they suffered shortages and hardships, a rain of rocket attacks and the loss of relatives. Unfortunately passions got out of hand. In 1989 four Tehran radio executives received prison terms and lashings for broadcasting a phone-in programme in which a sacrilegious caller said the show's uncomplaining heroine was a better role model for Iranian women than the daughter of the prophet Muhammad.

The odd thing is that, given the remarkable lack of foreign television programmes and the shortage of apparently normal foreign people on Japanese TV, the gaps in between the programmes – gaps bought by the advertisers who keep the commercial channels afloat – are jammed full of well-known foreign faces.

Certainly we are all grateful for weekend shopping hints, but when Sylvester Stallone looks you in the eye and says that Ito Ham 'is so delicious it is a gift of love', what do you make of it? The testimonial, not the man. And when was the last time Roger Moore, ex-British secret agent, suggested that you get with it and smoke Lark cigarettes? Would you like Frank Sinatra's advice on which Japanese airline to fly, or Richard Branson's on which brand of Japanese whisky to drink? When did Paul Newman's blue eyes last chuckle into yours and try to persuade you that only a halfwit walked around town without a certain bank's credit card in his back pocket? If you have never been to Tokyo it may be worth postponing buying that new central-heating boiler for a couple of years and flying to Japan just to gawp at which products your favourite movie stars are putting their names to over there. It may be the only way you will find out. Many are too shy to let the ads be seen anywhere else.

We all know that the Japanese feel uncomfortable paying less than twice as much for anything as anyone else in the world. They also do not seem to mind paying screen idols as much for a fifteen-second commercial as they might get for three months' work on a feature film in Hollywood. Eddie Murphy was paid $3 million for making his eyes pop out at the sight of a new Toyota saloon, although they may well have been popping at the sight of the cheque.

The same Japanese who guffaw uninhibitedly at foreign freaks on the box are polite enough, or desperate enough, not to pry into why so many of these stars are happy to work for Japanese advertising agents, selling everything from tyres to toothpaste, but then demand clauses in their contracts that guarantee that their fans in America and Europe will never see the commercials. It doesn't take Wittgenstein to wonder why appearing in an advertising campaign in Tokyo, mouthing some inanity or other, boosts a star's popularity in Japan but somehow disappoints his fans on the other side of the Pacific.

Well, some film stars are notoriously touchy. Many travel on location with their own rewrite team. If the film script calls for them to blow their nose, they might complain to the director that their character is not a nose-blower by nature and that, anyway, violent nose-blowing could revolt the fans. But when it comes to Japanese commercials, anything seems to go, as long as no one apart from 123 million Japanese sees the final result. Since the movie-loving Japanese comprise the second-biggest market for Hollywood films after America, cold feet about what fans in Boston or Birmingham might think seems doubly queer.

So here we have Roger Moore filling his lungs with Lark cigarettes. Like James Coburn, who also advertises the Lark brand, Moore isn't blunt enough to say, 'Go on, have a cigarette, why don't you' or 'Mmmm, tasty'. Instead, like Coburn, he urges us to 'Speak Lark', that peculiar command we came across earlier, but which we are still no nearer to deciphering. This demand must also baffle most Japanese, though they would probably be just as baffled if the request was to 'Smoke Lark'. Anyway, the chain-smoking Japanese light up cigarettes between

111

consecutive bites of sushi and seem to know what to do with Larks when they have them, so perhaps Moore and Coburn are getting their message through. Moore and Coburn are not alone. Anyone whose name has ever appeared on a film's list of credits in a position less obscure than 'Best Boy' or 'First Grip' seems to find work in Tokyo. Paul Newman earns an undisclosed but fat sum for performing on behalf of Fuji Bank. Alain Delon drinks Rémy Martin cognac. John McEnroe and Tatum O'Neal brush their teeth with Assess toothpaste. Arnold Schwarzenegger downs instant Japanese noodles to replenish himself after a workout. Micky Rourke looks steamy and says, 'It's my passion', although it's sometimes hard to remember whether the 'it' is a fast car or Suntory whisky. He advertises both rather passionately.

There is nothing unusual about famous actors putting on panstick to tell you which brand of bath cleaner they would find it jolly hard to live without. What is unusual is the 'Japan only' clauses that many of their lawyers weave into their Tokyo contracts. These slap huge penalties on the advertiser if a commercial that has been shot for a Japanese product gets seen abroad. Although the Japanese still rush in with their chequebooks, they are not completely blind to the slight. Japanese advertising executives complain that film stars want the cash but see no cachet in being in Japanese commercials. Many stars can make between $500,000 and $1 million from appearing in a Japanese ad, but the resulting film footage is something they would rather not advertise abroad.

If these foreigners are having a little laugh at the Japanese, the Japanese are sly enough to turn the rules to their own advantage as well. If what is seen in Japan has no impact on what goes on elsewhere, then presumably no one will object if Japanese companies hijack the faces of dead movie stars to put some zip into their product's tired image. Japan first began hoovering up American film stars in the 1950s, a golden age when America stood for baseball, hamburgers, Hollywood and everything else that a still poor Japan yearned for. Some of the stars from that golden age are still winking from commercials and advertising hoardings across Japan, even though they died years ago. Irritatingly for the estates of these actors, Japanese law does not oblige Japanese firms to pay royalties for 'portrait rights' of dead stars. So James Dean promotes just about everything in Japan from hygienic rubber gloves to high-tech robots. He is infinitely obliging. You have only to ask and he will personally endorse your noodle restaurant or petrol station. Marilyn Monroe's face also peers out of the unlikeliest posters in the unlikeliest places.

There are two reasons why Japan's advertising industry needs so many foreign stars. One is that although Japanese people may giggle at foreigners in the programmes, they like to see foreigners in commercials and Hollywood actors are the most famous foreigners that advertisers can find. Even the more hard-up advertisers fill the gaps between programmes with preppie Americans puffing cigarettes in New England settings with surfboards under their arms. This is another reason why, given the choice, advertisers prefer film stars. Film stars can act. The preppie young Americans who are sucked into Japanese commercials hold their cigarettes as they might if their fingers had just come out of plaster. Maybe they have. After each puff they look quizzically approving at this strange white tube in their hand, as if they were Walter Raleigh and were trying out this gimmick for the first time. The ads end with everyone laughing uncontrollably, which makes you wonder just what is in those Japanese cigarettes.

The other reason that Japan needs so many foreigners is that there are so many new products to advertise. Japanese business works on the principle of creating market share and then keeping it. So if you are a brewer and your rival produces a new red-coloured beer, you immediately produce ninety-nine new brands

113

of red-coloured beer. Thus, by the law of averages (providing that all red-coloured beers taste equally good or equally disgusting) only one out of every hundred beer shoppers will pick your rival's product off the supermarket shelf. Well, you've guessed it: the rival company then produces a few hundred more brands of red-coloured beer to balance out the averages again. It may sound like a fairly seat-of-the-pants business strategy, but it's what helped to make Japan stinking rich. The result of all this is that after almost every television commercial a little voice pipes up and says 'New product'. Most of these new products don't last longer than it takes to work out how to pronounce them. Red-coloured beer could be in the shops by June and out again by August. But in those three months, if beer drinkers desert traditional ales, then at least the same companies keep the business.

This huge advertising machine does more than keep Hollywood film stars in Lear jets and new Gucci loafers. It plays an enormous role in shaping the way Japan thinks and what it thinks about. Manufacturers need outlets to promote their products. Their advertising budgets keep Japan's thriving media afloat. Those advertising budgets have also made Dentsu of Japan by far the world's biggest advertising agency, with billings twice as large as those of its nearest international rivals even though almost all of Dentsu's business is generated in Japan. That, in turn, has given Dentsu the power to influence what is put out on the commercial television channels and in the newspapers and magazines that rely on its clients' advertising campaigns to pay the bills. Dentsu controls one third of Japan's commercial air time, one fifth of all advertising in Japanese newspapers and one sixth of magazine advertising. Roughly one quarter of all the money spent on advertising in Japan is spent through Dentsu. Because it sponsors television programmes, because it has shareholdings in Japanese TV stations and TV production companies, because its financial clout allows it to influence half the programming on prime-time television, and because it diplomatically peppers its staff with the sons of well-connected Japanese politicians and businessmen, Dentsu has become a powerful institution in Japan. It has cross-shareholdings with Japan's two biggest news agencies, Kyodo and Jiji. It even has a stake in Video Research, Japan's leading TV rating body. Dentsu can flex more muscles in Japan than some other countries have muscles. It looks after public relations for the Liberal Democratic Party, which has ruled Japan, almost without a break, since the war. Dentsu has been accused of using its leverage to prevent newspapers running stories that might hurt its clients. And because it controls certain prime chunks of air time, it can lure custom away from rival advertising agencies and then persuade a TV channel to produce a programme or a series that will complement its new client's needs. This close involvement with all sides of the business means that Dentsu can also offer its clients advertising tie-ins and merchandising based on the characters of the specially created TV series. Its jingles are hummed by salarymen and housewives. In his book, *The Enigma of Japanese Power*, Karel van Wolferen argues that 'Dentsu does more than any single corporation, anywhere in the world, to mould popular culture.' Others have called Dentsu Japan's 'Shadow Ministry of Information'.

But if the Japanese media are guided less by the principle of 'the public's right to know' than by the principle of 'the manufacturer's right to sell', and if the country's largest advertising agency is routinely referred to as the shadow information ministry, surely that can't make for a very vibrant press? It doesn't.

The Western world's newspaper barons would kill to have circulations like those of Japan's leading national dailies. The *Yomiuri Shimbun* sells 9.7 million copies every morning. The

115

Asahi Shimbun lags slightly with a sale of 8.2 million, followed by the *Mainichi Shimbun* with 4.2 million, the *Nihon Kezai Shimbun* (Japan's financial daily) with nearly 3 million, and the *Sankei Shimbun* with just over 2 million. The separate afternoon editions of those papers sell about half as much as their morning versions. These are not sensationalist tabloid newspapers, although Japan has plenty of those too. These are the country's respected, up-market broadsheets. They each employ as many as two to three thousand on their payroll to keep tabs on what is going on at home and abroad. Their reporters have day and night use of the newspaper's fleet of black company limousines that ferry them here and there, from assignment to assignment. For grander ferrying needs they might hop into the company's helicopter.

This press corps is technically very free. There is little in the way of strong libel laws, and no Official Secrets Act to offend. But rarely was so much money and effort put in by so many to produce so few articles worth reading. The Japanese press doesn't need official censorship because it censors itself. It censors the subjects it covers, and the way it covers them. Editorial comments are barely distinguishable, from one paper to the next, on any issue of the day. Front pages are usually identical, whether the lead story is the outbreak of the third world war or the quality of knicker elastic: strange as it may seem to an outsider, if one national broadsheet decides that the quality of, say, knicker elastic deserves front-page treatment, they all decide it deserves front-page treatment. No posh newspaper dares stray from the fold. Scoops are terribly bad form. Explaining what is going on in Japan or abroad on a particular issue is regarded as trying to be clever and ignoring the Japanese public's right not to understand fully what is really going on behind the headlines.

Of course this news is available to the public from other sources. Japan's racy weekly and monthly magazines deliver news, scandal and gossip by scatter-gun, sometimes hitting the truth, sometimes missing horribly; and sober, learned monthlies offer essays on newsy issues by academics and social-cum-political commentators. And for those who want the respectability of having the *Asahi* or the *Yomiuri* pushed through the letterbox each morning but a fun read on the way home there are the notorious sports dailies, which carry blaring headlines, are heavy on sport and pictures of naked women, run reviews and telephone numbers of the newest brothels in town, give advice on salarymen's worries (how to avoid breaking wind in business meetings was the subject of one column), even a cartoon strip on the adventures of an anthropomorphic penis. The sports dailies may not win any press awards, but perhaps the Japanese public is not completely satisfied with the nannying, we-know-best attitude of the uniformly dull broadsheets if they buy a sports daily like *Nikkan Gendai*, which manages to sell one million copies a day simply by writing headlines that are the complete opposite of those that appear in the quality papers. It slams the government and it even slams the Yomiuri Giants baseball team, which is about as close to blasphemy as you can get in Japan. Just how low-brow the Japanese will take their fare is highlighted by the staggering market for *manga*, the telephone-directory-sized comic books that most people, adults as well as children, read on trains and buses. One of the *manga*, called *Jump*, sells five million copies a week. Many of them are full of raunchy scenes or violent beatings and rapings of weeping women and of wide-eyed schoolgirls in uniform who eventually all realize that they revel in degradation. In fact *manga* cartoons are so much the preferred reading of Japanese adults that almost anything you can imagine is now published in comic-book form for easy absorption, from important instruction manuals issued by government departments and health authorities to history and economics books and Marx's *Das Kapital*.

117

But the broadsheets rarely trouble themselves with what appears in the weeklies, the monthlies or the sports sheets. They know their place, and it is not to be controversial. The tradition of the press in Japan is barely more than a hundred years old, and for most of that time it has been in the service of the government as a tool of propaganda. The American postwar occupation ended that nationalistic collusion without fully dispelling the comrades-in-arms spirit of the old days.

If you take a peep inside the hotel lobby of any international meeting or conference, say a world economic summit, Japanese journalists generally outnumber the rest of the world's press corps. They move in giant, anxious herds from one press conference to another, from one briefing to the next, from dawn till way past their bedtime. But when the readers back in Tokyo and Osaka open their newspapers the next day to learn what has happened they will read a short, factual account: no explanation, no background, no context, no comment. Facts, facts, facts. C.P. Scott, who stressed that comment is free but facts are sacred, might have approved of the principle, but not of its manner of execution. The facts will usually have come only from Japanese mouths. These mouths belong to men whose jobs in their Tokyo government ministries depend on putting the best possible gloss on the summit's outcome: anything less would be regarded as unpatriotic. So if the Japanese government's spokesman says that Japan won everything it wanted at the negotiating table, then that is what will appear in print, even if the rest of the world's press is writing editorials on Japan's humiliation at the hands of its fellow summiteers. The press in Japan is not there to agitate, to rock the boat.

Even so, such uncontroversial uniformity is a feat in a country that is not actually a dictatorship. How has it come about? The blame lies with Japan's 'reporters' clubs', a cosy cartel of about 12,000 journalists organized in about four hundred clubs that cover various government ministries, industries, companies, even individual politicians, in much the way that Britain's lobby journalists cover Downing Street. The difference is that lobby journalists can take or leave what they are told, can add perspective, can inject opposing views from opposition politicians, can at least try to give the reader some idea of whether the government is lying on such and such an issue or not. In Japan, information is funnelled only through these reporters' clubs, and then only to the élite newspaper and television journalists accredited to them. Regional reporters and muckraking magazine journalists who might not bite their tongues on request are left out in the cold to shiver along with the foreign press: government ministers, civil servants and industrialists in Japan seem to think that the sole reason that foreign news organizations send correspondents to Tokyo is to engineer the downfall of the democratically elected government of Japan. So their inquiries must be rebuffed whenever possible.

Obviously, no newspaper can afford to have its man kicked out of this or that club, so members of the reporters' clubs are chosen for their ability never to say boo to a goose. This self-control ensures that every newspaper gets the same news at the same time, but it also means that no one gets any troublesome scoops. Journalists who break ranks and publish something critical of the minister or the company, or expose some wrongdoing or other, find themselves clubless, which doesn't make them very popular with their editors. Those journalists who play by the rules find themselves with a permanent seat, sometimes even a permanent bed, in part of the ministry or the company's headquarters. These come with a steady supply of beer and whisky to keep him going through the long hours he spends in his pursuit of the official version of events that he is handed down at regular feeding times. He might even find a handsome gift waiting for him at home every now and then. If the services are not up to scratch, the reporters will complain. When Toshiki Kaifu became prime minister in 1989 he initially decided to carry on living in his central Tokyo apartment rather than moving into the grim and reputedly rat-infested official residence. But his reporters' club complained about their lack of facilities. They had to loiter around in the apartment building's corridors, with no specially assigned room equipped with TV sets, telephones, snacks or whisky. The nagging journalists finally hounded Kaifu and his reluctant wife into moving into their government-issue house, where the media camp could resume the life to which it was used.

Nevertheless, this symbiotic relationship ensures that politicians and business leaders get into the newspapers just what they want to get into the newspapers, rarely more or less. Interview questions are traditionally submitted to the subject for approval well in advance. Press conferences are more stage-managed than kabuki shows. The foreign reporters who stick their hands up with awkward questions are met with a look of what-shall-we-do-with-these-people pity: it is as if they were behaving as ungratefully as a wedding guest who after enjoying his host's hospitality then asks for a couple of bottles of champagne to take home as well. As Japanese journalists like to say, 'Nobody's scoop is everybody's happiness.' But don't tell that to the readers.

Yet every once in a while embarrassing revelations do get into the press. Sometimes it is by accident, sometimes by the hand of some determined, devil-may-care journalist, sometimes because Japanese newspapers like to register an occasional flicker of activity on the electrocardiogram to show that they are still alive, and sometimes because the foreign press has forced the pace. Probably the most dramatic instance of this happening was the 1970s Lockheed bribes scandal, which eventually toppled the prime minister Kakuei Tanaka from power, though not, of course, from grace or influence. It first came to light in a Japanese magazine. Yet it was only several weeks later, when foreign journalists had the chance to confront Tanaka with the allegations of his bribe-taking, that Japanese newspapers felt they could no longer afford to ignore the story. Until then they had deemed it discreetly un-newsworthy.

In the Recruit bribery scandal that brought down the government of Noboru Takeshita in 1989, the first evidence of corruption by a local official came to the attention of a reporter in one of the regional bureaux of the *Asahi Shimbun.* That thread eventually led back into the highest political and business circles in Tokyo. Had it first come to the attention of a senior political reporter in Tokyo, it might have just joined the many items of news and scandals that are well known in journalists' circles but never make it on to the page. The Recruit affair was also kept alive by a dogged Tokyo public prosecutor, who used his own reporters' club to leak information about his department's findings; he was worried that unless he acted quickly, justice ministry officials would use the leverage offered by their reporters' club to suffocate the dramatic story. Even so, Takeshita was far from disgraced. Like Tanaka, he remained a power behind the throne, certainly more powerful than the immediate successors he shochorned into office. Once they have been through the papers, scandals are once again swept under the carpet. When Margaret Thatcher visited Tokyo a few months after Takeshita was forced to resign over his links with the Recruit scandal, the British Embassy in Tokyo made sure that the British prime minister was seated close to Takeshita at dinner.

The strange behaviour of the Japanese media was paraded once more that year, when Takeshita's replacement was found wanting. It was again a Japanese magazine that carried the scoop and the foreign press which set the pace thereafter. The magazine, the *Sunday Mainichi*, published an interview with a former geisha who claimed that Sosuke Uno, the new premier, had 'bought' her body. In most countries, rival media would race to follow up such a tale, especially when it threatened to bring down two prime ministers in less than a month. In fact two broadsheets, wary of causing further political chaos, had refused her story before she turned to the *Sunday Mainichi*. So there was silence, even from opposition politicians, until foreign newspapers relayed details of the interview. That finally gave an opposition member of parliament the excuse to raise the subject, on the grounds that Mr Uno should either confess or otherwise scotch these stories that were condemning Japan to international shame. From there the drama picked up some momentum, but the prestige Japanese press still preferred to cover the story indirectly by concentrating on the foreign media's reaction to Japan's embarrassment. Even then, these papers could not bring themselves to do more than refer to it, as if with tongs, as Uno's 'woman problem'. Many of them preferred to see the story less as a political scandal, more as another instance of Japan-bashing by foreigners.

Just how hard it is for bad old habits to die was underlined in the autumn of 1989, when Sony, the Japanese electronics company, bought the Columbia film studios in Hollywood. It gave Japan its first major foothold in the foreign media and it gave many Americans sleepless nights. In a cover story on the takeover, the US magazine *Newsweek* touched America's nationalistic nerve by saying that the US was slowly ceding its economic destiny to Japan and that 'this time the Japanese hadn't just snapped up another building, they had bought a piece of America's soul'.

It doesn't take all that much nowadays to reawaken America's fears of the yellow peril. But surely Akio Morita, Sony's internationally minded boss, should have seen this coming and done what he could to prevent it? Instead, Sony announced its purchase of Columbia to a discreet Tokyo press conference of hand-picked, sympathetic Japanese reporters. American correspondents in Tokyo, excluded from a briefing about an issue of strong interest to their readers (and to their leader-writers), were not pleased. The hostility of America's reaction came as a shock to Sony and to Morita. Most painful of all was a front-page article in the *Asian Wall Street Journal* which said that while the private press conference amounted to privileged access to information, it managed to avoid violating stock exchange or government rules since both the Tokyo and New York stock exchanges were closed when Sony arranged its chat with Tokyo journalists. Nevertheless it feared that the problem of spoonfeeding Japan's domestic press and ignoring foreign correspondents could create more serious problems as Japanese companies made more acquisitions abroad. By shutting foreign reporters out of that crucial press conference, the paper added, 'Sony not only lost an opportunity to allay American concerns, it reinforced one of the concerns: the fear that a Japanese company controlling a major American communications medium might use that control to restrict the free flow of information and ideas.' Sony gained no advantage from its secrecy, but lost the good faith of its new host nation and the confidence of every foreign correspondent in Japan.

Yet it got Columbia. A year later, Sony was followed to Tinseltown by Matsushita, Japan's biggest consumer electronics firm, which bought MCA, owner of Universal Studios, for $6 billion. It was the largest single investment ever made in America by a Japanese company. Sony and Matsushita, fierce rivals at home, suddenly controlled more than a quarter of the American film business. The ironic thing about this move into one of the last big industries in which America has a clear lead, is that Morita was probably being completely honest when he assured America that he had no hidden motives in buying

Columbia. He did not buy Columbia so that he could have an opportunity to corrupt Americans or to teach them the discipline of paying all their credit-card bills on time. Both Sony and Matsushita moved in for the motive that inspires most corporate decisions. They did it for the money and for their own financial self-preservation.

Japan's own film output does not travel well. Foreign audiences would snore through most samurai westerns or the sickly sweet story about a pussycat that became a raging box-office hit a few years ago. But Japan's film-goers already do more to keep Hollywood afloat than the British or the Canadians do, by providing America with its biggest foreign market for films. The Japanese have also known that there is money to be made in the film business: the mansions in Beverly Hills say so. But the haphazard ease with which fortunes can be lost – over pricey flops like Michael Cimino's *Heaven's Gate* – made them hold back. An industry in which even star producers and directors are often mystified by one project's success and another's failure is an industry that makes most committee-minded Japanese businessmen wince with anguish.

But Sony and Matsushita were not seduced by the glitz or by the thrill of adding their hand prints to the pavement outside Mann's Chinese Theater. They saw buying a film studio as the next logical step for the world's leading electronics manufacturers. If you are making a mint from selling video cassette recorders (60 per cent of Japanese homes have them), why not sell the video tapes as well? The quickest way to get your hands on big film libraries and avoid the expensive auction to acquire video rights for US-made films is, of course, to buy the big American movie studios that own them. Columbia, the fourth largest studio in the movie business, owns a huge library of more than three thousand films, including *On the Waterfront* and *When Harry Met Sally*, as well as 2,600 television shows. Universal studios made such hits as *ET*, *Jaws* and *Back to the Future*, and the television series *Miami Vice*. Sony proved the attraction of such logic when it bought CBS Records in 1988, marking the first big takeover by a Japanese company in the entertainment business. In addition to earning money from CBS record sales, Sony has also used its new records arm to boost sales of CD players by filling shops with CDs. When Matsushita bought MCA it also acquired Motown Records as part of the portfolio.

Similarly, Columbia and Universal will help Sony and Matsushita produce new video products on new formats and to develop programmes for the new generation of high-definition television sets, which looks like being the next big battleground for Japan's consumer electronics firms. Matsushita, whose brand names include Panasonic and Technics, is known as one of Japan's most conservative and least glitzy firms. It overcame its fear of California's unfamiliar ways because it feared even more being left behind in the race against Sony to develop the audiovisual technologies that will dominate the next century. The immediate tussle is over video cassette formats. Sony has bet its future on 8 mm video cassettes, Matsushita on VHS. Video buyers and renters who want to see a Columbia-made movie may have to buy a Sony-made VCR if the video is issued only on 8 mm cassettes. Matsushita crossed the Pacific to make sure there would also be a steady supply of hit movies on VHS video tape. Whichever company can churn out more video tapes in its own format is likely to gain in the battle for sales of video equipment. Sony is especially keen to avoid the fiasco of its Betamax videotape system, which lost out to the rival VHS format. Not quite Sam Goldwyn and Louis B. Mayer, but the boys in Hollywood have been happy enough to take the Japanese businessmen's cash.

It will be interesting to watch how buttoned-up Japan, with its dry broadsheet newspapers and its fear of foreigners in their press conferences, copes with Hollywood's way of doing things. It will be just as interesting to see how Hollywood copes with the Japanese. Shortly before Sony moved into Hollywood, Paramount Pictures began shooting a gangster film called *Black Rain*, starring Michael Douglas, in Osaka, Japan's second biggest city. But the crew was finally beaten by Japan's exhausting bureaucracy. The location manager had to visit thirty committees just to get permission to film inside Osaka's fish market. The idea of make-believe also sometimes baffled officials in Osaka: Paramount said *sayonara* and left for home when problems arose over a scene in which a Japanese gangster knifes an American detective and pushes him under an Osaka underground train. Transport officials, fretting about the potential damage to Osaka's reputation, said the scene could only be filmed if the murder was cut.

7. The Quality of Life: Pay Now, Live Later

A widening gap between rich and poor – nature by telephone – a noisy nuisance – sinking under garbage – pollution – the environmental record: a low-key tune – wailing about whaling – warning: earthquakes

Wall-to-wall people and small houses are becoming less acceptable now that Japanese keep being told by foreigners how rich they are. Miniaturization may be attractive in a microchip but not in an apartment. Japan has money but lacks elbow room. More than 60 per cent of Tokyo residents say there are too many people in Tokyo. They want the total cut. Some people in Japan like to say it's a dog's life. But many dogs there pay an even higher price than their owners do for living at such close quarters. Some Japanese have their dogs' vocal chords cut or make their dogs wear anti-barking shock collars so that the animals do not disturb the neighbours.

But just how angry are the Japanese? They have uncommon reserves of patience and take much in their stride. As every year passes, they seem to be getting more and more fed up with belonging to the world's second richest nation, yet living at a level that makes many, much poorer, foreigners gawp in astonishment. Any quiver of rebellion puts the government in a flap. It wonders whether the growing disparity in income and assets between the well-off and the even-better-off will deepen feelings

127

of resentment within a nation that likes to think and act as one. Year after year, government surveys seem to show almost exactly the same thing: that the Japanese are unhappy with their long working hours, their brief holidays, the high cost of living and the shortage of parks, athletics grounds and other recreational facilities. They say they want to work less and play more. Even the countryside is crowded and the golf-courses are all full and expensive. Also, as more Japanese travel abroad, more of them realize that they are not enjoying the full benefits of the yen's strength against other currencies. Not only have foreign products not shrunk in price in Japanese shops, but Japanese-made cameras and videos are usually cheaper abroad than in Japan.

Increasing income disparities depress the Japanese not only because they cannot afford the things that Americans, Britons or Italians take for granted, but because they are creating new class divisions in a compact society, one in which the majority thinks of itself as middle class, middle income and middle of the road. The fear of no longer being part of the crowd is, for many Japanese, almost as uncomfortable as facing up to the fact that those of them not already on the property ladder probably have little chance of ever owning their own home.

But how *really* angry are the Japanese? It is difficult to avoid the conclusion that the debate about the quality of life is to the Japanese what the weather is to the British: everyone talks about it, but very little ever gets done about it. What the Japanese government tries to do about it is sometimes rather strange to foreign eyes. To set a new stamp for the caring 1990s, for example, the Health and Welfare Ministry published a thirty-eight-page guide to explain to Japan's corporate foot soldiers how to relax, how to stop treating the prospect of more time off as a threat and how to have fun. But isn't this what the foot soldiers have been seeking all along? Why do they need a government guide to tell them these things, especially a guide in which the basic kernel of advice is 'Go to bed early and get up early, always eat breakfast, forget about the job after hours and eat dinner with your family'?

Just how strongly the Japanese realized that the path to happiness might pass through the dinner table soon became clear. The arrival of the Health Ministry's guide coincided with the publication of the Ministry of International Trade and Industry's visionary goals for the 1990s, a regular and weighty once-a-decade prescription for Japan's future. It is drafted by some of Japan's most respected civil servants. There was the usual stuff about promoting the well-being of the individual, about making an improved quality of life the country's top priority and about Japan's desire to concentrate less on making money and more on making a humanitarian contribution to the world. But how will this be achieved? Well, one way, said MITI, will be through 'promoting eating space' in Japanese homes and restaurants so that 'the dining table will be a place where you can express yourself'. It is hard to see how expression at the dining table will allow Japan to fulfil MITI's goals of ending Japan's obsession with economic and industrial success, of cutting work hours and of shrinking the gap between the price of goods in Japan and those charged for the same products abroad. But at least MITI showed that the Japanese haven't lost their taste for inscrutability. Meanwhile, anxieties about the quality of life will top the Japanese people's list of professed worries this year, next year, and probably well into the twenty-first century. In 1992 the government handed the nation yet another five-year plan designed to boost the living standards of the country's workers, with a goal of 1,800 working hours a year by 1996 to bring Japan in line with the West and a promise to turn Japan into a 'standard-of-living superpower'. Much as they might welcome such a nirvana, few Japanese, working on average at least 200 hours a year more than their Western counterparts, are holding their breath.

129

Japanese consumers have neither the will nor the political clout to fight for their interests against farmers, shopkeepers, construction firms and the rest of the lobby groups who pressurize or bribe the government into seeing their point of view. Japan's rice farmers, most of them tilling paddy-fields the size of tennis-courts (often as tax dodges), produce rice that appeals to the Japanese palate but at prices several times what it would cost to import rice from, say, America or Thailand. Many housewives are keen to have the choice but are not influential enough to replace the rice farmers' lobby in the affections of a conservative government that culls millions of votes from rural areas. Japanese beef prices are also wildly out of line with world prices. It is not difficult to pay £30 for a pound of beef in a Japanese butcher's. It is very easy to pay much more. Japan's multi-layered distribution system, which steers every item through several hands (and several mark-ups) before it reaches the consumer, inflates shop prices too. Corner stores also have enough friends in high places to make it very difficult for supermarkets and large stores to open up in busy parts of town. Construction companies can persuade transport ministers to build motorways and bridges to nowhere. Politics, like much else in Japan, is expensive, and it is big business and the various lobby groups that help to pay the election bills. Housewives do not.

There is so little tradition of complaining in Japan that most people will not make a fuss even if they feel they have been cheated. Top sushi restaurants never have price lists. The bill is left to the chef's whim at the end of the meal. If a Japanese couple feel they have been wildly overcharged, they will usually just bite their lips, pay up and never return. Often, they will bite their lips, pay up and come back the following week, saying: 'That's how it's done in Japan. It can't be helped.' In recent years Washington trade negotiators, fighting to gain access to

Japan's markets for cheap American exports, have found themselves taking on the role of consumer champion on the Japanese consumer's behalf. But even they privately despair at the Japanese consumer's inability to stand up and shout, 'we're mad as hell, and we're not going to take it any more'. Actually just a whisper, now and then, would probably do.

Even more baffling to many Westerners than Japanese shoppers' willingness to pay through the nose, is their eagerness to pay in advance. Unlike millions of Britons who do not know how much they have spent until the Access or American Express bill arrives, the Japanese prefer to settle up even before they have written out their shopping list. Always keen to improve on any idea, even if the idea is cash, the Japanese have gone crazy for pre-paid cards. They do away with the bother of banknotes, which is the traditional method of payment in Japan for everything from shoelaces to washing machines, and they save the dread of being in someone else's debt, even if it's only until the credit-card bill arrives. This unusual fetish for paying now and living later began with the pre-paid telephone card (British Telecom got the idea from Japan) and has matured through train-ticket cards, taxi cards, amusement-arcade cards and supermarket cards all the way to McDonald's hamburgers cards.

Few Westerners can fathom why anyone would want to give a supermarket or a department store a fat interest-free loan by buying a pre-paid card. But credit-card companies are held in deep suspicion by many Japanese, who have traditionally preferred cash and will happily stroll the streets with enough money in their back pockets to buy into a Las Vegas poker game. The rarity of muggings helps. And the shoddy service that private (and uncomplaining) customers get from Japanese banks – only very rich people and pushy foreigners are allowed cheque-books – has made carrying cash a necessity. Distrust of debt puts many spenders off paying with plastic. Most Japanese do not have a credit card. Few have more than one. Pre-paid cards, on the other hand, are as common as chopsticks and twice as convenient. Watch someone open his wallet and, likely as not, an accordion of pre-paid cards will tumble out.

The love affair with these cards has grown so passionate that the Bank of Japan fears they will disrupt the country's monetary policy. The Japanese have applied all their usual skills in exploiting pre-paid cards. They come perfumed, they can flash holograms. A company that gives away pre-paid telephone cards inscribed with its sales pitch knows that it will be remembered at least until the card runs out. If a taxi company gives away a telephone card programmed automatically to dial the cab rank's number when it is fed into a telephone, it saves late-night drunks a headache and gives the taxi firm a ready source of customers. At election time, politicians hand out phone cards printed with their photos. The trouble is that the simple pre-paid card has become too successful for its own good. The cards are valid for only one purpose: it might be telephoning or paying for the dry-cleaning, but not both. Japanese brains are now perfecting multipurpose cards that can be used to buy from a broad range of vendors. But then companies issuing such cards would function as *de facto* banks, taking deposits from customers and running a settlement system to pay the vendors. If everything works out, pre-paid cards will effectively become a new currency that will compete with the yen. The Japanese will have reinvented money, and once again it will be the consumer who is out of pocket. Why do Japanese consumers make life so much harder for themselves?

Where the quality of life in Japan is changing, it changes in often unexpected ways. Nobody could call Tokyo one of the world's most beautiful cities. Among its ferroconcrete houses, overhead expressways and lack of parks, signs of nature are

difficult to find. But at least those Tokyo dwellers who are tired
of travelling three or four hours out of the capital to spot
anything greener than a supermarket lettuce or any bird more
tuneful than the screeching crows that monopolize the city's
telegraph wires can now enjoy nature in their armchairs by just
picking up the telephone. Instead of joining the weekend crush
to crowded country retreats, Japan's frustrated nature-lovers can
dial a telephone service that brings the soothing sound of birds
and insects into their homes. If they have a pre-paid telephone
card, they can also dial in from the shopping mall.

So along with widely available video tapes that turn their
television screens into small windows looking out on to a gently
swaying forest or on to the serene cone of Mount Fuji, Japan's
overworked city dwellers can come home, sit back, pick up the
phone and enjoy a safari without even the bother of mosquito
bites. Many people are obviously tempted by the convenience of
listening to nature while still being able to sit at their dining
tables at home, expressing themselves. So to prevent them becoming hooked on ersatz wildlife, the lady who hosts the skylark
and cuckoo recordings ends her telephone safari by urging
listeners to: 'Please go out and try to find the real sounds for
yourself.'

If you find this concept unappealing you may find the idea of
a telephone service that plugs diallers into the hubbub of an
airport, a train station, a crowded pub or just a busy family
kitchen even more baffling. Callers can choose one of these
locations as background noise for their conversation. The service
was not designed to give errant husbands convincing-sounding
alibis. Then for whom was this noise-on-tap dreamed up? Are
farmers desperate to tune in to the roar of traffic without all the
fuss of driving to their nearest motorway?

You could not imagine a more unnecessary service for a
country that has so much man-made noise pollution that many

people no longer regard it as a blight on the quality of their lives: they would feel eery if it was all suddenly switched off. The problem is not so much the Muzak in elevators and hotel lobbies, the noisy karaoke bars, sing-song hold buttons in telephones or the background babble from the television set that your host will switch on as soon as you enter a Japanese home. It is the chorus of announcements and nagging that punctuate the Japanese day. In some rural areas the loudspeakers attached to all the lampposts come alive at dawn to wake everyone up. They will often play music for the rest of the day. City streets are trawled by men in vans equipped with tape machines that sing their wares: hot sweet potatoes, or plastic poles for hanging out the laundry, or maybe loo rolls in exchange for old newspapers. Subway train rides are accompanied by a constant soundtrack of bells and 'train arriving soon' warnings on the platform and a stream of nannying from the guards once you are inside the carriage: 'We'll soon be arriving at the next stop, don't fall asleep, don't forget your belongings, don't lean on your neighbour, please don't spread out your newspapers if the train is crowded, sit closer together to make room for others.' Considering there is only a minute or two between subway stops, the conductors are speaking pretty well non-stop.

In red-light districts burly men use megaphones to hawk their ladies' attractions, in other entertainment areas young men use them to entice dancers into discothèques. Pinball arcades send clattering machine noises and carnival music into the street. Right-wing extremists drive around cities in armoured trucks blaring military music and anti-left-wing propaganda through giant loudspeakers. Police lecture pedestrians on traffic safety and crime prevention from megaphones on helicopters that hover above the traffic. The serenity of Kyoto's beautiful temples and Zen gardens is shattered by the screeching microphones of Japanese tour guides shepherding their flocks. Even on ski slopes,

134

trees are wired for sound, emitting wails from Barry Manilow as you zigzag down the mountainside. It is as if the whole of Speakers' Corner has flown from London's Hyde Park to Japan to accompany you day and night.

The other biggest source of urban pollution is trash. To hear it from the pessimists, Tokyo, which is home to a quarter of Japan's population, will sink under its own rubbish in just a few years as Japan's throwaway consumer society runs out of room in its rubbish dumps. The optimists are sure that Tokyo can hold back the tides of trash until the turn of the century. The government is going grey trying to find a way out of the mess. 'Tokyo's facing a major crisis,' says Soji Agata, the head of the Tokyo Metropolitan Assembly's sanitation committee. 'We and the sanitation department pray every day that our city will not end up buried in rubbish.' The government has come up with the idea of making manufacturers of things like TV sets, cars and fridges responsible for disposing of them when consumers throw them out, either by forcing them to collect the abandoned items or by making them pay the local council's collection costs. Appliance makers and car makers are not enthusiastic. Tokyo's governor urges Tokyoites to discard less and recycle more. He sets an example by using business cards made of recycled paper, maybe not that much of an ecological breakthrough in Britain, but a big paper-saver in a country where business cards are exchanged with every hello.

Tokyo produces five million tonnes of garbage a year. If things go on as they are Tokyo will very soon have more rubbish than it knows what to do with. Reclaiming land has been a convenient way to dump inconvenient rubbish and to gain a bit more elbow room in a congested country. But the government says there is a limit to how much of Japan's shoreline can be built on old tin cans and that limit is near. The capital's bureaucrats have even touted the idea of building a huge incinerator in the heart of

Tokyo's financial district. It assures bankers and stockbrokers that the processing plant will be odourless, but the financiers sniff at the plan. And there's that ever-present inventive streak: one of the more unusual ways of treating the family to a day out in Tokyo in recent years must have been the 'Trash Bash' organized by the government in the giant Tokyo Dome stadium. The aim of the one-day event was to get the capital's residents to think more seriously about rubbish. About 53,000 visitors turned up. They saw a 'trash fashion show' featuring recycled clothing, a display of rubbish trucks from around the world and several mock apartment rooms filled with shiny new furniture and appliances plucked from rubbish dumps, a sort of Ideal Home Exhibition for ecologists.

If you are not fussy about matching colours you could furnish a small apartment from what your neighbours leave on street corners for rubbish collectors to pick up. Some of the televisions, bicycles, washing-machines and tape decks may need a new plug or a couple of screws, since in Japan people prefer to buy a replacement than to bother with repairs. But most work perfectly. Many are just two or three years out of date, too old for many Japanese who are now rich enough to afford the latest hi-fi and whose flats are too small to warehouse anything that is not in everyday use. Manufacturers indulge their customers, and boost their profits, by bringing out new models almost every year. Sometimes retailers have to throw away the previous year's stock to make room for new items. The government's challenge seems to be to persuade everyone to hold on to still usable household goods for a little longer.

But no one ever accused the Japanese of being the most passionate guardians of the environment. Even Mount Fuji, which brings tears to emotional Japanese eyes whenever they see it, turns into a giant *al fresco* rubbish dump during the summer climbing season. Most people who climb Mount Fuji do so at night, with the aim of reaching the peak in time to see the sun rise. Hungry and thirsty as they march, they eat the pre-packed rice balls and drink the cans of Pocari Sweat that they brought with them in their backpacks, discarding the debris on the way.

Yet a mess on Mount Fuji is a relatively modest stain on Japan's ecological reputation. Japan's environmental copybook has been blotted so often and so badly that it tops the Bad Boy league of most international environmental campaigners. A United Nations survey concluded that Japanese were less willing to take action on the environment than people in most developed and even some developing countries.

Perhaps the worst tragedy to have struck Japan was the Minamata pollution case, in which thousands of Japanese suffered organic mercury poisoning as a result of industrial waste discharged by a chemical factory into the Bay of Minamata and the Ariake Sea in southern Japan. The discharge continued from 1932 to 1968. Victims of the poisoning suffered irreversible and progressively more debilitating corrosion of their central nervous systems. The first cases of Minamata disease were officially diagnosed and catalogued in 1956, when two sisters, aged three and six, were taken to hospital, unable to speak or walk properly and showing signs of mental instability. They had eaten fish caught in Minamata Bay. They died shortly afterwards. It is possible that more than 16,000 have been struck by Minamata poisoning, many of them already dead, although it is unlikely that it will ever be possible to make an exact tally. Compounding the tragedy is the government's refusal to discuss an out-of-court settlement with the victims, who are seeking compensation from the chemical company that discharged the industrial waste and from the local and national governments, who failed to stop the pollution after its effects began to be realized. The chemical company and the local government are willing to start discussing an out-of-court settlement. It is the central government which is

137

putting its foot down, even though several court cases have found it liable.

Japan retains a reputation for having little regard for its own environment or the ecological balance of the rainforests and the oceans which it ravages, and for caring even less what international lobby groups think of its behaviour. If there is anything approaching an environmental movement in Japan, it is very difficult to see it twitch, let alone move. Greenpeace Japan has managed to round up three hundred members. After a decade of preaching, Friends of the Earth collected just five hundred members.

It is hard to think of an environmental issue for which Japan is not in the doghouse. Japanese builders use disappearing tropical hardwoods as moulding frames when building concrete walls. The wood is then discarded or burned. More wood goes in the bin in the form of disposable chopsticks. Millions are thrown away every day. After years of international outcry, Japan finally relented in 1989 and agreed to join a world ban on ivory trade. Japan accounts for about 40 per cent of world consumption of ivory, which is mostly used to make the signature seals used to sign documents and authenticate deals. Less successful has been the world's campaign to make Japan think twice about dealing in endangered species. Japanese journalists who have investigated Japan's taste for exotic animals will tell you that if you stroll into a pet shop in Japan and tell the man behind the counter that you are interested in buying a rare animal, the chances are that he will lead you into his backyard and offer you a choice of exotic monkeys, parrots, tropical fish – and several other species that are ranked as endangered by conservation groups. The trade in endangered species has flowered under a curious canopy of laws which make it illegal to import protected species, but impossible to confiscate those which have slipped through; which make it illegal to sell a protected animal, but legal to own one. Japan imports more of the world's most threatened flora and fauna than any other country. It has a reputation as an animal smuggler's paradise. Chiba Zoo, just east of Tokyo, had to brave the wrath of the World Wide Fund for Nature when it paid a record price of eighty-six million yen for a pair of endangered lowland gorillas and then put them on show despite evidence that they had been imported illegally. Every year customs officers at Tokyo's Narita airport force travellers to hand over thousands of rare animals, fish, fur and various mounted animals whose trade is banned under the Convention on International Trade in Endangered Species, CITES. Not all get caught, though. In a typical case, a Japanese dealer was allowed through customs at Narita with fifty slow loris, an endangered south-east Asian monkey. The export permit was later found to be fake. Bought in Bangkok for pennies, the loris were sold in Japan for more than 150,000 yen each. Another dealer's plan to smuggle in nine leopards and two white-handed gibbons from Thailand went awry when the drugged animals, hidden in false-bottomed suitcases, woke up unexpectedly in the customs hall. A favourite Japanese import is the arowana fish which swims in the waters of Malaysia and Indonesia. Brought in inside whisky bottles, the fish sell for anything from 200,000 to one million yen.

Of course lowland gorillas and white-handed gibbons are the least of Japan's public-relations problems. The one activity that has made it the pariah of the world's ecologists is its refusal to stop whaling. Japan officially stopped commercial whaling in the 1986–7 season after hauling home 1,941 whales that year. Since then, its fleets have sailed to the Antarctic for research purposes only, usually coming home with a little over three hundred whales. They might manage a few more were their harpoonists not dogged by Greenpeace activists. Wildlife campaigners scoff at Japan's argument that its whaling research programme is designed to collect population data that will show that there are ample enough stocks to lift the moratorium on commercial whaling imposed by the International Whaling Commission. Japanese scientists say the information they need on age, sex, diet and health can be got only by killing the whales. They say non-lethal methods, such as skin samplings and sighting studies, do not give reliable data. Ecologists reply that Japan's scientific whaling programme is just a mumbo-jumbo ruse to skirt the IWC's ban. Their suspicions are roused by the swift sale, at fancy prices, of the whalemeat caught by the research boats. The scarcity of whalemeat has made what was a dull school-lunch staple into a luxury for Japanese diners. Anti-whaling lobbyists also suspect that research whaling is at least partly designed to keep the country's commercial whaling industry and its skills alive until the IWC ban is lifted. Japan, meanwhile, sees the criticism and abuse hurled at it from abroad because of its fondness for whalemeat as something between insensitivity to another country's traditions and unashamed Japan-bashing. The issue arouses such fierce passions that the Japanese deserve a chance to have their say, to state their case for the defence: here is one of their witnesses.

Wataru Kohama, now in his sixties, used to harpoon whales in the Antarctic when Taiji was a busy Japanese fishing port and whalers gathered in its bars to tell of minke that got away. After the IWC moratorium on commercial whaling Taiji – Japan's oldest whaling port – lost its bustle, Kohama lost his job and whalers now meet to gossip about which factory needs odd-job men.

Whaling is still in Taiji's blood and the people of the town hope that one day soon the world will stop looking on them as ogres and will allow them to return to the livelihood that has supported them for four hundred years. In the meantime Taiji, a remote speck on the mountainous coast of southern Japan, earns a steadier income from its whaling museum than from whaling. The Moby Dick restaurant in the town still serves a big menu of whalemeat. But the prices have changed. In the early 1960s, when whalemeat was a staple food in Japan, steak for dinner was usually whale steak. Today, the bill at Moby Dick for whale sukiyaki makes it a place for a treat, not a lunchtime snack.

After nearly forty years manning the harpoon guns, Kohama was told by his boss in 1987 that the IWC's ban on commercial hunts meant there was no more work for him. With the bruised confidence of outcasts, he and the rest of Taiji's population hope that the IWC will not kill Japan's whaling skills altogether by banning the controversial research whaling programme. In the 1960s Taiji had more than 250 whalers. They provided one third of Taiji's income. Now the ten whalers who hunt in the waters off Japan's coast and the six more who work for the government's research programme are lonely statistics among the four thousand or so people who live in Taiji and they constitute barely 3 per cent of the town's revenue.

'There are lots of people who gave up at the same time as me,' says Kohama. He is amiable and bright but has found it hard to pick up work since losing his job on the whaling boat. He knows that whaling stirs up emotions and that many foreigners think him a barbarian, but still he dreams of returning one day to peering across the Antarctic through the gunsight of his 90 lb explosive-charged harpoon. 'I was in the business from 1948 to 1987. I stopped after the IWC ban on whaling took my job. My company disappeared. It was a whaling firm headquartered in Tokyo. At one time we had 2,300 employees all over Japan. It was hard for me suddenly to join the other unemployed fishermen in small coastal whaling ships, or in boats fishing for tuna. It's just not the same.

'I used to be a gunner, the harpoonist. It took me ten years to become an expert. It took a lot of skill. Apart from right whales, which were protected even before I started in the business, I used to catch all types. But by the time I quit, I was catching only minke whales, because the IWC had slapped bans on all the others: I caught about nine out of every ten I spotted. It's a matter of experience. I would love to return to whaling if the IWC lifted its ban. I chose whaling as my career for life. I miss the sea. I think the way Japanese people look at things is 180° different from Americans, Britons and other Westerners. In the States, whaling was a job for low-class people. You only have to read novels like *Moby Dick* to see that people involved in this business were looked down on. But in Japan it was regarded as a job which required courage. Whalers commanded the same respect as samurai.

'Since giving up whaling I've been on the dole. But the dole will run out. Younger people who lost jobs at the same time found work outside the town because they have to support their families. Some of them got jobs on oil tankers and freight ships. Most who found jobs in factories are working on a temporary basis. If the IWC lifts its ban this town could revive the whaling business. The people who acquired the traditional skills are still alive. But time is running out.

'I think Japan is very misunderstood. Western people see whales only as cuddly, cute things. Also whales have become a symbol of the environmental movement to save the earth. But Japanese people traditionally regarded whales as just another kind of food. We deserve to win our fight to have the IWC ban lifted.'

Naturally, the people of Taiji are prickly and defensive about Western criticism of the way they would prefer to earn their living. Yoji Kita, who looks after whaling affairs at Taiji's town hall, said, 'We're really proud of our whaling tradition. Japanese people are called barbaric because they eat whales. When I protest that you eat cows, the answer is that cows are bred to be

142

eaten. But that is just Western people's arrogance. Britain, America and Holland also used to go whaling until they no longer needed whale oil. The West's reaction is another example of Japan-bashing. We should have the same treatment as Eskimos, who are allowed to hunt whales because it is part of their tradition and livelihood. It's the same for us.'

Ironically, while Japan gets lashed by environmentalists for its alleged crimes against nature, one of the world's biggest environmental threats faces Japan itself. Worse, it is completely out of Japan's control as to when the havoc will be wreaked.

So far this century, about one in every ten of the earthquakes around the world that have registered more than seven on the Richter scale have struck Japan, an unlucky draw for a country that accounts for only one hundredth of the earth's surface. Japan is also home to about one tenth of the world's active volcanoes. It is a pretty inexact science, but Japanese seismologists are convinced that another powerful earthquake will strike the Tokyo region in the near future. Not the sort that Tokyo residents very soon get used to, the ones that make the crockery rattle a little and make you wonder if the living-room walls will hold up, but the sort that kills thousands and which triggers International Red Cross appeals.

The details of the great earthquake in 1923 that razed Tokyo and killed 140,000 are as familiar to most Japanese as cherry blossom. Surveys find that 95 per cent of Tokyo residents are afraid of earthquakes and that 40 per cent of them believe there will be a large tremor within the decade. Seismology experts say that Japan is hit by a massive quake every sixty-five to seventy years, which means that the clock is ticking.

Recalling his schoolboy memories of the 1923 earthquake in his autobiography, Akira Kurosawa, the Japanese film director, wrote that the centre of Tokyo was veiled in a dancing, swirling dust whose greyness gave the sun a pallor like that during an eclipse. The people looked for all the world like fugitives from hell, and the whole landscape took on a bizarre and eerie aspect ... The burned landscape as far as the eye could see had a brownish red colour. Amid this expanse of nauseating redness lay every kind of corpse imaginable. I saw corpses charred black, half-burned corpses, corpses in gutters, corpses floating in rivers, corpses piled up on bridges, corpses blocking off a whole street at a crossroads.

The 1923 earthquake registered 7.8 on the Richter scale. The Japanese government has calculated that if a jolt of similar size struck the Tokyo area today, 150,000 people would be killed and 200,000 injured. Something like 39 per cent of the buildings in greater Tokyo would also be destroyed. As a result, most Japanese have safety helmets, torches and fire extinguishers ready, and most Japanese department stores have a 'disaster section' that sells these items along with emergency food rations and first-aid kits. Once a year, on 1 September, evacuation drills are held in parks and baseball grounds to prepare the nation for an earthquake: children run through tunnels of smoke, old women hose down burning buildings, planes drop emergency medical supplies. To drive home the seriousness of the threat and the need for everyone to take part in practice drills, government leaflets are dropped through everyone's door announcing details of the forthcoming drill under headlines like, 'Are You Ready for the Big One?' But how much can you prepare? Sceptics say that when the time comes, Tokyo's fire-engines and other emergency rescue teams will get caught up in Tokyo's notorious traffic jams and will be all but useless in helping anyone.

Japan has changed so much since 1923 that it is difficult to measure how much damage a major earthquake will inflict on the capital. On the one hand, there are fewer wooden homes. On the other, Tokyo Bay, once barren, is now peppered with gas tanks and chemical containers. One estimate, made by Japan's Tokai Bank, of the damage that would be caused by a killer Tokyo earthquake runs to 80,000 billion yen. And a quake would not only be a catastrophe for Tokyo. The world would suffer, too. If the Tokyo area were an independent nation, its gross national product would be the sixth biggest in the world, larger than that of Britain. As Japan sucked back its wealth to finance its reconstruction, the flow of Japanese capital that helps to keep the US afloat would dry up, sending Wall Street and the American economy into a spin, triggering a world stock-market crash and knocking a few points off the world's GNP.

As always, however, the Japanese expect to come out on top. Here is Kaoru Oda, a research analyst at the Tokai Bank: 'After a few years, business is likely to be rather brisk because of the reconstruction boom. I think it shows the strength of the Japanese economy.'

8. One of Us: Unique Japanese and the Outsiders Looking In

Aliens – racism – the outsiders – the uniqueness of the Japanese – the hidden underclass – riots in Osaka

British cabinet ministers and American presidential hopefuls must sizzle with jealousy at the way Japanese politicians regularly manage to insult 'inferior' foreigners – Americans in general, blacks and Asians in particular – without being hounded out of office or even producing more than a passing paragraph or two in the local newspapers. That is not to say that the xenophobic or racist or patronizing comments do not often cause outrage abroad, among the people who are the butt of the insult. They do. But at home in Japan, the comments raise little fuss. If apologies are offered, it is because the Japanese politicians who voiced the insults are embarrassed for having led Japan into a critical international spotlight, not because they realize that what they have said is regarded as unacceptably racist abroad.

Just how differently Japan and, say, Britain react to such controversies was highlighted in 1990. In Britain, Nicholas Ridley, the trade and industry minister, was forced to step down from Margaret Thatcher's cabinet after making disparaging comments in a magazine interview about Germany and its leader Helmut Kohl; essentially that Germany was threatening to dominate the European Community, and hence Europe, and that anyone who knew anything about German politics and

146

Germany's past knew that we had better all be on guard. In Tokyo, just shortly after Ridley had tendered his resignation, Japan's newly appointed justice minister saw no reason to step down after comparing black people to prostitutes: the minister, Seiroku Kajiyama, said both destroyed neighbourhoods once they had moved in. He made his matter-of-fact remark after accompanying police on a round-up of foreign prostitutes in Tokyo's red-light district of Shinjuku. He said the young ladies from Thailand, Korea, Colombia and Brazil would destroy Shinjuku just the way blacks did when they moved into a community in America. 'Bad money drives out good money, just like in America, where the blacks came in and drove out the whites,' said Kajiyama. Americans, especially black Americans, were not pleased, and Kajiyama made the usual murmurs about misunderstandings and about how he wasn't expecting his comments to be broadcast to the world.

Even ignoring the fact that Japanese prostitutes far outnumber foreign ones in Tokyo, or that it is Japanese gangsters who import most of these foreign girls with promises of waitressing jobs before confiscating their passports and forcing them on to the streets, the fact that Kajiyama could voice such a view without being roundly condemned inside Japan seems breathtaking to people in Europe and America, where even gaffes must usually be atoned for by some sacrifice or other. But not in Japan. What Kajiyama's opinion, and similar ones expressed by other cabinet ministers in the past (and since), makes clear is how insular Japan remains even now that it is among the world's richest and most powerful nations and now that its products are famous from London to Lima. When Japanese MPs voice such views in Japan, which is still a largely mono-racial and little travelled society, they think they are talking about something as obvious and uncontroversial as the laws of gravity. Their local audiences think so, too.

On average, a cracking international howler seems to drop from a Japanese politician's mouth about every two years. Two years before Kajiyama made his contribution to international diplomacy, Michio Watanabe, a big power broker in the ruling Liberal Democratic Party and a future prime minister, announced that, unlike Japanese people, American blacks had few qualms about going bankrupt. He also implied that they walked away from their debts, whereas Japanese would rather commit suicide than live with such a stain on their character. America fumed, especially because Watanabe's outburst coincided with the reappearance in Tokyo department stores of Little Black Sambo toys and beachwear. But perhaps to show that he did not look down only on Americans, Watanabe also declared that same year that in modern China 'many people still live in caves'.

Two years before that it was the turn of Yasuhiro Nakasone, then prime minister and still regarded as the most internationalist premier Japan has ever had. He raised a chorus of protest in America but few eyebrows in Japan when he said that the overall level of Americans' intelligence and knowledge was low because it was pulled down by the presence of a 'considerable number of blacks, Puerto Ricans and Mexicans'.

Then again more recently, two years after Kajiyama's trip through Shinjuku in fact, another Japanese politician, this time the speaker of the powerful Lower House of Japan's parliament, shared his views on the world with his constituents. The speaker, a man called Yoshio Sakurauchi, described American workers as lazy and illiterate. Only three in ten of them could read. Moreover, he added, America had sunk to such industrial depths that nowadays it was little more than Japan's subcontractor. All these views are not uncommon in Japan and are traded quite openly between Japanese over an evening drink. What seems odd to non-Japanese is not only that senior Japanese politicians do not realize that such views will not endear them to their allies

– who might not regard them as indisputable laws of nature –
but that they have not grasped that Japan is no longer closed off
from the rest of the world, that a huge foreign press corps is
relaying news from Tokyo back to America, Europe, Australia
and Africa, that they cannot expect to say things in television
interviews 'for Japanese ears only'. It is one more aspect of the
country's clinging insularity and awkward unworldliness.

Such insensitivity can cause as much pain inside Japan as it
does abroad. Particularly notable was the time the Japanese
police rather than politicians had to do the apologizing, to the
Pakistani Embassy in Tokyo, after issuing an internal official
staff manual that said 'Pakistanis have a unique stink' and 'do
nothing but lie in the name of Allah'. The manual also instructed
police officers to wash their hands after questioning Pakistani
suspects for fear of catching a contagious disease. 'There are
some points which might invite misunderstanding,' a senior
police officer told the press after the manual came to light, 'so
we are going to revise it.'

The suspicion with which Pakistanis are greeted in Japan
partly reflects the fact that they are fairly recent arrivals. Korean
families who have lived in Japan for three generations still feel
like unwanted outsiders. They are regarded as foreigners and,
like all aliens in Japan, they have been forced to have their
fingerprints registered and to carry a special alien's pass at all
times, on pain of a fine or even a jail sentence. After years of
diplomatic pressure from Seoul, Japan finally softened its stance:
from 1993, all permanent residents – mostly of Korean and
Chinese origin – were allowed to skip the fingerprinting ordeal
and get through life by promising always to carry a document
bearing their snapshot, signature and family history. Non-
permanent residents are still forced to have their fingers inked.
But Western aliens have a relatively easy time of it in Japan,
although some landlords and bar owners, particularly in country

areas, will still turn their backs. And after all, most of the Westerners living in Japan choose to live there. Many Koreans were forced to move to Japan when Korea was ruled by the Imperial Army and colonized Koreans were made to speak Japanese. Many people of Korean descent now living in Japan have never been to Korea, cannot speak Korean, and regard themselves as Japanese. Although they make up around 70 per cent of the million or so foreigners living in Japan, Koreans are sometimes hard to distinguish, and not just because they speak Japanese so well. Many of them change their name to a Japanese one. They fear they will not be able to find a job or a Japanese spouse otherwise. Potential employers and pukka parents-in-law usually trace official family records anyway, just to make sure.

In a more peculiar position are Japanese who have lived abroad and are ostracized by their countrymen when they return because they have apparently lost their 'Japaneseness', that quality that makes Japanese stand out as a unique and generally superior race. These returnees complain that employers refuse them jobs when they see a spell in London or New York on their CVs, saying 'you are no longer Japanese'. This often means little more than that you might disrupt the routine by bringing in foreign ways of doing things or by refusing to wait patiently for your promotion like your colleagues. Children of such families are often bullied by Japanese classmates, sometimes just because they speak English so well, sometimes because they raise their hands in class, forgetting that Japanese schoolchildren do not ask questions or discuss a point with teacher. The process of reassimilation has been so troublesome and upsetting for many returnees that dozens of support groups have sprung up to help returnees readapt to their home country.

Sometimes this Japanese sense of their superiority or their 'otherness' reflects a yearning to distance themselves from their Asian neighbours in China and Korea, even though all sprang from the Mongoloid race and even though many of the things that define Japanese society – from kimonos and kanji script to Zen Buddhism and scroll paintings – were imported into Japan from China or Korea. Sometimes it reflects a hangover of the ignorance that fermented through centuries of isolation but which still breeds fantastical theories about the outside world, such as those that trace most of the world's troubles to an international Jewish conspiracy of one sort or the other. Masao Uno, a former Japanese schoolteacher, has become a rich man by churning out a string of anti-Semitic bestsellers that blame Japan's economic problems on a conspiracy by 'international Jewish capital', that allege that Jews run just about every major American corporation from Ford and General Motors to IBM and Exxon, that many of Japan's political bribery scandals were triggered by Jews, that believe the 1992 Barcelona Olympic Games were somehow orchestrated by Jews, even that the 1992 market integration of the European Community was a dastardly Jewish plot designed to take over and rule the world. Uno's books have sold more than a million copies in Japan, which must give the Japanese an odd insight into a people most have never come across in their lives.

Sometimes this striving by the Japanese to prove their superiority reaches hysterical proportions. In a particularly fantastic thesis laid out in an article for the Japanese magazine *Voice*, Kimindo Kusaka, managing director of a big research group called the Softnomics Centre, argued that those who moan that 'high prices, inadequate housing and long working hours' make for a grim standard of living in Japan have failed to understand that 'many so-called obstacles to a better life are actually assets. These disguised benefits constitute a distinctive Japanese lifestyle'. Kusaka points out, for example, that 'American families transferred to Tokyo are astonished to learn they must pay $7,000 per month for an apartment that seems impossibly cramped,' but they soon learn to appreciate the advantages: 'Because there is less space, they are easier to clean and maintain. No yard means no lawn to cut or leaves to rake.' It seems obvious now, doesn't it? Lack of space also means that Japanese entertain in restaurants rather than at home, thus 'Americans living here are spared the expense and bother of US-style social- izing at home' and executives' wives are spared the twin burdens of being good hostesses and interior decorators to boot. As if foreigners were not already chastened to hear how much better off they would be living in tiny, gardenless, easy-to-clean apart- ments, Kusaka reminds them that some non-Japanese are already seeing the light: 'Many countries have adopted Japanese norms of cleanliness, for example. (Daily bathing is a ritual here . . . People put on clean clothes each day)' and that very soon 'the world will beat a path to our door'. An exposition like this is greeted with nods of assent in Japan: the majority, who never doubted the superiority of Japan's ways, or the lackadaisical bathing habits of others, are heartened to see that the rest of the world is learning that, along with microchips, Japan also leads the way in lifestyle; those who harboured doubts about living in cramped houses and working all day and night are reassured that it all does make sense after all, so much sense that even foreigners are following suit and will soon be selling off all their spare bedrooms and doing all their entertaining in hostess bars.

If all this seems hard to swallow, there is more; and it is, if anything, even lumpier. It has to do with Japan's sense of its own uniqueness, which is the foundation stone for the Japanese people's belief in their racial specialness and hence – it's only logical – their race's superiority over others. The oddest things are unique in Japan. Japan's special snow once prevented a baffled French ski manufacturer from entering the Japanese ski market on the grounds that its skis would not be able to take a grip on the unique brand of snow that fell on Japanese mountains. Japanese people's unusually long intestines have been one reason for Japan's reluctance to import foreign beef: the unique intestines make American-raised beef tricky to digest. Some Japanese believe their brains work in a unique way. There is even the case of the unique Japanese head that conspired to thwart a British sweater manufacturer: the unnamed British company apparently tried to sell pullovers to the Japanese but failed because Japanese heads are disproportionately large in relation to their bodies and could not fit through the head holes in the sweaters without tearing them asunder. The story was told by Hiroya Ichikawa, deputy director of the Keidanren, Japan's equivalent of the Confederation of British Industry, who used it to explain why foreigners who complain about Japan's supposed import barriers should not always assume that Japanese are being deliberately obstructive. Nevertheless, you can't help wondering why their disproportionately large heads do not prevent Japanese tourists in London loading up with cashmeres at Harrods.

A Tokyo correspondent of the *New York Times* relishes the story of the day he asked a Japanese meteorologist 'why so many Japanese, even in big cities, seemed preoccupied with the weather. Probably, he replied, because Japan used to be an agrarian society. It apparently never occurred to him that every country was once an agrarian society.'

This fetish for their own uniqueness, and a conviction that the Japanese way is intrinsically best, spawns racism, and not only against foreigners. Japan's biggest racial problem is working out how to deal with the Burakumin, historically the outcasts of Japanese society and still all but ignored by respectable society. They have always been among the worst-treated communities in Japan, forced to live in segregated ghettoes whose names appeared on no map. They are descended from those men and women consigned to the lowest caste of society because of their work. They did 'unclean' jobs – they were butchers, leather tanners, shoemakers, grave-diggers, they cremated the dead – and they evoked little sympathy because Buddhists believed that being born an untouchable was punishment for misdeeds committed in a previous life. Although nowadays Burakumin no longer have to wear special clothes and shoes to distinguish themselves from their racially identical fellow Japanese, and although they were officially emancipated by the Japanese government in 1871, they are still shunned by polite society, and discriminated against in jobs and marriage. Supposedly illegal lists of Burakumin still change hands for folding money in Japan, among employers and prospective in-laws seeking to avoid making an embarrassing social mistake. There may be as many as three million Burakumin in Japan, but their third-class existence is barely acknowledged, even by their neighbours; their problems rarely provoke the interest of book publishers and newspaper editors. They are part of the underbelly of the Japanese economic miracle, out of sight, out of mind, and mentioned as infrequently as possible.

Not surprisingly, Burakumin often conspire in this social sleight of hand. They are as keen as the rest of society to pretend they do not exist, if only to improve their access to better jobs and better pay, to friends and to spouses. Many, though, have not succeeded and many others have tried and failed. They are concentrated in no-man's-land ghettoes around Osaka, Kyoto and Kobe, as well as in pockets in other parts of the country. The worst-off live a precarious and painful existence in slums, exploited by the police, by the *yakuza* gangsters who milk them of their last yen and by anyone else they might happen to come into contact with. Occasionally, but rarely, the patience of the day-labourers and itinerants who live in these Skid Row communities snaps. Polite society does its best not to notice, but sometimes the explosion of fury is so great that it cannot be entirely ignored.

The last time real mayhem erupted was in the autumn of 1990, in Osaka. It was the first time in nearly twenty years that the homeless day labourers of Osaka's slum quarter had rioted against police corruption, bullying by *yakuza* gangsters and against their own dismal lives. After the 1970s outburst, tidy-minded local councillors responded to the crisis by changing the name of the awkward area from Kamagasaki to Airin, which means 'love thy neighbour'. It may have kept the mapmakers in business, but the week-long explosion of anger in October 1990, which left more than two hundred policemen and protestors injured, and which left Airin in flames, showed how little the re-naming had done to cheer up the bleak, secret lives of Airin's 20,000 down-and-outs. Many are believed to be Burakumin, some are vagrants, others are those who have made a mistake – perhaps a theft – that makes them rejects of a society which has no convenient place for those who do not conform. Their days and the streets they sleep on at night are so different from the rest of prim, modern, middle-class Japan that entering the area is like walking into a sort of Disneyland in reverse. There are flophouses offering uninviting beds for 900 yen, the price of a couple of coffees in Japan. The capsule-shaped rooms are so grim and rat-ridden that many men prefer cheap liquor and a cardboard blanket on the grim and rat-ridden pavement. There are Orwellian video cameras on street corners keeping an eye on the inhabitants. The place stinks of urine and dirty clothes. Street stalls sell frayed shirts and trousers, a jolt in Japan, where nobody buys second-hand anything.

Yet many Japanese do not even know that Airin exists. Those that do rarely talk about it. A week of stone-throwing, petrol-bombing and rioting was brought to an end by typhoon rains, tiredness and a 2,500-strong police presence. But it left a train station, several shops, dozens of cars and more than a hundred vending-machines wrecked or burning. It was more like South

Korea than Japan. Yet the Japanese media gave the story less space than they might give to a provincial street festival. Had the same thing occurred in a European or American city, it would dominate the headlines and the evening news broadcasts. Even in Seoul, where riots happen almost daily, the camera crews would have been patrolling the streets. Yet here, in the second biggest city of a country famed for its social cohesion, for its well-behaved and disciplined citizens, there were burning train stations and wrecked cars and looting and the chaos barely troubled the media. When the story became too big to miss, NHK, the state run TV channel, gave it a mention twenty minutes into its half-hour main evening news bulletin, where it was preceded by the sort of news items that might make the inside page of a provincial newspaper on a very slow news day. When one asked Japanese for their reaction to the carryings-on in Airin, many of them, even the well-educated and well-read ones, seemed to know nothing about it. The vagrants' outburst seemed to be regarded as rather vulgar and un-Japanese. When I visited Osaka to see for myself, the taxi-driver who took me from Osaka station to as near the centre of Airin as he was willing to go, told me that he had heard that something or other had happened, but most people in Osaka knew little about it, and probably cared less.

Evening shows the citizens of Airin at their most exploited. As dusk falls on their urban leper colony, they return in twos and threes from another day on another building site and settle down for a drink. When they drink, they often gamble and when they gamble the police often make a raid. The labourers get arrested and, they say, kicked and beaten. The *yakuza* gangsters who organize the poker and dice games get away. The labourers say that this is because the mobsters get tipped off by the police in return for lining the policemen's pockets. That makes the gamblers angry and the tension in the streets swells once again.

It was the arrest of a policeman for taking eleven million yen in bribes from *yakuza* that helped to trigger the riots of 1990. But the Osaka police say that although they have a reputation for surliness and corruption, they are not on the make. 'We regret that there was a bad apple in the barrel,' Inspector Rentaro Atake at Airin's local police station told me. 'There's no excuse for that. But it's ridiculous to say that this whole police station is taking bribes.' As we chatted through the afternoon, Inspector Atake chain-smoked his way through a packet of cigarettes and watched the glaziers repair windows that had been smashed by the 1,600 rioters who had lain siege to the station. Riot shields were still stacked against the walls. He had the distracted, itchy look of someone keen to end an unwanted telephone call. Asked why the riot had started, he turned to ask a colleague, as if it were the first time he had stopped to wonder about it.

'It's a hard place to be posted,' Inspector Atake said between lighting another cigarette and inking colleagues' time-sheets with his personal name seal. 'I only came here a year ago. I was sort of shocked. For a start, the police-station building is not even clean. Look at it. Also the crime rate is high. And the area is disease-ridden. Our relationship with the locals wasn't bad. But it wasn't too good either. There are about 20,000 migrant workers here, mostly from rural areas. Only about 10 per cent are dangerous, always getting drunk. The police have been strict with them. But others are cooperative and we get on well. We sometimes play baseball against a labourers' team. I don't think the police here are corrupt.'

It is not the story you hear on the streets. 'We're taken to the police station and the police beat us up,' said one grey-haired labourer. 'It happens every day.' His front teeth, top and bottom, are missing, leaving a neat hole. His dental problems made him difficult to understand, but he was not dim or illiterate. He was waving a broadsheet newspaper. 'The police discriminate against us. Whenever we're drunk, or we lie on the street, the cops take us in and beat us up. Also, all the labourers are getting fed up with being ripped off by the *yakuza*. It was this resentment, coupled with anger against the police, that exploded and triggered the rioting.'

Yoshio Dan, who looks after the Kamagasaki Day Labourers' Union office in Airin, barely fifty metres from the police station, said 'this area is like a concentration camp in an open space. When we're not getting beaten up by the police, we're getting fleeced by the *yakuza*. The people who hand out the day jobs on construction sites every morning are all *yakuza*. The wage for unskilled manual labour is 11,500 yen a day, but we reckon the operators who hand out the jobs get 15,000 yen from the building-site foremen. So they're taking 3,500 yen a day off our wages. Also when we need cash for gambling or drinking, the *yakuza* lend us money, but at 10–15 per cent interest per day, which is illegal. We gamble and we get arrested, but the *yakuza* rarely do. They seem to know when there is going to be a raid.'

Yoshio Dan shares a tiny room with busy cockroaches and fading photographs of Lenin and Che Guevara. He knows that there is as much chance of any kind of revolution in Japan as there is of the moon being made out of tofu. He settled for looking after the interests of the local community and making sure his fellow down-and-outs have medicines. 'There are homeless people all over the world. They exist in Japan too. The Japanese press doesn't want to throw any light on this dark side of Japan.'

Around the corner, Inspector Atake was lighting up a cigarette, marshalling the glaziers and stamping his red signature seal on more time-sheets. 'I think the incident has died down for the time being. But the same thing could happen again. Some of these labourers get really drunk.'

This Japanese ability to look around themselves at a country which is home to three million descendants of Burakumin, to hundreds of thousands of 'aliens' of Korean descent who are now almost indistinguishable from Japanese, to thousands more whose grandparents came from China but who now also regard themselves as all but Japanese, to a nation whose incomes stretch from the £50-a-day itinerant labourers of Airin to the billionaires like Yoshiaki Tsutsumi and Japan's rich new Picasso-owners, to well-organized clans of *yakuza* gangsters, and to believe that Japan is a racially pure, culturally homogenous nation in which everyone thinks and behaves alike and in which more than 90 per cent of the population belong to the middle class, is a triumph of their will to cherish notions about their uniqueness against overwhelming empirical odds.

The Japanese reluctance to embrace anyone who might be considered a foreigner into their inner circle, for fear of diluting the national bloodstream, can produce some awkward hypocrisies. When Alberto Fujimori, a Peruvian whose father came from Japan, was elected president of Peru in the summer of 1990, the irony of his victory at the polls escaped most Japanese, who saw his triumph only in terms of another export success story. Front-page headlines in Japanese newspapers celebrated the 'world's first president of Japanese descent' in much the same way as those newspapers relay news of a world-beating new Japanese laptop or fridge-freezer. Japan took a motherly concern in the faraway Peruvian vote. Television newsreaders, throwing impartiality to the wind, openly supported a victory for Fujimori throughout the campaign. Yet many Japanese bristled at reports that Fujimori's candidacy had uncovered pockets of anti-Japanese sentiment across Peru and that some of his opposition critics thought that Lima was not yet ready for a first-generation Peruvian as its president. Here was just one more incident of Japan-bashing, they thought out loud, apparently forgetting that in Japan, Korean descendants whose grandparents came to Japan before the Second World War and who speak only Japanese cannot get jobs as junior civil servants. For them, the idea of a Korean descendant ruling Japan would be a fantasy.

9. *Japanese Bearing Gifts: It's Never the Thought That Counts*

Present indicative – the debts of obligation – being Japanese means always having to say you're sorry – death by satellite – catholic beliefs, but not in Catholicism

In Japan it's never the thought that counts. The Japanese may weep to see a sprig of cherry blossom, but the dinner guest who wants to be invited back would do best to take along a £50 musk melon or a £50 bottle of malt whisky. Socially nervous types might consider taking both, to be on the safe side.

Learning algebra is easier than cracking the art of gift-giving in Japan, which in addition to run-of-the-mill presents for birthdays and graduations, is celebrated in two annual frenzies of present-swapping when debts are repaid, customers coddled, bosses indulged, teachers pampered, politicians wooed. Politicians woo back, of course, especially near elections. One of these big showcases is in the middle of the year, the other is at the end of the year: the motives, the recipients and usually the presents, too, are the same. In between these two binges there is no shortage of other opportunities for generous Japanese to bear gifts. But the rules are complex. Bringing the wrong present – too cheap, too small, too large, too late, too expensive – is often worse than coming empty-handed. And don't, for goodness sake, give four or nine of anything: the Japanese word for four also means death and the word for nine is the same as that for agony. It really is best to stick to a melon.

In certain circumstances the act of giving a gift obliges the receiver to reciprocate with another. Sometimes immediately. When you go to a wedding, for example, make sure your car boot is empty. You will be leaving at the end of the party with carrier bags from your hosts full of cakes, cut-glass bowls, towels, maybe a toaster, or even a vacuum cleaner if the couple is out to impress. This is a sort of swift thank-you for the present you brought for the bride and groom, which will have been at least £150 in cash – no cheques, just new unfolded 10,000 yen notes – slipped into a special wedding envelope you must buy from a stationery shop. If you are actually quite close to the bride or groom, or you are one or the other's office boss, you will have been rather more generous than that.

A present for a newborn child must be repaid with a gift equal to a third or half of that received. Table mats or teacups will sometimes do, sometimes liquor goes down better, which is why gift catalogues from Japanese babywear shops begin with the usual range of pink romper suits and blue sailor outfits and suddenly descend into household goods and lists of whisky prices. This gives the uninitiated the generally unfounded impression that Japanese babies are either very house-proud or like a little nightcap in their final bottle-feed of the day.

If you have been ill, your first duty on leaving hospital is to send presents to all those who visited your bedside with fruit or flowers (though not to those who were insensitive enough to bring you a potted plant, which carries the curse that your illness, too, might take root right there in the ward).

The popularity of the expensive musk melon and the bottle of rare single malt is due to the fact that their prices are known to everybody. That makes it easier to calculate the degree of obligation the receiver has been put under. A fancy whisky maker who cuts his price is a fancy whisky maker who will lose business among Japanese who usually give someone a present worth exactly £50. This is exactly what happened when the marketing team of the Canadian owners of Chivas Regal thought they would steal market share by trimming the price of their whisky to undercut their rivals. They lost market share until they put their prices back up to where the rest of the herd was gathered.

And don't even THINK of wrapping the present yourself. The wrapping is at least as important as what is wrapped. Its job is to show that the present comes from a swanky department store (*the* place in Japan to shop for everything, from picture hooks to Picassos). Strip your garden of every flower, but your bouquet will not thrill as much as a bunch of daffodils swathed in the 'right' florist's cellophane. Fortunately, most Japanese are spared this dilemma because they don't have the size of gardens that throw up enough flowers for a bouquet, and a few bonsai clippings do not fill a vase, however inventive your way with ikebana.

The average family in Japan gives or receives a gift at least once a week and probably spends more than £1,000 a year on presents. Between them, they spend about £50 billion a year on gifts. It is a pivotal part of the country's economic and social structure, intricately woven into the Japanese sense of obligation. To get an idea of what this sense of obligation means, and the lengths to which Japanese will go to cement personal ties, bear in mind that when the new president of Nippon Telegraph & Telephone – Japan's British Telecom – takes up his job he spends pretty much the first three months greeting and thanking ten thousand NTT employees, customers and suppliers.

To maintain the social momentum through the year, the Japanese give gifts on occasions for which other people don't even have occasions. Weddings and birthdays are pretty straightforward. But don't forget to find something suitable for the woman who becomes five months pregnant, or the baby who has just eaten its first solid food, or the child who has just entered school or the person who has landed that dream of a lifetime – lifetime employment. Mourners at a funeral will give cash to the bereaved family and go home with a present: perhaps a set of towels, or some rice wine. Gifts are expected by those whose houses have burned down. When you move to another area, your new neighbours will also expect a little something.

Every Japanese who goes anywhere, even for the weekend, is obliged to bring back suitcases full of local souvenirs – cakes and biscuits go down well, so do pickles – for family and friends. It is a hangover from the days when a traveller was given spending money for his journey and the souvenir was a return gift. Now it's just a headache for most Japanese. To help them out, kiosks in Tokyo's central train station stock a range of souvenirs from all over Japan, including local wrapping paper, so that tourists can do all their tourist shopping within a short taxi ride of home and avoid humping parcels up and down faraway train platforms. Japanese tourists who travel abroad are not offered the same courtesy on their return to Tokyo's Narita airport, which is why they are always frantically buying up tins of tea at Fortnum's. What with picking up the Burberry raincoat, the Hermes scarf and the Chanel shoulder-bag at non-yen prices and then buying several dozen souvenirs for friends, relatives and workmates, many Japanese tourists have little time left to see the sights. In fact Japanese tourists are the biggest spenders in Britain, even though most don't stay a single night in a British hotel: the British leg of their European tour gives them just enough time to do some shopping in Bond Street before flying off to Paris.

The reason why Japanese people log all gifts given and received is that it is hard to keep count just in your head, unless you have the mental agility of an experienced currency dealer. The worst times, of course, are the summer and end-of-year gift-giving fixtures – which are known as *o-chugen* and *o-seibo*, respectively – when department stores give over whole floors to servicing gift-pickers and when Tokyo becomes a blur of delivery men. It is a bit like the first day of the Harrods sale. But much worse. And it lasts for about three weeks at a time, at full tempo throughout.

Now, a peculiarity of these mid-year and end-of-year jamborees is the choice of present. Bottles of cooking oil, jars of instant coffee, blocks of processed cheese, all these are considered very acceptable, if dullish presents. They hark back to an age when Japan was poor and such things as instant coffee and vegetable oil were undreamed of luxuries. Nowadays, Japanese people are a bit better off and cooking oil no longer makes their mouths water. But it has become something of a tradition. The trouble is that cooking oil is not that expensive and nobody is out to skimp when the whole point of the exercise is to make a good impression. The result is that you are likely to get a fancily packed case of three bottles of cooking oil (remember, never four) and six packs of Eezyspread processed cheese. For this you are now deep in someone's debt.

Naturally, anyone of social prominence begins weeping come late June and early December as each new department-store delivery man deposits one more box of ham chunks or peanut oil. All this unimaginative generosity has created room for a new breed of pawnbroker. They buy unwanted summer and winter gifts at 30 per cent of cost and try to resell them at 50 per cent. Business is booming, especially now that the Japanese, who panic if a year passes without their having found a new occasion on which to swap presents, have sucked Christmas into their calendar. One of these modern-day pawnbrokers claims that he once came across a very indulged household which threw out five hundred gifts at a stroke. Sometimes the piles of discarded boxes include Rolex watches and Tiffany bangles, still unopened, which at least shows the danger of expecting cooking oil in every parcel. The advantage of the otherwise monotonous range of presents, of course, is that few people suspect when you recycle your own unwanted gifts next time around. Inventive department-store executives do try to drum up something out of the ordinary. For example, a golf insurance policy against a hole-in-one (presents expected all round, I'm afraid, at the club, at home, at the office). More spicy was the offer by the Daimaru department store at the height of the Latin American dance craze: they would send ten South American Lambada dancers to anywhere the gift-giver chose for 550,000 yen.

What makes all this furious present-swapping seem a little barmy to the casual foreign observer but as natural as breathing to Japanese is that giving gifts is just one part of a complex map of obligations across which every Japanese must steer his life. Being Japanese means always being in someone's debt for something, which in turn means always having to say sorry or thankyou to a parent, a boss, an emperor, a teacher, a friend, a victim of your stupidity, a lender, a relative, just about anyone you come across. The Japanese child is born with obligations it began accumulating while still in the womb and one of the trickiest tasks of growing up is learning the spread and depth of your various obligations – which include an obligation to make sure that your own good name is never dragged through the mud as a result of your own or anyone else's actions – and then learning how to meet all these debts diligently and elegantly. Your duties in this area as a Japanese person will include thanking your child's employer at every opportunity for being considerate enough to hire your offspring; avoiding making someone feel ashamed – not telling him to his face that you think he is talking bunkum, or that the product he is trying to sell you is garbage, and telling him instead that he has a very interesting view on such-and-such a subject, or that you will naturally think very carefully about placing an order for this item he has so thoughtfully brought to your attention; making sure that you back the majority wherever possible, whether in your choice of government or baseball team, because while supporting the underdog or the outsider might be noble, it can leave you feeling a shameful and isolated fool if he does not win; making sure that you do not force someone to admit that they are ignorant on a certain subject, even if it is just the plumber and your house is slowly filling with water, because you will leave that person with an intolerable sense of shame; resigning your position as chairman, without a second thought, to take the blame for an underling's mistake or misbehaviour in a bid to rehabilitate your company's name in the public's eyes; and committing suicide if that is the only option left to repay a debt or clear your family name of shame.

It is an occasion for despair when a foreigner asks a Japanese to explain the ground rules of obligation in Japan, because the rules are so complicated. Even something as simple as not counting your change is something that a foreigner must learn and a Japanese knows instinctively, since to do so might imply that you do not trust the change giver. One foreigner who has succeeded better than most in translating the rules is the famous American anthropologist Ruth Benedict, in her study of Japanese culture, *The Chrysanthemum and the Sword*. She describes how a son's obligation to his mother, to pick one example, will mean that he will remain silent as she relentlessly finds fault with everything her daughter-in-law does, to the point where the mother might even break up what is, to her son, a rewardingly happy marriage. This maltreatment of daughters-in-law – who effectively become the possessions of their mothers-in-law after they marry and move into their husband's parental home – is a common theme of Japanese novels. It is also one reason why young women today say they would prefer to wed a second son, who is not the heir obliged to look after his parents. They are thus spared the torment of sharing a roof with a harridan of a mother-in-law. Benedict explores the particularly onerous form of obligation known as *giri,* and argues that it is impossible to understand the way Japanese behave without taking it into account, for its bear-hug embrace takes in everything from gratitude for an old kindness to the duty of revenge.

'No Japanese can talk about motivations or good repute or the dilemmas which confront men and women in his home country without constantly speaking of *giri,*' she writes.

Phrases are full of resentment and of emphasis on the pressure of public opinion which compels a person to do *giri* against his wishes. They say, 'I am arranging this marriage merely for *giri*'; 'merely because of *giri* I was forced to give him the job'; 'I must see him merely for *giri*'. They constantly talk of being 'tangled with *giri*', a phrase the dictionary translates as 'I am obliged to do it'. They say, 'He forced me with *giri*', 'he cornered me with *giri*' ... All these usages carry the implication of unwillingness and of compliance for 'mere decency's sake'.

Giri clearly gets about in Japan. Benedict tries to pin down its flavour a little more by comparing it to her fellow Americans' attitude to repaying money they have borrowed.

We do not consider that a man has to pay back the favour of a letter received or a gift given or of a timely word spoken with the stringency that is necessary in keeping up his payments of interest and his repayment of a bank loan. In these financial dealings bankruptcy is the penalty for failure – a heavy penalty. The Japanese, however, regard a man as bankrupt when he fails in repaying *giri* and every contact in life is likely to incur *giri* in some way or other. This means keeping an account of little words and acts Americans throw lightly about with no thought of incurring obligations. It means walking warily in a complicated world.

168

It is one of the more relaxing pleasures of being a foreigner in Tokyo that one can happily give and receive gifts with no thought beyond the pleasure they bring, and that one feels under no social pressure to resign one's job or to commit suicide if one has chosen the wrong colour flowers or bought a box of chocolates, quite unknowingly, for a diabetic.

Even more taxing, in many ways, than *giri* towards others is *giri* to one's own name, that is, making sure you either stay clear of any shaming trouble or, if you fail to do so, perform whatever acts are necessary to atone for the misdemeanour and rehabilitate your name among your fellow citizens. That's bad enough if you have one name to look after. Some Japanese have several. Kabuki actors, for example, go through life with a clutch of vaunted names, all of which must be protected from dishonour. Take the elaborately named kabuki actor Koshiro Matsumoto IX, a huge name in Japan, where kabuki stars are so important that theatre programmes do not even bother to mention the authors of the plays that are being performed. Koshiro – kabuki performers are known by their first names – comes from a line of kabuki kings going back three centuries. He used to call himself Somegoro Ichikawa. In fact his real name is Teruaki Fujima. All this may be disconcerting to the accounts department at American Express but it is standard in the kabuki business. Each of the handful of top kabuki families has a closetful of historic stage names which it can bestow on rising stars. They punctuate an actor's career. A child making his debut is given a minor name, a sort of kabuki teething-ring. As he (it's all men in the kabuki world) grows up and learns the ropes he gets a more exalted title. The top names, like Koshiro Matsumoto, are the most prized heirlooms. Some names are passed on automatically when the holder dies, the plusher ones are awarded for special merit and are occasions for huge and glorious celebrations in the theatre, when the actor and the audience weep for the joy of it all.

'The succession of names is different from family to family,' Koshiro told me. 'I was born into a kabuki family. My father was a kabuki actor. Two of my father's brothers were kabuki actors. I am Koshiro Matsumoto IX, which means that there were eight before me. Koshiro Matsumoto I lived three hundred years ago. Wherever you cut me you will find kabuki in my blood. But I was never told by my father that I ought to inherit his name. My father thought it was not right to force someone to do something if he didn't want to do it. According to my father it is not just a name-succeeding ceremony, although there is a ceremony. You are actually succeeding the life of your father. When I was three years old I was Kintaro Matsumoto II. At the age of six I became Somegoro Ichikawa VI. In 1981 I took the name of Koshiro Matsumoto IX, but I still don't feel I have succeeded my father's life. My son is now seventeen. He is called Somegoro Ichikawa VII. He is also training to be a kabuki actor.' Koshiro makes his inheritance sound fairly relaxed, quite take-it-or-leave-it almost, but he also gives the strong impression that if any shame or dishonour were brought on to his dynasty's various names and titles, perhaps by a son refusing to pick up the baton and succeed his father's life on stage, Koshiro Matsumoto I's spirit would probably want to know why.

It is this pressure to avoid shame or, failing that, to show fitting penitence that spawns the legendary stories of headmasters who took their own lives after a fire had started in their schools – not because they started the conflagration, but because the flames threatened the picture of the once divine emperor that used to hang in every school. Benedict tells the tale of a man who, in Hirohito's reign, committed a huge social gaffe by inadvertently naming his son Hirohito. Instead of just thinking of a new name, the man killed himself and his child, which shows just how young the burden of obligation begins in Japan. If there is no other way out, suicide has the advantage of being a recognized and respected way of clearing your name in Japan. The big disadvantage is that it is just a bit drastic and leaves no room for second thoughts.

Of course, it is a great deal more convenient if you can get someone else to do your dying for you. It is a job that many minions seem quite willing to take on, when they do not actually feel obliged to do so. Just one day after Noboru Takeshita announced in April 1989 that he was stepping down as Japan's prime minister because of his links to the Recruit bribery scandal that was raging through the government's ranks, his chief aide went quietly to his modest flat and selflessly slit his wrists and hanged himself. Ihei Aoki had been Takeshita's main confidant and fund-raiser for more than thirty years. It was his job to make sure that there was always enough cash at hand to meet the expensive costs of playing politics in Japan and for Takeshita to dispense enough patronage among junior MPs to remain at the top of the ruling Liberal Democratic Party. Part of Aoki's unwritten job description was to make sure that however unsavoury the sources of finance were, the deals and channels through which it arrived were kept at arm's length and camouflaged enough to guarantee that Takeshita's sleep was never troubled by the taint of financial suspicion. Aoki felt responsible enough for Takeshita's disgrace to take the blame for his boss's downfall on his own shoulders.

Almost every scandal that has rocked Japan has claimed similar casualties. When Kakuei Tanaka, one of Takeshita's more colourful predecessors in the prime minister's seat, was under the spotlight in 1976 for accepting bribes from America's Lockheed aircraft company, the dutiful chauffeur who had driven Tanaka to various secret meetings where envelopes changed hands committed suicide: reluctant to be quizzed about his boss's comings and goings, Masanori Kasahara nobly gassed himself in his car. In 1979, Mitsuhiro Shimada, executive director of one of Japan's biggest trading companies, leapt from his seventh-floor office window after having first tried to cut his carotid artery with a pencil-sharpening knife. Shimada's company, Nissho-Iwai, had become entangled in another aircraft bribes case, this time involving the American firms McDonnell Douglas and Grumman. A year later, allegations that KDD, a major Japanese telecommunications firm, had bought the favours of bureaucrats at the Posts and Telecommunications Ministry prompted two of the KDD's president's aides to take their own lives. Just as dramatically, General Maresuke Nogi and his wife killed themselves on the day that Emperor Meiji was buried in 1912, their useful mission on this earth completed. Courtiers of monarchs and feudal lords have traditionally committed suicide on their master's death, so as to be able to accompany them out of this world and continue to serve them in the next.

All these deaths just lengthen the list of obligations of the average Japanese, since funerals are a prime currency for settling debts and repaying favours. And because businessmen and politicians feel that it is impossible not to attend when asked, funerals have become a nightmare. Busy executives and MPs are obliged to pay their respects at the funeral of a colleague, a corporate ally or a constituent almost every day of the week. The obligation has become so taxing that a new service has recently been invented that marries the country's tradition with its knack for high-tech. Instead of attending all those funerals in person, grieving mourners can now console themselves more pragmatically by offering incense to a flickering Sony television monitor. The amount of corporate time saved could be huge. Japanese salarymen's funeral obligations are not limited to their own bosses. Because of the web of cross-shareholdings that mesh a company to its suppliers, its bankers, its stockbrokers, sometimes even its rivals, a corporate heavyweight could draw several thousand mourners. Many of them will never have clapped eyes on the recently departed one. Their obligation, instead, may be to their own boss, who might in turn be directly under obligation to the deceased tycoon. The subordinates of a dead man's nephew, for example, might feel duty-bound to attend the funeral of their boss's uncle, even though that uncle worked for a different firm and even though they might never have seen him alive.

Mitsui, one of Japan's giant trading houses, hit on the idea after it had to organize the funeral in 1989 of Tatsuzo Minakami, a senior adviser to the Mitsui board of directors. Instead of hiring a stadium to host the nearly 20,000 mourners, it decided to rent satellite space and transmission equipment and to broadcast the service on closed-circuit television. The death, at around the same time, of Konosuke Matsushita, founder of Matsushita, the world's largest consumer electronics empire, also forced his funeral arrangers to resort to the novelty of a satellite broadcast for those paying their respects.

Masahiro Mizuno, who spends his time at Mitsui thinking up new commercial ideas like this one, reckons that of the 800,000 Japanese who might die in any year, 100,000 – all of them men – are the sort who could benefit from a corporate TV funeral. Company-arranged funerals, which are usually held about a month after the family service, have been limited to five thousand guests. Mizuno reckons that without space worries, the president of a blue-chip company could easily attract 50,000 closed-circuit mourners who would be spared the headache of flying all over the country, from funeral hall to funeral hall, while their in-tray piles up with work. Even the lowliest salarymen attend two or three funerals a month. MPs, who are expected to show their face at constituents' weddings and funerals if they expect to get re-elected, joke about always having to carry a white tie for the former and a black tie for the latter: the MP's gang of aides go too. You might think it a bit cold bowing respectfully to a

173

television monitor. Mizuno cannot see a problem: 'In Japan we have a tradition of worshipping something special from a distance. For example, people worship and bow towards Mount Fuji from Tokyo, or even more distant places.'

Japanese are not always so serious and long-faced that they cannot occasionally limit their acts of atonement simply to resigning or taking temporary pay cuts rather than committing suicide. The resignation of a company's president or chairman or senior executive is seen as an acceptable course of public breast-beating to show a company's customers that it is contrite. The action does not necessarily mean that the executive has actually left the company. In most cases he carries on doing the same job, though perhaps with a slightly different title: the company's bankers, suppliers, and so on, would expect little else. But the action is supposed to draw a line under the misdemeanour: no more retribution is exactable.

The Japanese know these rules, but foreigners do not. That is why Toshiba Corporation was so baffled after its president and its chairman had both done the decent thing and resigned in 1987 to shoulder the blame for a trading scandal. The scandal erupted after Toshiba Machine, a subsidiary, was accused of selling high-technology secrets to the Soviet Union in violation of international restrictions. Toshiba's chairman, Shoichi Saba, admitted in his resignation statement that Toshiba owned only about half of Toshiba Machine and was not involved in the sale of precision machinery to Moscow. But he added, 'I failed in my responsibility to ensure that none of the companies in the Toshiba group violates regulations.' That, he thought, was that and he was dumbfounded when America then demanded sanctions against Toshiba. In spite of his resignation, though, Saba continued to go to his office at Toshiba every day. Nor did his resignation do anything to jeopardize his position as deputy chairman of the Keidanren, Japan's equivalent of the Confederation of British Industry.

When a Japan Air Lines Boeing 747 crashed into a mountainside in August 1985, killing 520 people, the airline's president, Yasumoto Takagi, stepped down as a sign of the company's atonement. The chairman of Sumitomo Bank, Ichiro Isoda, resigned in October 1990 after a former branch manager was arrested for arranging illegal loans to a group of stock-market speculators. He did not even know the former branch manager's name, but did not think twice before taking the decision to go. If this sort of behaviour caught on in the West, the chairman of British Rail, the head of the precarious Italian postal service and the person in charge of repairing Manhattan's potholes would all be resigning their posts at least once a fortnight.

Because it is notions of shame rather than of guilt that shape Japanese society, because the culture of Japan has not sprung from Judaic–Christian tradition, because the absence of moral absolutes of right and wrong make it acceptable to, say, lie if that is what is needed to meet a more pressing obligation, you might expect Japan's relationship with religion to be unusual. It is. There is a native religion, Shintoism, culled from ancient animist beliefs. It was the state religion until the American forces which occupied Japan after the Second World War introduced a new constitution that separated religion and state: the idea was to stop Shintoism being hijacked by empire-building ultra-nationalists, who used it as a tool for promoting the virtues of Japaneseness and as the religious basis for their militaristic adventures abroad. Shinto shrines cater profitably to that part of a Japanese person's soul that seeks comfort in small but expensive mascots that promise success in such things as passing exams, childbirth, driving tests and making piles of money. Flamboyantly dressed Shinto priests will accept commissions to bless new buildings, new babies, new products and anything else that might benefit from spiritual protection. Buddhist temples also dot country hillsides and city street corners. Buddhism came to Japan from Korea in the sixth century. Ten centuries later, the Jesuits brought Christianity to Japan, but Christian missionaries have probably had less success in Japan than almost anywhere else in the world that they have tried to plant Christ's teachings. There is even a Jewish Community Centre in Tokyo, but it caters largely to expatriates who wish to attend Sabbath and Yom Kippur prayers or who wish to use its open-air swimming pool on sweltering summer days. Most Japanese say they are not religious.

The real novelty about the Japanese way of religion is the people's pick-and-mix approach to different faiths. The choice is based not so much on any muscular belief as on a religion's suitability to meet a particular requirement. The combined number of believers in Buddhism and followers of Shintoism in Japan totals 220 million, even though Japan's population is only 123 million. Japanese who claim to believe in Shintoism commonly marry in Christian churches and are cremated as Buddhists. In fact, so rare are Shinto funerals that even many Shinto priests have Buddhist funerals. This is not a system of religious belief that is readily comprehensible to Western outsiders.

This is why it is often difficult to gauge the temperature of Japan's periodic bouts of religious soul-searching. In the teeth of protests from Christians, civil rights groups, Japan's main opposition parties and constitutional experts, the government managed to draw up quite a religious Shinto menu of funeral ceremonies when Emperor Hirohito died in 1989. Critics said the government had buckled to pressure from the uglier fringes of Japan's extreme right-wing nationalists, whose goal is to restore the emperor to his pre-war eminence. The government got away with it all by arguing that although world leaders who had flown in for the rites would be watching religious funeral ceremonies, they would be doing so at the invitation of the imperial household, not of the government, and thus the separation of state and religion would be intact – a loophole that one constitutional scholar said 'barely succeeded in not violating the constitution'. In the autumn of the following year, when Hirohito's heir was formally enthroned, a similar rumpus surrounded the legitimacy of a controversial Shinto rite called the Daijosai. In this ceremony, according to Hideaki Kase, author of a book called *The Mystic Emperor* and an enthusiastic nationalist, the emperor-to-be must enter a special shrine to lie down beneath an eiderdown and await the arrival of the gods. 'The emperor-to-be shares the bed with his great ancestress, Amaterasu. The prince enters Amaterasu's womb, emerging as the new emperor.' The Daijosai went ahead in spite of the hullabaloo, and what at the time seemed close to a constitutional crisis has been forgotten. Had most Japanese noticed that there had even been a brawl?

Since the Japanese, through Shinto, already descend directly from god, one can see why strict, more demanding religions like Christianity have found it tough to make a mark among the take-it-as-it-comes Japanese. This might also explain why many young people are turning more and more to fringe religions for guidance: some of them seem to be rich youngsters trying to sate their thirst for the meaning of life after Versace, while others are failures and drop-outs from Japan's competitive education rat-race, looking for a place where they can fit in and be loved. So-called 'new religions' are mushrooming and claim millions of followers. Many of them promote the power of the occult, or psychokinetics or faith-healing. They fire their TV-generation followers through videos rather than through written religious tracts. There are more than 180,000 religious sects in Japan, all of them carrying lucrative benefits in tax write-offs. Religious corporations are being bought and sold like some form of celestial debenture.

One of the new breed of cult leaders who has keenly exploited the potential of the new fervour by blending religion, business and politics is Shoko Asahara, a maverick Buddhist sect leader who makes devotees drink his blood and sip potions brewed from his long black hair. Asahara's notoriety swelled after police quizzed him about the disappearance of a lawyer who fought for families that had lost children to his cult, the Aum Supreme Truth sect. It swelled further in 1990 when he offered himself to the voters of Japan in a general election. Asahara, a tubby, bearded man in his late thirties who looks like an oriental version of the singer Demis Roussos, claims he is 'the only priest in Japan who has ever reached the ultimate nirvana' and that he has 'descended from a legendary Utopia to this secular world as a saviour'. Many Japanese know him better as a fraudster who was arrested in 1982 for selling fake medicines. He fleeced about a thousand ageing sufferers from rheumatism of forty million yen. Few outside his secretive inner circle believe in his powers. He claims to be able to levitate and to hold his breath and meditate for hours under water. Photographs are the outside world's only proof and darkroom experts say the pictures are clumsy photo-composites. The one levitation photo that looks vaguely passable shows him cross-legged with his long hair trailing upwards and an anxious look on his face, suggesting that rather than rising from the ground he has been crudely snapped falling from a height. When he was on the hustings, Asahara offered the Japanese salvation from what he predicted would be a US–Japan economic war, a surge in nationalist fervour and a revival of militarism. He said he could protect Japan from these plagues if he were voted into parliament. He did not explain why he would not use his mystical powers to save his countrymen even if he lost at the polls and had to remain an ordinary Buddhist preacher. Asahara's premium course of yoga meditation and psychic power costs around a million yen, although that sum includes a swig of what is said to be the Master's blood. The magic does not always work. Some leave when they find the blood transfusion has no effect, others when they are asked to write a will leaving all their property to the cult. Still, Asahara retains a troop of devoted followers, who say they have found truth, enlightenment, the secret of rejuvenation and even learned how to conquer cancer under his guidance. With such powers, you might have expected Asahara and the twenty-four disciples who ran with him for seats in parliament to find electioneering a doddle.

They all lost.

10. A Modern Mikado: Now the Politicians Hold the Reins

Hirohito and after – wistful nationalists – from deities to democracy – the politicians who have taken over the reins – city of scandals – who will trust the Japanese?

Emperor Hirohito of Japan, once revered by his subjects as a god and a man who is likely to remain one of the twentieth century's most controversial figures, died after a long battle with stomach cancer as dawn broke across Tokyo on 7 January 1989. The thread of Japanese history that still tied modern Japan to its militaristic imperial past seemed to snap. Mourning was mixed with a sense of relief and a fear of what now lay ahead. The man who had changed from being a living god to being a no-longer-divine symbol of a defeated but democratized postwar Japan and a bridge that camouflaged the bewildering gulf between the backwater Japan was and the muscular world power it is today, had finally, after sixty-three years as emperor, gone. How would the country cope without him?

Crown Prince Akihito, who was at the emperor's bedside when he died, immediately ascended to his father's throne. But in keeping with palace ritual, he was not formally crowned until the autumn of 1990, after a year of official mourning by the imperial family. Government officials began six days of mourning and the nation was urged to wear sombre clothes and to refrain from entertainment for the weekend. The news of Hirohito's death was broadcast live from the Imperial Palace in central Tokyo to a television audience that watched and gawped and cried in their living-rooms, in their offices and in coffee bars. This was a measure of how far Japan's still fusty imperial institution had come from the days of Hirohito's father, who died in 1926, when such a glimpse inside the palace walls would have been as unthinkable as a glimpse of the emperor himself.

Newly unfurled Japanese flags began flapping from office buildings and from the doorways of elderly Japanese, who felt that the emperor had shared their experiences through the century. The palace's moated grounds were immediately fringed with thickets of weeping mourners, some who had made the journey specially to pay their respects, others who had just been passing by and, suddenly frozen into a snapshot of history, decided to go no further. Television stations pulled all commercials and national newspapers stripped their pages of advertisements. On the Tokyo stock market, dealers fell silent as their trading screens switched to news of the emperor's death. The market then closed. Thousands of companies across Japan, uncertain of the protocol but wary of being found wanting, put in motion already-drafted plans to keep business to a minimum and to carry out necessary activity in a solemn enough manner to deflect charges of disrespect. The national carrier Japan Air Lines, for example, cancelled in-flight films, provided sombre outfits for stewardesses and issued staff with black armbands. One distraught ex-soldier, eighty-seven years old, the same age as Hirohito on his deathbed, hanged himself in his shed. He left a note which read: 'I go together with the emperor in death.'

It is one of those quirks of history that the funeral of Hirohito – at one time perhaps the most hated man in the world – drew more kings, presidents and VIPs to Tokyo than went to mourn the passing of President Leonid Brezhnev of the Soviet Union, President Josip Tito of Yugoslavia or of President John F.

Kennedy of America. It was a statistic not lost on the statistic-obsessed Japanese. They were proud and, privately, very pleased. It seemed to confirm Hirohito's passing as the start of an era untainted by the memories of the last war.

Hirohito reigned longer than any of his predecessors in Japan's 2,700-year imperial line. He also led – and sometimes was manipulated by militarists to lead – his people through the most traumatic somersaults in their history, including a nuclear holocaust and their first military defeat. But as long as his familiar, shambling figure waved twice a year from the balcony of the Imperial Palace to receive birthday and New Year wishes from his subjects, the Japanese could conveniently forget about how much Japan had changed and about how well equipped it was to cope with the responsibilities and challenges that burden the world's rich superpowers. That change, masked by Hirohito's longevity, has not always been easy to measure. It might have been harder elsewhere too if, say, Churchill were still in 10 Downing Street, de Gaulle still in the Élysée Palace and Stalin still walked the corridors of the Kremlin. To say that, unlike them, Hirohito held no executive power under the American-written postwar constitution, or that he was not officially head of state, or that his portrait did not hang in Japan's embassies or stare out from the nation's stamps, or that his speeches were dull and stilted, belies his role as a cosy grid reference at which the Japanese could take their bearings. The millions who queued across Japan to sign registers wishing Hirohito a speedy recovery – he was four months on his sick bed – testified to his standing in a country which was forced suddenly to rethink how it should behave towards its monarch: in neighbouring Korea, where many still recall Japan's brutal reign as their colonial master, people shuddered at what they feared was a nostalgic lurch back to the heady days of Japan's Asian commonwealth.

Japan does not deal well with uncertainty. It likes to plan in

182

advance. The emperor's longer-than-expected illness gave government ministers and bureaucrats a chance to organize their funeral drills and gave his subjects time to graduate from panicking to preparing for a new era. The transition was smoother as a result. But it was still far from seamless.

Hirohito was very nearly indicted as a war criminal, probably only saved by General Douglas MacArthur, then head of the occupying American forces in Japan after the Second World War. MacArthur realized that the emperor would offer a rallying point for the devastated Japanese after their humiliating defeat. Part of the deal was that Hirohito should renounce his divinity – or 'de-god himself' as the Americans put it – and tell his people that they were not a master race. His power withered. Yet most Japanese, even those too young to remember the war, had been happy to have Hirohito as a symbol of continuity both of the imperial dynasty and of a fast-changing Japan. Given a second chance by MacArthur, the emperor put it to good use, ending his days as an enlightened constitutional monarch. He commanded respect, if not reverence. Historians still quibble over his precise part in the events that led to Japan's disastrous immersion in the Second World War and brought the proud Japanese to their knees. But given the opportunity to start afresh, the emperor did his best to make amends. He helped to redirect Japan on to a pacifist, democratic path and through an economic renaissance that has brought it more riches, power and prestige than conceited militarism ever delivered.

The death of Hirohito created both an opportunity and a risk. Would it breathe new life into a political machine that looked too cranky and old-fashioned, too provincially minded to steer the powerful economy that Japan had become? Would the Japanese be happy to see the uncontroversial but colourless Akihito take on his father's mantle? Would Akihito's own unstuffiness – he married a commoner, sent his sons to study at a foreign university and occasionally still joshes with foreign correspondents – encourage those in Japan who are glad to see the emperor take even more of a back seat? Or would the new monarch's modernity rattle Japan's nationalists, who still yearn to restore the emperor's pre-war eminence as a head of state, perhaps even a sacred one, and to rewrite the American-written constitution of 1947 to allow Japan to rearm and defend itself, rights renounced to MacArthur after the war?

Nationalists in Japan still believe that 're-godding' the emperor is vital if Japan is to hold up its head as a nation that controls its own destiny rather than one that lives by rules written by Americans in language that some dismiss as pidgin Japanese. They want the emperor restored to his former glory as a Shintoist priest-king. One of the most provocative and eloquent of the emperor-worshippers is Hideaki Kase, a confidant of senior Japanese politicians, who panders shamelessly to the myths of Japanese uniqueness that General MacArthur tried to extinguish. He argues that the beliefs of Shintoism – Japan's native and once its state religion – are based on blood and race, making it 'hard for Japanese to see foreigners as human beings like themselves'. Reinstating the emperor's supremacy, he says, is vital to Japan's survival. Most Japanese are happy with the system that has given them half a century of peace and, more recently, riches. Fringe fanatics enjoy no real resonance in the body politic: most Japanese are more interested in watching television than in dressing up in khaki or rewriting the constitution. But Japan's nationalists can still cause havoc on the streets and can intimidate those who would steer Japan into more modern, more democratic, more cosmopolitan waters.

Even in his coffin, Hirohito's name was defended by right-wing fanatics. A year after Hirohito's death the mayor of Nagasaki, Hitoshi Motoshima, discovered the price of angering Japan's menacing nationalists when he was shot – by chance, not fatally – through the chest by a right-wing activist. His crime was to break the Japanese taboo and suggest that the late emperor bore some responsibility for the Second World War. The Catholic mayor had made his controversial remark fourteen months earlier, in December 1988, a time when Hirohito's failing health had reopened a worldwide debate about his war conduct. The remark drew a battalion of angry rightists in army trucks to Nagasaki. They patrolled the streets, flying the Rising Sun flag and blaring military music through loudspeakers, and bullied the mayor with death threats and random gunshots at his office windows. Motoshima had been under twenty-four-hour guard by police but, tiring of the security, he had asked for the police guard to be called off just one month before his shooting. It was a chilling reminder of how nationalists use shock and shotguns to give them a threatening voice that they cannot muster by numbers alone.

Japan's National Police Agency reckons that there are about 840 right-wing groups in the country, with 125,000 members. Police keep a close watch on only fifty of the groups, with a total of just 22,000 members, which they label extremist. For such a small band, these nationalists have an intimidating profile. Their convoys of armoured trucks regularly disrupt traffic and shatter eardrums in Tokyo. When their threatening tactics fail to silence their targets, they turn to force. In 1960 they stabbed and killed Inejiro Asanuma, chairman of Japan's Socialist Party, but they will just as readily intimidate conservative politicians they feel have besmirched Japan's name: for example, bribery scandals that dirty the names of ruling conservative politicians anger them. In 1987 they shot dead a journalist of the *Asahi Shimbun*, a leading national daily whose modestly liberal views make the nationalist fringe faint. Even a report in the *Asahi* that Hirohito, then on his deathbed, had cancer (a fact that had, until then, been discreetly hidden from the public) earned the newspaper a

185

broken window and a smoke bomb. The newspaper was told in a message that it had been attacked for being unpatriotic. In 1961 a publishing company infuriated rightists by publishing a novel satirizing the imperial household: a rightist youth broke into the publisher's house, stabbed a housemaid to death and seriously injured his wife.

But Japan's rightists do not have to maim to spread a sense of terror. During the long illness that preceded Hirohito's death, big Japanese companies cancelled their traditional end-of-year bashes and politicians postponed their fund-raising parties for fear that celebrations while the monarch's life was slipping away would offend the rightists. Some cynical commentators said that young people went to the imperial palace to sign get-well registers and, later, condolence books because they wanted to leave evidence of their support for the emperor just in case the rightists ever seize power in Japan.

It is not hard to see why some of Japan's nationalists, though they would be devoted to any emperor of Japan, are chewing their nails over the easy-going Akihito. They fret that he would be too weak to fight should anti-monarchists attempt to bury the imperial ideal. 'I know the crown prince well,' a senior Japanese diplomat confided over lunch shortly before Hirohito died. 'Akihito's reign will be more democratic, less stuffy than his father's. The imperial family still leads a very sheltered life. He'll try hard to make the whole institution more open, providing the old guard at the imperial household let him. I think he will probably succeed.' Akihito had long hinted that, when his time came, he would try to teach his father's courtiers some basic lessons of life in the twentieth century and to shrink slightly the gap between himself and a nation that still refers to him, respectfully, as 'the honourable one across the moat'. He appears to see that he has a chance to redefine the image of Japan, both for sceptical foreigners and for the Japanese.

Akihito is well educated, speaks English, has travelled widely abroad and, as well as taking on the burden of Hirohito's ceremonial duties, he has long shared his father's passion for marine biology. He is sensible, but stiff. He is willing to be a modern mikado, if Japan has use for one. He made clear just how open he was prepared to be with his new subjects when, within a week of his father's death, he gave the *Asahi* newspaper a catalogue of his tastes and habits, providing the Japanese more information about the private life of their new monarch in one newspaper interview than they had picked up about his father in all the eighty-seven years of his life. Moreover, they were given a glimpse of a family man who thinks more like them than they might have hoped or expected. The candid disclosures were a clear symbol of the airier, more democratic monarchy that Akihito would like to create. Hirohito's chamberlains would have trembled at such frankness, even though it was far from 'kiss-and-tell' stuff.

The new emperor confessed that he eats bread for breakfast and has a weakness for curry and rice, but rarely demands special meals to be prepared for him. He reads newspapers before and after meals, watches the morning news on television and video-records documentaries. He owns three dark suits, two grey ones and six blazers. Like many men, most of the ties in his fifty-strong collection – some of them thirty years old – were birthday presents. Sometimes he wears Japanese clothes, at night.

You might well think, 'So what?' But just how extraordinary all this is for a Japanese emperor is highlighted by the paraphernalia that Akihito immediately did away with. He ordered that his food need no longer be tasted before it reached him and, unlike his father, he would no longer require his pre-bedtime urine and faeces to be analysed. This is a far cry from the days of Hirohito, whose culinary habits leave most people breathless. All Hirohito's tableware was sterilized before use. Everything he ate was analysed by scientists. Meals were weighed before and after and records were kept of the emperor's daily dietary intake: the records are now part of the imperial palace library. Such was the aura that surrounded Hirohito that a chauffeur who had the misfortune to be driving the emperor in 1947 when the car's engine failed was contemplating suicide until the monarch sent him a note telling him not to worry about the incident.

Akihito has done much else to humanize both the institution he inherited and the once remote inhabitants of the palace. The new emperor's chauffeur stops at traffic lights, under Akihito's orders, and slows down for ambulances. Security has become more relaxed: the royal couple wave at crowds through open car windows rather than from behind the thick bullet-proof glass favoured by Hirohito. Instead of the large, custom-designed limousine used by his father, the new monarch travels in sedans of the sort used by company executives. Friends still make informal visits. When he meets the press, he likes to bill it as a press conference rather than an audience. As far as his thumbnail political beliefs go, he says he stands for freedom of speech and advocates a system in which the emperor is a figurehead without political power. Once again, you say, 'Big deal!' But Japanese find the accessibility of an emperor who mingles in crowds and who talks to them in polite but everyday Japanese, rather than the near incomprehensible aristocrats' jargon used by Hirohito, rather novel and refreshing. After seeing Akihito's first-ever press conference as emperor broadcast live on television, one sixty-year-old remarked, 'In our generation we regarded the emperor as up in the clouds, someone untouchable, but it was clear that the new emperor and empress are trying to be more relaxed, more normal.'

Akihito's first brush with modernity was his decision in 1959 to spurn his courtiers' advice and marry Michiko Shoda, the beautiful daughter of a rich flour merchant and the first commoner to marry into the 2,700-year-old imperial dynasty. Ever since, they have done what they could to crack conventions. Akihito was torn from his family at the age of three to be reared in isolation by five guardians. His friends were hand-picked and even examined for disease before playing with him. He and Princess Michiko decided that their children would live at home, not with servants and chamberlains. Their sons were the first imperial children to study abroad, at Oxford University. The fact that Princess Michiko had studied at Sacred Heart College, a Christian school and university in Tokyo, also suggested that they were nudging the imperial entourage to become more accommodating towards other religions. Everything Akihito has done, from reaffirming his commitment to Japan's democratic postwar constitution to talking more openly to his subjects, seems designed to warn the country's dreamy nationalists that the glory days are not about to be revived and to reassure anxious left-wingers that democracy and pacifism are safe in his hands.

What more promising start could Japan have hoped for at the dawn of a new monarch's reign? Here was the best opportunity in decades to spring-clean Japan's corrupt political machinery and adapt it for modern times. But within months, Japan's elected leaders again proved how, through their customary blend of corruption, cupidity and crassness, they will always manage to make Japanese politics a source of baffling wonderment to even the greediest, most venal and most ambitious politicians the West has to offer.

In the days when Japan was one large paddy-field, the shenanigans of Japanese politicians might have raised a titter among its Western partners, who dismissed all this pocket-lining as one more oriental eccentricity. There were plenty of trade disputes, but few major worries about international diplomacy or security because Japan did not roll the dice on those big tables. Now that is changing. Tokyo's allies might be less ready to swap opinions with Japanese officials if they feel these officials have been sold to corporate interests. Even in America, where pressure groups and the political fund-raising that goes with them have ballooned, there is a seam between politics and business. In Japan there is usually just a blur.

Akihito's first year as monarch was one of the spiciest for political scandal that even Japan has seen. By the autumn, voters were getting to know their third prime minister of the year as one premier after the other was fed to the lions in a desperate attempt to save colleagues who remained in office. There was talk that the upheavals would change, once and for all, the way Japan plays politics. So great was the shame at home and the alarm abroad that some political pundits even raised the fantastical possibility that the conservative Liberal Democratic Party, which has ruled Japan for nearly four decades and is effectively the only serious political party in the country, might have to make way for an opposition administration.

Corruption is endemic to Japanese politics, but the scale of the bribery scandal that brought down the first prime minister that year shocked even Japan's cynical electorate. Centring on a property and information group called Recruit, it began as such a parochial affair that at first it seemed to surprise few Japanese, whose rock-bottom respect for their politicians could not be pushed any lower by revelations that a former prime minister, several cabinet ministers, dozens of MPs and several civil servants had been lavished with cut-price shares and cash by a pushy, self-made millionaire looking to buy friends and influence in high places. After all, when more than half of a country's postwar prime ministers have at some time in their careers been investigated for alleged corruption – as Japan's have – scratching backs in high places is business as usual.

But when it became difficult for the prime minister of the time, Noboru Takeshita, to rustle up a twenty-strong cabinet untainted by the Recruit affair, it began to strike many Japanese that influence-peddling had grown out of control. Needless to say, the scores of politicians, bureaucrats and businessmen who made a killing on the cheap shares they bought from the Recruit group never thought the deals would come to light. They knew that Japan's was not a Watergate culture: traditionally, scandals are strangled at birth by a whisper in the right ear. This semi-feudal system of control suits the long-governing Liberal Democrats and the voters have tended to tolerate it because, well, that is the Japanese way: even now, when Japan's economy flourishes, schoolchildren are still taught that they must work hard and work together or Japan's wealth will evaporate as quickly as it grew. The Japanese move in quiescent crowds and they know that wheels need to be oiled. They do not stick their necks out, especially when everything is going well. And things have been going very well for the Japanese, many of whom still remember the rubble that was Japan after the last war.

Japanese voters are at least partly to blame for the corruption that haunts their parliament. Hiromasa Ezoe, the now disgraced former chairman of Recruit, built it into a mighty empire in a drive for a respectability denied him by his humble background. The bargain-priced Recruit shares he handed to friends soared in value when the company later went public. The aim was to catapult Ezoe into high society and it worked. Ezoe numbered among his friends Yasuhiro Nakasone, who was prime minister when the questionable share deals took place and who is still probably the best-known Japanese politician outside Japan. Nakasone and his cabinet – which included Takeshita, who was premier when the scandal came to light – did very well out of

Recruit shares. Takeshita pocketed 151 million yen in donations and cheap shares from the Recruit company. Ezoe also donated regularly to a long list of MPs, who were grateful for the cash: politics in Japan is pricey.

A major factor behind political corruption is the country's multi-seat constituency system, which means that to win an election a party has to win many seats in the same constituency, and that candidates from the same party have to fight one another. This makes politics an expensive choice of career. MPs who want to hold their seats have to raise ten times their official salaries to make ends meet and to keep voters sweet. MPs must attend constituents' weddings, funerals and parties, always carrying a substantial present. They must find jobs for their constituents' sons, entertain fund-raisers' wives who want to visit Tokyo and pay for the wives' hotel bills as well. Most MPs are helped in these tiresome tasks by a dozen aides, whose salaries they also have to pay. Most MPs need a hundred million yen a year just to stay afloat. A minister might need five times that. In an election year, both sums balloon. Politicians complain, with some justice, that voters cannot demand favours from their MP and then cry foul when that MP scavenges for money to pay the bills. Without improbably huge political donations; without friendly stockbrokers who will ramp up certain shares to provide a cash-strapped MP with a quick, fat return on his investment (even though this trick naturally leaves smaller, unsuspecting speculators with a loss when the price of the over-hyped shares returns to earth); and without men like Ezoe, the country would soon creak to a halt.

Ezoe got much in return for his outlay. He was put on some powerful committees by Nakasone. He also had the ear of senior civil servants whose ministries covered areas, such as employment law, that dovetailed with Ezoe's own interests in job-vacancy magazines. For the most part, there was nothing illegal in what

Ezoe did, although he did it on a rather grand scale. Privileged share deals are common currency in Japan. But the Tokyo public prosecutors who investigated the case felt that in some instances the generosity may have tripped into bribery. Arrests were made, but few big names (and certainly not the powerful politicians like Nakasone and Takeshita) were foolish enough to be caught with smoking guns. Although Takeshita was forced to resign – more because of a clumsy lie told by his aide than because of direct proof of his own links to the scandal – he remained the kingmaker in the wings of Japanese politics, effectively choosing the three politicians that succeeded him in office and making sure that none did anything to hurt his own interests. It was much the same as the aftermath of the 1970s Lockheed bribes scandal that preceded it. Kakuei Tanaka, who stepped down as prime minister after it was found that he had accepted bribes from America's Lockheed Corporation to favour the company's Tri-Stars over its rival's DC10s, also continued to reign from the shadows well into the 1980s and was only nudged into the background when he suffered a stroke. Tanaka has never served the four-year prison term to which he was sentenced in 1983: he was released on bail and has remained on bail ever since. It is the Japanese way of ensuring that as far as political corruption goes, although justice need not be done, it must be seen to be done.

The Recruit scandal caught the Japanese at an awkward time. Although generally tolerant of their politicians' corrupt ways, the public was shocked at the blatant way Recruit sought powerful friends and it envied the ease with which tax-free cash flowed into influential pockets when suddenly breath-taking property prices were making the middle classes feel poor for the first time in their lives. Japan's élite forgot one of the basic rules for a peaceful life: leave a cut for everyone, however small, and everyone will be happy. The Recruit revelations also coincided with the introduction of a much-hated sales tax: the public seemed to be venting its fury over the government's new tax by getting angry about Recruit. It was unusual that the Recruit scandal swelled so large and ended up causing such chaos in Japanese politics. That it did owed less to any crusading zeal by Japan's press and more to the discreet spoonfeeding of incriminating evidence to journalists by the same dogged public prosecutor who pursued Tanaka over Lockheed.

Just how short memories of such scandals can be was underlined by the fact that the idea floated by Liberal Democrats to replace Japan's multi-seat constituencies with single-seat ones – which would eliminate the need for members of the same party to canvass against each other, thus making politics less expensive and, therefore, less dependent on businessmen's cheque-books – has quietly withered and died. There were no mourners at its funeral. Just as characteristically, less than three years after he became the first high-level casualty of the Recruit mess, Kiichi Miyazawa was installed as Japan's prime minister. Miyazawa was forced to resign as Takeshita's finance minister after failing to satisfy parliament about how his name got to be on some Recruit share certificates. Then, Miyazawa had barely settled into his new job when it came to light, in 1992, that the Tokyo public prosecutor was investigating yet another bribery scandal. This time it was a parcel-delivery company called Sagawa Kyubin which was reported to have filled the wallets of hundreds of politicians in return for favours that might boost Sagawa's business prospects. Spreading their largesse, Sagawa executives also made shady and unauthorized loans to friendly companies and, just to make sure everyone was kept happy, to a top gangster syndicate.

The second scandal to scar the dawn of Akihito's reign in 1989 seemed, at first, to be very un-Japanese in flavour. Sosuke Uno, the amiable, toothy politician who had been plucked from the ranks to keep the prime minister's seat warm until the Recruit heat had died down, quickly fell to a sex scandal, the unlikeliest of plots for melodrama in Japanese politics. The trouble started within a fortnight of Uno taking office. In a rare breach of Japanese etiquette, which turns a blind eye to sexual infidelity, a respected weekly magazine ran the allegations of a former geisha who claimed that Uno had paid her a total of three million yen to meet her in Tokyo hotels over a five-month period in 1985. Even the *Asahi* newspaper, which eventually urged Uno to step down if only to save Japan possible embarrassment when he went abroad and faced questions from a less buttoned press corps, conceded in an editorial that there had always been in Japan a certain 'leniency among the public and the media regarding the private lives – and especially love affairs – of politicians. The Japanese political community appears to be perplexed by this latest event. And Uno may want to complain about why he is being singled out for criticism.' But the leader writer added that times, and the public's attitude, had changed. The scandal also tarnished Uno's clean image, one of the main reasons he had been chosen as premier after the havoc of Recruit. The rest of the press, which had so recently been sniffing out impropriety among politicians involved in the Recruit scandal, had retreated into its shell. Even the boisterous opposition MPs who had spent the previous few months taunting the government's senior leaders over their links to Recruit, decided they were not going to make an issue of the geisha's allegations against the married Mr Uno.

His accuser said her motive for revealing her affair was Uno's rude, selfish, vain and bullying behaviour and her desire to protect the country from such an 'immoral man'. Nevertheless, for many Japanese the practice of keeping concubines is too commonplace in politics to ignite a scandal. Indeed, a man's ability to cope with the financial, emotional and logistical problems of juggling a wife, a mistress, two homes, often two families, and a complex social timetable, and then to be powerful and charismatic enough to ensure that everyone from wife to waiter does not blab, is a skill that traditionally has been admired in Japan as evidence of a man's virility. They use a different slide-rule for morality. Although foreigners thought that Uno had been felled by a sex scandal, he had actually been brought down because the Japanese sneered at his inability to handle a geisha well enough to ensure that she did not spill the beans to the press. They could see no good reason for such a fumbler to be prime minister. As soon as was politically polite, Uno made way for a new man, Toshiki Kaifu, another puppet whose strings were pulled by Takeshita.

Thus, after what to the rest of the world seemed to be a tumultuous period in Japanese politics, little has changed. Money is still the lubricant that keeps Japan's political machinery churning today. MPs are still as greedy for cash as they ever were. Voters still expect their MPs to turn up to weddings with a present in their pockets, preferably £200 or so in cash. Politicians still philander shamelessly and often. It is sometimes difficult for Westerners to understand. They ask themselves, is Japan as black as it is painted by the scandals that periodically dirty its name, embarrass its politicians, throw an unflattering light on its shadier corners and send its political machinery into a temporary spin?

Well, perhaps, perhaps not. It rather depends on whether you are looking from the East or from the West, and what you were expecting in the first place. That one of the world's richest and most powerful countries could get into such a mess that it needed three prime ministers in less than a year would probably rank as a crisis in London or Washington (though maybe not in Rome, come to think of it, where the Italian cabinet changes as regularly as chic Milanese hemlines, and Italy cannot even boast an economy as vigorous as Japan's. A puzzled Italian journalist in Tokyo told me that the 151 million yen that Takeshita received from Recruit would barely buy a few local councillors in Italy). In Tokyo it is seen as the sort of clumsy tomfoolery that politicians – who are viewed with even less respect than most Japanese would show to a vending-machine – get up to every now and then. But, like eating with knives and forks, the Japanese are getting used to Western ways. Many see the loss of prime minister after prime minister, to one scandal or another, as something of a crisis because they know the West will see it as a crisis and then Japan will lose face, a currency whose value is far more familiar to most Japanese.

Everyone in Japan knows that bureaucrats and businessmen decide the nation's policy, not politicians, who lack true power in the Western sense. Only now are the Japanese realizing that many Westerners, who are used to seeing different parties in power every now and then (unlike the Japanese devotion to the Liberal Democrats) and who are drawn (or repulsed) by strong political philosophies like, say, Thatcherism, are shocked at how different Japan is from the West. Whose fault is that?

What jolts the Europeans and Americans who tut-tut about how readily Japanese politicians take cash from pushy and generous tycoons and how the Japanese traditionally turn a blind eye to the often flagrant adultery of their MPs is that they always thought that the Japanese were hard-working, wealthy, efficient, honest and made jolly good television sets. Western leaders sometimes think that Japan, a relatively new member of the family of leading industrialized nations, is learning Western ways so fast that it is threatening to become more royalist than the king. And then every time Washington is about to urge Japan to take on a bigger share of the burden of being a superpower, to donate more aid and help sort out the world debt problem, all this political chaos keeps breaking loose.

Worse still, promises on trade deals are made by Japanese ministers who are just trying to be polite and who do not expect to be kept to their word, because trade deals are in the hands of civil servants in Tokyo. That causes more confusion, more bad feeling and more bafflement.

In the opposite corner, the Japanese who worry about how to cope with the West's shock are often the slightly insular ones who have been unwilling to look abroad for immigrant workers, inspiration or ideals. It is true that the Japanese have done well enough economically without letting outsiders take root in their country, without letting foreign financiers invest heavily in Japanese firms and without letting Western morality and etiquette dictate their behaviour. This reluctance to mingle is hard to define but easy to detect. We have already met the Japanese trade negotiators who said that they could not import more American beef because Japanese intestines differ from American ones and would not be able to digest it. Japanese company directors break into a sweat at the idea of foreigners infiltrating their clubby world. Ask the Texan businessman T. Boone Pickens. When Pickens turned up in Tokyo one day and asked for seats on the board of a Japanese company in which he had just bought a one-fifth stake (a pretty normal procedure elsewhere), the firm's directors smirked at his gaucheness and ignorance of 'the Japanese way'.

The departure of prime ministers like Takeshita and Uno are the product of this clash of cultures and Japan's rapid education in the ways of the twentieth-century West. The Japanese know their politicians need well-fertilized bank accounts to meet their expenses. They also know that their MPs sometimes need a comforting new lap to lie on. The Japanese are tolerant of extramarital affairs and admire men who can handle them well. Japanese women know what is expected of them. It has been expected of them for a very long time. Is it Japan's fault that the

West has been so ignorant of its ways? On the other hand, is the West willing to confide in Japanese leaders who apparently have no clout, peddle their influence among entrepreneurs in return for cash and who womanize shamelessly because traditionally there has been no shame attached to this?

More and more Japanese are saying that the country's political machinery is out of date and too expensive. More and more women are saying that extramarital affairs should not be smiled on by discreet wives. More and more newspapers and magazines are investigating once matter-of-fact subjects like corruption and marital infidelity in high places. Japan, confused by the sudden changes in social ground rules, is slowly adapting to how it thinks the West expects it to behave – or at least wondering whether it needs to. What has accelerated the pace of change is criticism by foreigners, particularly by friends of Japan in the West. Japan gets embarrassed by headlines in foreign newspapers depicting it as a haven of corruption and loose morals.

But the real world moves at a more languid pace, especially in Japan. Two factors in particular make any dramatic change in political behaviour unlikely in the near future.

The first is the unchanging complexion of the ruling Liberal Democrats. Faces may change after a Japanese election, but surnames remain reassuringly familiar. The son also rises in Japanese politics. Hereditary succession is a comfortable part of everyday life in Japan, like the trains which run on time. The worlds of industry, high finance, show business and even sport are family affairs. But nowhere is nepotism more flagrant than in the world of politics. The Liberal Democrats' stranglehold on power has made the transfer of seats from father to son as routine as handing down the family silver. Since neither politicians nor voters feel they have much to gain by abandoning this cosy relay race, newcomers have a tough time getting a hand on the baton. At any time, about 40 per cent of the ruling party's

MPs will owe their seats to daddy, fathers-in-law or to grandpa. Often half or more of the cabinet will be hereditary politicians. Propitious marriages between the sons and daughters of MPs help to make the network more watertight.

If this closed-shop arrangement suits Japanese politicians, it suits voters just as well. Having invested heavily in making their local MP a mover and shaker in Tokyo, voters are reluctant to squander the investment. Voters assume, usually rightly, that hereditary politicians can take advantage of their bigwig relative's pre-existing network to tap favours and pull strings for their constituents. The MPs who benefit from it certainly feel no embarrassment. There are so many second- and third-generation Liberal Democratic MPs that they even have their own parliamentary group. Its name, loosely translated, means that members owe seven eighths of their success to their parents, and one eighth to themselves. All this political in-breeding – Japan's opposition parties suffer from it too – increases political laziness and makes a political spring-clean unlikely.

The second factor militating against any big political change is the lack of a credible political opposition in Japan. Japan's opposition parties, who have spent most of their lives moping around like Cinderellas in the scullery of Japanese politics, go through the motions of pretending that one day they, too, might be invited to the ball. But they are not holding their breath. The biggest, which used to call itself the Japan Socialist Party until it joined the world bandwagon of social democrats after the collapse of Communism, does not even field enough candidates at general elections to grab a majority in the key lower house of parliament, even if all its candidates were to win. It also lacks a clear political agenda on such issues as defence, and there is not enough common ground with other parties to make an opposition coalition a serious runner. The socialists have also in the past accepted contributions from companies, which were said to they marry and move into their husband's parental home – is a have been funnelled towards rebuilding the party's headquarters in central Tokyo. And the Liberal Democrats, in one of those peculiarly Japanese conventions, has a habit of donating funds to opposition MPs in return for their help in nursing bills through parliament: it is not that they need opposition votes to secure a majority for their intended legislation, just that it is deemed rather bad manners and offensive to the idea of consensus if the ruling party bulldozes bills through in the teeth of opposition protests.

The only real opposition in Japanese politics is provided by the Liberal Democrats themselves, whose five warring factions, each led by a powerful baron like Takeshita or Miyazawa, rotate power among themselves: cabinet seats are fought over after each general election and ministerial posts tend to be distributed in proportion to the relative strengths of the rival tribes. That is one more reason why Liberal Democrat candidates wage costly election battles against constituency rivals from their own party. Obviously, by expanding the size of their cliques, faction leaders like Takeshita can boost their political muscle; and they expand the size of their factions by giving financial help to promising new candidates who will repay them with their allegiance. That puts the warlords under even more pressure to amass huge political war chests. The circle is vicious or virtuous, depending on your point of view. Takeshita's fund-raising skills are legendary. They have allowed his faction to call the shots in Japanese politics for the past two decades.

Should all this change? Perhaps. Will it? Slowly at best. Does it matter? One day it might.

11. Crime and Punishment: Everybody's Safe, Even the Gangsters

Yakuza – knocking on Tokyo's door – taking a share of shareholders' meetings – arrival of the drug dealers – policing the streets – who polices the police? – new mobsters on the beat

For an idea of just how easy it can be to make crime pay in Japan, take an envious glance at the case of Seiichi Kawaguchi. He picked out the names of more than four thousand rich people at random – not all that tricky in a country in which even the moderately well-to-do might only have to save for a few months to buy a Matisse – and then sent them all blackmail letters threatening to expose their guilty secrets. He hit the jackpot. Well, he hit a decent enough jackpot for a job that didn't require very much more than gall, a sharp pin and an up-to-date Tokyo telephone directory.

By the time the police tracked him down, Kawaguchi had already picked up 5 million yen from over 130 people who could not rest easily on their futons at night for fear that their extramarital affairs, their graft, medical malpractices and other dirty deeds were about to be exposed. Some Japanese might not be all that surprised by Kawaguchi's success: Japan is so overcrowded that it is quite possible to commit five blackmailable offences just getting off a subway train. Even so, the cheek of the scam is breathtaking. 'Even though I had no proof at all, I hit on a lot of people with a guilty secret,' Kawaguchi told police when he was finally caught. Business was so brisk that Kawaguchi had to hire part-time help to address and put stamps on his blackmail letters.

Kawaguchi was not even a member of the *yakuza*, Japan's famous organized-crime syndicates, who have turned large-scale extortion into just another of several inventive fund-raising schemes. Japanese police reckon that nearly one in three Japanese businesses pay up when *yakuza* racketeers come knocking on their executive suite doors asking for cash. Sometimes these 'donations' are as much as a million dollars, which is an awful lot of money for, say, a phoncy newsletter that the gangster might offer the businessman in return, just for appearances' sake. The more sophisticated hoods turn up at companies' annual shareholders' meetings and threaten to disrupt the proceedings or to expose embarrassing details about the company's book-keeping or the president's bedmates. Cash buys their discretion.

Such nimble racketeering makes the crooks in *Miami Vice* look rather heavy-handed. But now Tokyo is worried that it might have to brace itself for a more clumsy gangland war as Japan's biggest crime syndicate tries to spread its wings and swoop on the capital, a rival's lucrative turf. Police are in a panic. They are worried that shoot-outs that have been cracking the calm in other big cities in Japan in recent years may soon be on their way to Tokyo and could spread over the next decade, as gangs compete to fasten or tighten their grip on the capital. That would bring a peculiar sense of threat to a city where women roam without fear after dark and where even pickpocketing is rare.

But the mammoth Yamaguchi-gumi gang, which is running out of opportunities in its home base in Kobe, a busy port in western Japan, is not coming to Tokyo purely to hawk loans and hookers. A base in the financial capital will enable it to keep a closer watch on its investments. It has only recently come to light that the gang, far and away Japan's biggest, is also a huge investor on the Tokyo stock market. Until Japanese share prices started sinking faster than a thermometer rammed into a snowdrift, at the start of this decade, stock-dealing was more reliably rewarding than gambling or drugs. The stock market's plunge happened to coincide with the introduction of a new rule by Japan's finance ministry, forcing anyone holding more than 5 per cent of a company's shares to declare their stake. This is common practice in most Western nations but a novelty in Japan, where the Dickensian level of corporate secrecy would make New York's more imaginative stock arbitrageurs green with envy. The result is that Japanese boardrooms have begun frantically to decode shell companies and other camouflage tactics to try to discover whether mobs are on their share registers, too, after one big Japanese textile company discovered that the Yamaguchi syndicate was its biggest shareholder. Police still haven't a clue whether the mob is just investing or laundering dirty profits. They would probably prefer not to know. They like to let the gangs get on with it.

In a rare crackdown on organized crime, police raided Yamaguchi-gumi offices in 1990 after a spate of shoot-outs between rival gangs in Osaka, Kobe's big neighbour. Police have traditionally turned a blind eye to underworld activities as long as mobsters did not settle their rivalries in the streets and visited their mothers at New Year. But a younger generation of gang bosses seems less finicky about keeping a low profile when the rewards can be so high. Police fear that Tokyo will be the next battleground, particularly as Japan becomes an increasingly attractive target for international cocaine traffickers. They believe the Yamaguchi-gumi is inviting trouble by breaking a long-standing secret pact not to trespass on the Tokyo mobsters' territory. As one of Tokyo's long-time gangsters put the problem to a local reporter: 'The Yamaguchi-gumi has disturbed the prosperous coexistence of local syndicates in Tokyo. We must take action.' He may make it sound like mopping up a small milk spill at a ladies' coffee morning. But when the Japanese take someone on, they take the job very seriously. However long it takes. Ask Detroit. So mobsters' crime, and the *yakuza*'s influence in Japan, is likely to grow in the coming years, not contract.

There are nearly 90,000 *yakuza* members, famous for their tattoocd bodies, tightly permed hair, their flashy white suits and their big American limousines. Even at a conservative guess, organized crime is an $11 billion a year business in Japan. That is roughly $120,000 per gang member, or nearly four times what the average Japanese salaried office worker earns a year. Of course, some estimates put the *yakuza*'s income at perhaps four times as much. Although they only make up one tenth of 1 per cent of Japan's population, the *yakuza* have a wide reach. At least one quarter of all homicide arrests and two thirds of extortion-related arrests involve *yakuza* gang members. Selling drugs, running illegal gambling dens, making books illegally on horse-racing, setting up language schools, organizing sex tours of Asia, importing young Filipino and Thai girls into Japan and forcing them to work as prostitutes (for pathetically little money and after having confiscated their passports to stop them fleeing back home), lending their muscle (literally) to important occasions, smuggling arms, even just driving into innocent passing motorists and then forcing them to pay hefty out-of-court compensation, all these services are available from your local *yakuza* franchise; that franchise still generally operates its office quite openly and is manned by members who proudly wear their gang's tie-pin in their lapels and who hand out business cards which state clearly their syndicate affiliation and their rank. A new law was brought in in the spring of 1992, supposedly designed to crack the whip by allowing district governments officially to designate mobsters as, well, mobsters. But once designated, the gangsters can more or less carry on doing what they did before, providing they do not break the law, a restriction that has never particularly troubled or thwarted them. Aware that more and more people are beginning to regard them as a bit of a nuisance, especially if they start shooting at each other on the streets, many *yakuza* offices have become a bit less brazen since the new law was passed and have traded in the brass nameplates outside their high-street offices for new, more discreet, brass nameplates that refer to them as this or that corporation rather than merely a local office of, say, the Yamaguchi-gumi. It is an easy switch, for the world of commerce is one which *yakuza* hoods know well. This is because when their other streams of income run dry, *yakuza* gangsters are not averse to marching into a stockbroker's office, declaring that they have been sold shares that fell in price and that they are so upset by this awkward turn of events that the stockbroker had better buy them back at the purchase price. Preferably right now.

One of the peculiar services that gangsters can offer is their unrequested attendance at the annual shareholders' meetings of publicly quoted companies. The men who make a nuisance of themselves are professional hecklers-cum-extortionists known as *sokaiya*. In a country where consensus is king, and where directors refer to 'our company' when addressing shareholders, never 'your company', the *sokaiya* earn their keep by intimidating anyone who might be thinking of asking the board an awkward question and thereby prolonging the meeting beyond the planned fifteen-minute formality. They are equally willing to intimidate managements who fail to pay.

It has been illegal since 1982 for a firm to pay off *sokaiya*, though that has not weakened their presence or their bullying power. Companies hold their annual meetings on the same day in an attempt to spread the *sokaiya* more thinly. But there are more than enough of them to go round. Thousands of police attend the annual meetings to try to prevent the racketeers causing trouble, but they make little dent on this odd aspect of Japanese capitalism. And now that *yakuza* gangs have turned to share-dealing as a way of recycling and swelling their earnings from crime, they no longer even need the pretext of blackmail to get angry about a firm's balance sheet. Police and stockbrokers say the *yakuza*'s influence is now big enough to start buying sprees if word gets out that they are filling their pockets with a particular stock. They have been stung by the stock market's doldrums, but they are not the sort to stay at home and weep into their knitting. Many Japanese mobsters have turned to art. They lend money at high interest rates to art buyers and take the painting as collateral. When borrowers fail to pay up, the *yakuza* gets a valuable canvas at a bargain price. Some aesthetically minded crime syndicates have collected so many paintings that they have opened their own art galleries.

The toll of those *yakuza* who operate in the related field of loan-sharking is not just measured in percentage returns. Newspapers commonly report cases of men, women, sometimes whole families who have committed suicide because they have been unable to pay off a *yakuza* loan shark, known as *sarakin*. The *sarakin* plays on the borrower's fear of social shame should his debts become the talk of his neighbours. Those who fear they might never be able to meet their repayments take their lives instead. Some just disappear, abandoning their families.

More and more *yakuza* are turning to dealing in hard drugs. As rich young Japanese look for new thrills and as Colombia's cocaine barons look for markets after Manhattan, Japan is realizing that its years of insulation from the drug menace that has dogged America and Europe may have come to an end. Cocaine hauls, though still measly by the standards of other rich countries, are ballooning. Prices for the drug are outrageously high: four times as much as American street prices. The police, unused to tracking down cocaine-pushers, find it tricky to cope with, especially since the drug is drifting through new channels: *yakuza* gangsters who handle the methamphetamine stimulants that keep truck drivers and housewives happy were slow to get involved in the cocaine traffic but have now joined the trade after seeing just how lucrative it could be. The fact that Japan's banking secrecy laws make it difficult to expose drug-money laundering, makes drug trafficking all the more attractive. But even before cocaine arrived in Japan, the *yakuza* had secured the reins of Japan's drugs trade. Methamphetamine, commonly known as 'speed', is sold fairly openly on Tokyo street corners. The trade is controlled by *yakuza* and is said to be worth up to 1,000 billion yen a year. Only 20,000 or so users are arrested every year, but police estimate that there are more than 200,000 injecting the drug. Since the police tend to err on the side of caution in such matters, the real figure is probably very much higher. Methamphetamine coursed, quite legally, through the veins of many Japanese soldiers, kamikaze pilots and arms-factory workers in the Second World War and remained legal in Japan for several years after the war's end. But many young, fashion-conscious Japanese do not care for such a fuddy-duddy drug. Cocaine offers them a needle-free fix and more cachet than speed, the suburban housewife's choice. The *yakuza* has adapted along with modern trends, becoming more and more like the Mafia as it seeks to strengthen its influence beyond Japan's borders.

Violent crime is low, robberies relatively few, muggings rare and rape, though wildly under-reported, is still probably far less common than in many other countries; but given all this gangland racketeering and drug-pushing, all this pimping and loan-sharking, all this gun smuggling and blackmailing, how did Japan get its reputation for being cosy and comparatively crime-free? Why don't the police do something about the 90,000 or so instantly recognizable *yakuza*? Largely because the *yakuza* do quite a lot for the police, not just in terms of giving policemen bribes and backhanders for turning a blind eye to bathhouses where the diligent female assistants like to run up a vigorous lather; *yakuza* also do much of the policing that Japan feels it needs.

Peer pressure helps to keep the crime rate low in Japan. So does a degree of intrusiveness into personal lives by anyone vaguely in authority – even the local postman – that would make most Westerners scream for privacy. Police routinely drop in on new families who have moved into their patch and take down details of their habits and lifestyles that British market researchers would kill for. Cramped housing helps everyone to keep an eye on their neighbours. A car more than one or two years old is already heading for the scrap heap in Japan, so stealing cars is not a rewarding route to riches for any would-be criminal. As a result, many Japanese policemen are still viewed the way British bobbies were forty years ago, people whose basic job is to nod to the local residents, help children across the street, lend bus fares to housewives who have lost their purses, and lend an ear to problems. They have the time and freedom to do all this because the *yakuza* are policing the streets on their behalf.

A new hood on the block has little chance of establishing himself in Japan if he is treading on the lucrative stamping ground of a local mobster. Pickpockets will be hunted down by *yakuza* if they are causing such a nuisance that customers are no longer frequenting an amusement arcade or street market protected by *yakuza* gangs. As long as the *yakuza* do not thrust their activities under the police's noses, the police will happily look the other way. Cynics say that gangsters would have to carry a warm corpse into their local police station for the police to intervene in *yakuza* affairs. Even then, the gang would offer up a sacrificial junior member to take the rap and serve the prison sentence as part of his apprenticeship, so sparing a more senior gang member, and the police would regard the unfortunate matter as closed.

Gangland shoot-outs on the streets do, however, upset the police a little, particularly if innocent bystanders get hurt. Shoot-outs make the police look as if they have been lax. To show that they are in control, the police will then swoop on *yakuza* offices and arrest gangsters, having first given the gangsters enough warning so that gang bosses can escape and incriminating papers or drugs can be secreted elsewhere. In return the gangsters will leave a few guns around the place that the police can seize and display before the television cameras. A few days later most of the *yakuza* mobsters arrested will be released for lack of evidence or charged with minor traffic offences.

In their book *Yakuza* about Japan's criminal underworld, David Kaplan and Alec Dubro give a flavour of the give-and-take palliness that bonds police and *yakuza*:

In keeping with the unusual openness of the gangs, there is a great deal of personal rapport between the *yakuza* and the police; local cops know local gangsters by name, and there is an easy familiarity between them. Such amicable relationships help form the bridge to police corruption. Departing precinct captains, for example, traditionally collect cash gifts from local merchants ... For the police chief, however, this can mean substantial gifts from local operators of massage parlours, gambling halls, and other gang businesses – but not if he has made life too uncomfortable for the community's wealthier 'businessmen'.

Japanese police chiefs can often be seen dabbing their eyes along with other respectful mourners at the funeral of a local *yakuza* chief.

Oddly, those criminals who lack a *yakuza* business card in their wallet can find police custody an altogether grimmer affair.

Japan has an impressively high clear-up rate for criminal offences, well over 90 per cent for murders, and above 70 per cent
for crimes like robbery, arson and assaults against women.
Those who do not find these figures impressive are critics who
feel they reflect a haphazard attitude to justice by Japanese
police, who sometimes assume that an arrest also means proof
of guilt. These critics say that police brutality and bullying in
detention cells, aggravated by the police's ability to hold and
interrogate a suspect for twenty-three days before filing any
formal charges, often results in forced confessions. Lawyers have
no right to be present while their clients are interrogated in these
pre-trial detention cells. There is no jury system to act as a
buffer in the courtroom. Some of the guilty verdicts based on
confessions extracted under pre-trial interrogation have been
overturned after the 'criminals' have spent more than twenty,
sometimes more than thirty years on death row. In a report on
Japan's system of police custody, the Japan Federation of Bar
Associations said, 'In Japan, police officials become so maniacal
about interrogating suspects that they tend to take advantage of
the situation, compelling the suspects to "confess". This system
has thus resulted in severe violations of human rights and led to
forced confessions.' The federation detailed how suspects are
bullied, monitored closely twenty-four hours a day even while
they excrete, deprived of food, sleep and privacy, told of threats
to their family if they do not confess. The result is that of those
brought to trial, 99.8 per cent are found guilty by judges. It is as
if the Japanese have quietly agreed a Faustian deal: unfettered
freedom for the police to behave as they wish, with no account-
ability to anyone, in return for a low crime rate. If that occasionally results in a miscarriage of justice, it is a tolerable price to
pay for keeping the streets safe. But there is no proof that the
two are related. And there is less and less tolerance among
Japanese lawyers and Japanese human rights groups for a pre-

trial detention system that sometimes resorts to a lottery to find suspects to pin to unsolved crimes.

One typical case involved Chisako Tezuka. She was so distraught that people outside Japan might not realize what went on during these interrogation routines that she collared a *New York Times* reporter and told of her ordeal after being arrested on suspicion of obtaining a loan fraudulently: she was taken to a police station, strip-searched, subjected twice to genital search and forced to urinate while policemen watched. She was questioned for twenty days, handcuffed and roped around the waist. Tezuka was never indicted and the police discovered she had paid back the loan two months previously. The police later acknowledged that the questioning and genital search took place, but denied that what happened constituted mistreatment.

Others have been less lucky. Yoshimitsu Umeda spent nearly nineteen years in prison for a murder he did not commit until a retrial in 1986 found him not guilty. Umeda says police led him through his confession, telling him what to say he had done, kicking and punching him for days until his statement matched their already drafted outline of his role in the crime. After a long and dogged campaign on his behalf by lawyers, journalists and Amnesty International, Masao Akahori was released in 1989 after serving nearly thirty-five years on death row: he had been wrongly convicted of murdering a six-year-old child. Later that same year Kenjiro Ishii was released at the age of seventy-two after having served forty-two years in jail for a murder he did not commit: during his incarceration Ishii had requested five retrials, contending that his confession had been forced out of him by police. These are not isolated cases. Lawyers suspect that many whose death sentences have already been carried out were probably also innocent, framed for the sake of judicial convenience and the police's self-respect.

It is not surprising, given all the interrogating they have to do and confessions they have to take down, that the police have been happy to leave the *yakuza* in relative peace, letting them creep under Japan's legal radar. But here too the police may have to accept a change to the cosy status quo. As money becomes harder to come by, competition between *yakuza* syndicates is swelling, and a younger breed of gang bosses, with far less regard for the old social niceties, is emerging. And as the turf wars between rival gangs grow, both police and the victims of gangsters' mischief are beginning to question the old saw that organized crime is at least better than disorganized crime.

Tokyo police officials who track gang activity say the Yamaguchi-gumi is opening dozens of new offices in Tokyo every year, now that they have expanded as much as they can in western Japan and other parts of the country where they are strong. They are going out at night to Tokyo bars and other nightspots and handing out their name cards, which is a recognized code for seeking protection money. Foreigners should be wary. Japan is a country where even your doorman swaps business cards. If you come home at night and you haven't got at least fifteen new name cards in your wallet, most people will think you have spent the day in social purdah. So be wary next time a thuggish-looking man, with maybe the end of a finger missing (a common sacrifice made by younger gangsters needing to show repentance to the boss), hands you his card. And think very carefully before handing him your own. Yamaguchi-gumi bosses, chauffeured in a fleet of twenty luxury stretched limos, occasionally gather at favoured restaurants to discuss strategy for expanding their Tokyo operations. Although the gang has about 30,000 members, only a paltry 500 of them are in Tokyo. One senior member of the gang told a reporter for Japan's *Yomiuri* newspaper, 'We can absorb smaller syndicates in local areas. But it's difficult to do that in Tokyo, where all the smaller syndicates are affiliated with larger organizations. So we have poured into Tokyo so that the Yamaguchi-gumi can take root here by itself.'

The syndicate's headquarters in Kobe give 5–10 million yen to gang members to set up new 'business offices' in Tokyo. The seedcorn money from HQ covers start-up costs. Once the office is running, it starts sending at least 300,000 yen a month back to base. Nevertheless, you can't stroll around town dropping quietly threatening business cards unless you have a lot of eager youngsters to do the dropping. So the syndicate is recruiting new members in Tokyo. They approach people who hang out in bars, buy them a sharp suit, tell them how good they look in it and urge them to join the band. Usually they do. The new recruits earn a regular monthly salary of 150,000–200,000 yen, just as if they had been hired by Mitsubishi or Nissan. And they get a lapel pin.

The gangs that control Tokyo are not happy about their rival's expansion plans. The powerful Tokyo-based Sumiyoshi-rengokai gang is building a war chest, buying guns and sending members to the Philippines for shooting practice. Both rival gangs are seeking to increase their numbers and recruitment is made easier by the romantic image many still have of *yakuza* as modern-day samurai, living life to an honourable code.

But once inside the gang's embrace, many might find the life harsher and less comfortable than they imagined. Even some foreigners fantasize about joining the *yakuza*. It might sound up your street. But not everyone is suited. If you are the sort of person who would generally sooner coat your skin in massage oil than in tattoo ink, or the type who thinks a man's best friend is more likely to resemble a golden labrador than the Osaka police force, then a life in the *yakuza* is probably not for you.

12. Education: Not as Sudden as a Massacre, but as Deadly in the Long Run?

School after school – never too young to start – examination hell – making the ideal Japanese – playing by the rules – no doubts about discipline – no Nobel – whitewashing history

What most Japanese children do after a day at school is to go to another school, which probably teaches them an awful lot about plankton and the annual rainfall in Chile but doesn't leave very much time for running and jumping. A country that chooses rice as its staple food and chopsticks as the implement with which to eat it is a country that is not hungering for an easy life. But even so, does dawn-to-dusk education show how keen and bright Japanese children are? Or is there something wrong with an education system if regular school hours are not enough to produce Japan's next generation of Toyota engineers?

America still manages to produce some of the world's liveliest brains even though in many American inner cities high-school education has become more or less optional. And it doesn't take long in the real world to twig that, outside a classroom, securing a last-minute table at a fashionable restaurant impresses the hell out of people more than reciting rainfall figures for any Latin American state you care to name.

Even Japan is beginning to question whether an education system that prizes facts more highly than Dickens's Mr Gradgrind, and exam success above everything, is the best way to produce

215

leaders who can run the world's newest superpower and explain Japan's views to allies who sometimes still find 'the Japanese way' as mysterious as the Milky Way. Now the Japanese government – traditionally guided by education ministry bureaucrats who dream of 'the ideal Japanese', someone diffident, accommodating and who thinks of Japan first, second and last – has joined parents and educationalists in wondering how Japan can break the grim habit of forcing children to spend hours after school going to yet another school, an expensive cram school. It is a timetable that produces a 99.7 per cent literacy rate but which makes family life pretty well impossible.

At a time when government leaders in America, Britain and other parts of Europe are calling for a little less *laissez-faire* in the classroom to repair the cracks in their children's knowledge, Japan's education machine looks enviable. Talk of any kind of crisis in education in Japan makes many other countries gawp in disbelief. Japan's scientists produce some pretty brainy microchips. The country's business acumen is evident in its trade figures. Shop assistants in Tokyo do not reach for the pocket calculator to tot up two 100 yen purchases, as they might in London or New York. Over 95 per cent of Japanese children go to school until the age of eighteen. Then 37 per cent carry on swotting at university or go on to some other form of tertiary education. But young children in Japan, often out till ten or eleven every night at one of the country's 35,000 cram colleges, are suffering from the same stresses as office executives. Like their parents, they are complaining of sleeplessness and muscular tension. Unlike their dads, they cannot wind down with a whisky and a geisha.

Every year, several hundred children commit suicide in Japan. As many as 15 per cent of them are younger than fourteen. Police reckon that between a quarter and a half of these child suicides are the result of educational pressure: the children have failed an exam, are ashamed at not living up to their parents' hopes, maybe they just got behind with their homework. Suddenly, for these children, the life cycle of plankton and the amount of rainfall in Chile no longer seem that pressing.

Japan's education ministry has concluded that there is too much pressure on students, that school rules are too rigorous, that there is too much emphasis on cramming and on learning everything parrot-fashion, and that children are, to put it simply, not getting enough out of life. To show how seriously it takes the problem, the ministry even published a white paper in which it relayed its findings that children rarely have a chance for such enjoyment as 'coming in contact with nature, feeling awe and respect for life, experiencing the importance of hard work and learning from difficulties'. Translated into non-Japanese, this means that even the notoriously stuffy conservatives in Japan's education ministry have realized that spending all the waking hours of your formative years in a classroom has its drawbacks.

Ask any Japanese and you will hear complaint after complaint about the gruesome Darwinian struggle that begins at pre-kindergarten age. At the same time, every parent knows that he or she is not powerful enough alone to break a well-signposted system in which the right school leads to the right university, which leads to the right job (still usually for life), which carries the sort of social cachet and financial benefits that could lead to securing the right spouse.

For instance, almost anyone of any muscle in Tokyo's political world or in the foreign and finance ministries (the most snobbish in the bureaucracy) graduated from the law department of the University of Tokyo, Japan's top seat of learning. It is still the most reliable passport to the Japanese establishment. The University of Kyoto will also do nicely enough. A spell in one of Tokyo's other prestigious, albeit slightly less prestigious, universities such as Waseda and Keio will allow many of their graduates to rub shoulders with the boys from Tokyo and Kyoto universities. The list goes on, in decreasing order of social glamour and job-grabbing power, until you get down to the last of Japan's five hundred or so universities.

But the truly baffling paradox about going to university in Japan is that after all the pointless facts you have learned to recite and after all the tears you have shed to get a place at university, once you are past the front gate it is a life of leisure. Even the education ministry admits that students understand only about half their lectures, that they read fewer than three books a month and that they see their university years as a time to make friends, drink, meet members of the opposite sex and generally to reward themselves for all the sweat they expended getting there. Graduating is usually a formality and bears little relation to the quality of a student's work or his or her intellectual ingenuity. Most companies prefer to submit new employees to their own in-house training programmes anyway, so they are not too fussed over whether or not their newly hired staff can chat comfortably about existentialism. And since students at the best universities are wooed so fiercely by employers, many have secured blue-chip job offers well before their final year, the time when hiring is officially supposed to start. That leaves plenty of worry-free time to relax on the campus.

With those kinds of rewards, guaranteed for a lifetime, it becomes easier to see why Japanese mothers devote their lives to shepherding their sons and daughters through exam after exam. When it comes to the university entrance exams, many mothers will travel to the examination hall in Tokyo with their child. They might spend the preceding night in adjacent rooms in a nearby hotel doing some last-minute revision, with the mother also making sure that early morning alarm calls and taxis are arranged so that there will be no possibility of a hiccough on the way to the examination room. So you can appreciate why

218

Japanese mothers feel it pays to start nurturing their offspring young. Very young.

'This is my first baby, and I didn't know how to play with her or help her develop,' says an anxious thirty-year-old mother who takes her six-month-old daughter to a pre-pre-school in Tokyo. At another pre-nursery crammer – The Growing Bud in Tokyo – the headmaster explains, 'The institute operates for babies one year or older, developing their curiosity through tangerine-peeling or collecting and colouring snow.' Well, you can understand why a mother might quiver at the responsibility of guiding her own children through tangerine-peeling and decide to hand them over to the Growing Bud.

When these children grow up, their mothers will continue to do their best to secure a place in a good school by helping them with their homework. This help might consist of allowing junior to swot in the parents' bedroom, so that rival parents passing by in the evening will see junior's bedroom light off and the sitting-room light on. Naturally, they will assume that junior is lackadaisical about his studies and spends all his free time watching garbage on the telly. Mummy will be in the sitting-room watching the latest soaps, the plots of which she will later relate to junior. At school the next morning, junior will talk animatedly about last night's television to reassure his pals he has not been boning up on Chilean rainfall. The idea, of course, is to trip up junior's pals so that when the school entrance exam asks just how wet it gets in Santiago, junior nabs one of the few places vacant at a famous school.

Traditionally it has also fallen upon schools to nurture Japanese values into Japanese youth, especially 'group spirit', the glue that binds Japanese society. Schoolchildren are taught that 'the nail that sticks out must be hammered down', that haunting phrase that every Japanese can quote so readily that suspicious immigration officials could use it as a test of Japanese nationality. At its most ludicrous, this maxim results in a stifling conformity. At its most harmful, this relentless beating down of unsightly rogue nails, this philosophy of the factory production line, discourages individual thinking as something disruptive and disloyal to classmates.

Students at most schools in Japan carry rule books that would make their European and American counterparts faint. The books dictate their lives down to the smallest detail, stipulating the exact width of trouser turn-ups, the colour of underwear, the length of boys' crew cuts, the colour of a girl's gloves, the correct number of eyelets in a pair of school shoes. Children whose hair is not naturally jet black – as is that of most Japanese – must bring a letter from home certifying that they have not dyed it. Girls who perm or colour their hair can find themselves caned, often expelled. Some schools demand that pupils wear their uniforms on Sundays as well. Others ban children from going out at night, or dating, or going to fast-food restaurants without the school's permission.

Just how strict some of these guidelines can be was exposed by the weekly magazine *Shukan Asahi*, which relayed what it discovered about the rigid regulations of a well-known Tokyo high school, which runs a points system for its students.

Under the system, each student is given 100 points on being admitted. The student can't advance to the second year unless he or she has accumulated another 100 points and this process continues yearly. Students need 400 points to graduate. Each student must carry a small notebook entitled 'Student's Record of Acts', in which teachers add or subtract points according to the student's behaviour. Points are subtracted when the student violates the rules. Students must not have on their person cigarettes, key chains, sweets, cosmetics, etc., contact with the opposite sex is forbidden, and so on. It's minus five points for long hair, perms, dirty slippers, or socks with holes. Five points are subtracted for going to a café (plus suspension from school for two weeks) and for associating with the opposite sex (which also carries a two-week suspension). Sometimes points are added: five points for perfect attendance for a month, helping to sweep at a nearby railway station one Sunday a month, acting as group leader on a school trip, taking part in a student committee activity or helping a teacher. Students can earn even more points by turning informer, for example, reporting that a certain student went to a disco. Teachers encourage this.

You might now begin to understand why Thomas Rohlen, a professor at Stanford University who has written an acclaimed reference book on Japanese high schools, compares school life in Japan to life in the army, right down to the identical black Prussian military-style uniforms and peaked caps that all Japanese schoolboys have to wear.

Because of the structure of Japanese society, teachers have enormous power over their charges, and they use it. Parents will often not complain when their children tell of beatings by teachers, even though corporal punishment is illegal. Japanese are taught to bow to authority and many traditionally minded parents feel that teachers are doing what is needed to mould their children for life as adults in a tightly packed society that thrives on conformity. The rules they have broken are often trivial, especially to non-Japanese. Every now and then children die from such scholarly beatings. One student died after being thrashed for taking a hair-dryer on a school trip.

One of the most chilling stories told by Seiji Fujii, a campaigner for children's rights in Japan who has written several books on school discipline, is of a girl who went to school in Aichi, central Japan. Her mother packed her off to school each morning, ignoring her daughter's protests about a teacher who regularly beat and humiliated her. One day the mother and daughter were summoned to the school and the teacher took the girl into an adjoining room for a beating. The mother listened to the daughter's screams but would not enter the room. 'The purpose of practices like this,' says Fujii, 'is to convince students that it is futile to resist. And it works, sometimes well enough to make them give up on living altogether.'

Just how far some Japanese teachers go in their mission to stamp out waywardness was brought home by two harrowing incidents that might have passed with barely a mention had they not occurred within weeks of each other in the autumn of 1990 and persuaded some parents that things were getting out of hand.

In the first incident, seven teachers took two of their pupils off to a remote beach in southern Japan and buried them up to their necks for twenty minutes as punishment: the teachers believed the boys had wheedled money out of their classmates, but the boys refused to admit it.

The second incident was a tragedy: Ryoko Ishida, a fifteen-year-old schoolgirl, died when a teacher slammed shut a heavy school gate on her, apparently trying to teach her a lesson for being a few seconds late for school. It was the first time that Ryoko had missed the 8.30 a.m. curfew. She died within two hours. While local police began an investigation to see whether Toshihiko Hosoi, the teacher who trapped Ryoko's head between the school's 500 lb metal gate and a concrete gatepost, was professionally negligent, the headmaster of the school in Kobe told his students matter-of-factly that while the incident was regrettable, the schoolgirl had partly herself to blame. 'This grievous accident would not have happened if you all had arrived at school only ten minutes earlier. If you come ten minutes earlier, teachers wouldn't have to shout, "hurry up, don't be late".'

Even many compliant Japanese parents felt that this was taking discipline a little too far. Hosoi, who eventually resigned from the school, was later indicted by the public prosecutor for criminal negligence. Even so, a survey conducted by the *Asahi* newspaper found that fewer than half of high-school principals were strongly critical of the school involved in the tragedy. One headmaster of a Tokyo school responded to the survey by saying that 'It is an ordinary procedure at schools to close the gates at a set time in the morning as a guidance to students. There shouldn't be an easing of the disciplining of latecomers just because of the incident in Kobe.'

As if to prove that such heavy-handedness is far from freak behaviour, just one year later, Japan was thrown by another grim incident of a teacher who didn't know where to draw the line between discipline and death. The headmaster of a private reform school on a small island in the Inland Sea, off the coast of Hiroshima, detained two teenagers in an airtight railway freight container. With temperatures outside topping 90°F, and temperatures inside the makeshift prison cell at least thirty degrees higher than that, the children died of heatstroke and acute dehydration. The fourteen-year-old boy and the sixteen-year-old girl, both handcuffed, had been locked up in the steel box for forty-four hours because they had been caught smoking. The headmaster, Yukio Sakai, was charged with unlawful detention and manslaughter.

When Japanese classroom discipline is not heavy-handed it is often bizarre. One school makes pupils practise screaming in order to improve speech delivery. Throat specialists say the children develop sore throats and could suffer permanent damage if their voices are just breaking. The headmaster dismisses all this moaning on the grounds that 'It's important to be able to speak with a loud voice, so I intend to continue the training.' At a kindergarten in Kawasaki, three-year-olds spend winters in chilly classrooms and freezing playgrounds dressed only in gym shorts. The school's perceptive masters say they think that the children do probably feel the cold, but they do not want to be defeated by it, and that is what is important.

Is it surprising that more and more Japanese children do not want to go to school? A survey conducted by the Tokyo metropolitan government found that just over half of the capital's schoolchildren hate going to school. Worse, another survey by the education ministry discovered that a growing number of Japanese students are skipping classes rather than face the brutal discipline and nail-chewing competition that has taken root in Japanese schools. Around one in seven junior high-school students is a hard-core truant – skiving off for more than fifty schooldays in an academic year – still a relatively modest amount but four or five times more than a decade ago. And education experts reckon that since children may turn up at school long enough to register as present before slipping away again, the number of truants could be three or four times higher than the official government tally. It is to reimpose some sense of discipline on such wayward pupils that many parents pack their children off for short spells of 'correctional behaviour' to the sort of reform schools run by the overzealous Yukio Sakai.

If rule books and examination pressure do not put children off school, then bullying often will. Bullying goes on in all schools, but has achieved an almost institutional status in Japan. Victims suffer not only from incessant teasing but from isolation through being excluded from the group. The herd instinct is so strong that when someone has clearly become a victim even his own friends will desert him. Victims are too thin, too fat, too puny, too strong. Children who return to Japan after living abroad for a while because of their parents' jobs often find themselves jeered at or abused for no longer being 'completely Japanese', even if they have spent all their time overseas in Japanese-run schools. Schoolchildren who return to Japan speaking fluent English can find themselves bullied not only by their classmates but by their English teacher, who may find it uncomfortable to coach a student whose English is better than theirs. (Indeed, so strong is the Japanese reluctance to endanger group spirit, that when a Japanese man I know was hired as a graduate trainee by one of Japan's top trading companies, he was forced to attend the heavy timetable of English conversation classes prescribed for all new employees even though he had been brought up in Australia and America and spoke English with ease. His bosses were worried about the effect his absence might have on his fellow graduate trainee entrants.) Just how serious a problem school bullying has become was made clear when, in 1990, a Japanese court ordered a city government to pay eleven million yen to the parents of a fourteen-year-old boy who hanged himself because of bullying at school. It was the first time that a Japanese court had ruled that a school bore responsibility for a student who committed suicide due to being bullied. The boy's classmates forced him to eat grass on the roadside on the way home from school, extorted money from him and poured harmful chemicals on his body. The school did nothing and said in its defence that it could not have known that the victim would kill himself.

Given Japan's cultural background, it is perhaps surprising that a debate is taking shape at all on what sort of education system the country really needs to cope with a changing world.

What has stung Japan into discussing the drawbacks of its own education system are fears that it will not be able to jump from a nation of car and television producers to an inspired co-leader of the free world if it does not start producing opinion formers who have original things to say as well as the courage and the latitude to say them. Students who are discouraged from asking questions in the classroom, who are trained largely to shuffle unrelated pieces of statistical information in their heads for the sole purpose of passing exams, are students who are ill-equipped to dream up new and cogently argued solutions to old social, economic or political ills. As Stanford's Professor Rohlen puts it, Japan's education machine was designed with the aim of

225

'shaping generations of disciplined workers for a techno-meritocratic system that requires highly socialized individuals capable of performing reliably in a rigorous, hierarchical and finely tuned organizational environment'. Not exactly what you might call a particularly enthusiastic or glowing reference.

What also irks a country that now has most things money can buy is that snide foreigners still dismiss Japan as a nation of mimics, making money out of others' inventions, a country that has yet to produce a reliable stream of science and arts Nobel laureates, as the West has done. Much of the carping is unfair. But in a country obsessed with what others think of it, the remarks sting just the same. As an anguished leader writer for the *Japan Times* put it:

Between 1890 and 1910, Budapest's top three high schools alone produced seven of this century's greatest scientists. Their alumni also included two giants of social thought, a great composer, a major novelist, the acknowledged inventor of the computer, at least two economists of the first rank and an international film director and producer. The list could continue. Nothing would help us overcome our national inferiority complex about classroom creativity better than a similar flowering in Japan. How is it that America can transmute an often poorly served high-school student into a brilliant postgraduate scientist or historian? That is the educational magic we still need to learn.

The case was put more stingingly in a speech to the Asiatic Society of Japan by Stephen Platzer, when he was a visiting fellow at Tokyo University's department of education. Platzer, a former lecturer at the University of Chicago, could not fathom why some Westerners envy Japan's education system. He feels it is leading the country into a crisis. 'Japanese society will be in deep trouble in the twenty-first century because of the way the education system is cultivating the intellectual abilities of its young,' he warned.

If the government continues to educate the children of its citizens in the rigid way it is now doing, I am afraid that by the time the facts become fully apparent, it may be too late to do anything about it . . . The crisis Japan faces is the consequence of more than a hundred years of a system of education designed to teach people to accept uncritically the truthfulness of knowledge passed down by those above them . . . There is still the notion that there is a correct answer for every question and that it is something that must be fixed for the people [by the Ministry of Education] and never by them.

Platzer argued that to remain a leader in the twenty-first century Japan would need just the sort of people its school system stifles. 'Japan's education system makes it extremely difficult for such creative and independent individuals to flourish. The schools go to great lengths to convey the message that they are not the kind of people desired by the society.'

The most glaring example of the Japanese Education Ministry's stultifying interventionism is its vetting of textbooks in order to distort history. The battle against the ministry's rose-tinted vision of Japan's past has been waged almost single-handedly by Saburo Ienaga, a former professor at Tokyo University, who has been pursuing the government in court for forcing him to delete references in a textbook to Japan's brutal invasion of China. The celebrated case, which has been ricocheting through a series of appeals in Japanese courtrooms since 1967, is not only a constant reminder of the state censorship that still dictates what Japanese students may be allowed to learn; it has also become something of a litmus test of the new Japan's thinking on its military future and its remorse over the Imperial Army's past excesses.

So far, courts have always found in the ministry's favour and effectively ruled that Japanese textbooks must soften references to such events as the 1937 Rape of Nanking, when 200,000 Chinese were shot dead or buried alive by the Japanese army.

Japan's education ministry, which screens all textbooks, asked Ienaga to change phrases such as 'Japan's invasion of China' into 'Japan's advancement into Asia' and to revise sections covering the Nanking massacre and the Imperial Army's notorious Unit 731, which specialized in chemical and germ warfare. Ienaga claims that such requests amount to whitewashing Japan's wartime history by distorting facts. Similarly, it was only recently – fifty years after the event – that the Tokyo government grudgingly admitted that Japan used thousands of young Korean, Filipina and Chinese women and schoolgirls as sex slaves during the Second World War. Their duty was to keep the troops sexually comforted after a hard day on the battlefield: Korean survivors, who are now seeking compensation from Tokyo, claim that they were expected to service up to fifty soldiers a day and that colleagues who were unfortunate enough to contract venereal diseases were dispatched with a soldier's bullet through the vagina. Tokyo refuses to consider compensation. The government says that while it has belatedly found evidence that comfort women did accompany Japanese troops in the theatre of war, it has found no evidence that the women were forcibly conscripted into service. The few Imperial Army soldiers who have spoken out about how the young girls were wrenched from their homes and how callously they were abused have found themselves exiled from Japanese society and evicted from their old veterans' associations. One consequence of this state censorship is that many young Japanese who visit Peking and Seoul for the first time are puzzled by the hostility and suspicion that greets them from Chinese and Koreans who still remember the brutality of Japan's soldiers and former colonial administrators.

Fears of nationalist rustlings in the education ministry were fanned further when it introduced new curriculum guidelines designed to bring up children 'with the necessary qualities to carry our country into the twenty-first century'. What worries teachers and parents in Japan, as well as the victims of Japan's militaristic past in Asia, is that the ministry's idea of progress is a step back to the traditional patriotic values of pre-war education. On the pretext of developing a curriculum to match Japan's new economic and political strength in the world, the Education Ministry now asks pupils to venerate the emperor, salute the Rising Sun national flag and sing the unofficial national anthem, once regarded as a prayer for the emperor's long life. Neither the Japanese flag nor the national anthem, both stained by past associations, have been rehabilitated fully since the Second World War. Neither has any status in law. Venerating the emperor has been constitutionally dubious since the American occupation force stripped Emperor Hirohito of his divinity after Japan's defeat. Another ministerial leap back into the past is the revived study of controversial war heroes like Admiral Heihachiro Togo, whose ships sank the Russian fleet in 1905. Togo, who came from the finest traditions of Japanese patriots willing to lay down their life for emperor and country, disappeared from Japanese classrooms after the Second World War because of his militaristic ways. Takeo Nishioka, the education minister who brought in the new guidelines, was philosophical in dealing with those who were anxious about the changes. 'There are many things to reflect on in connection with the Second World War,' he explained, 'but it is not constructive to drag it on for ever.'

The task facing educational reformers is daunting. Changes come slowly in Japan and individuality is uncomfortable for many Japanese. Worse still, even defining the problem is a headache. According to Ikuo Amano, Professor of Education at Tokyo University, 'The very meaning of "to think" is not well understood in our culture. To us it means something like "to find an answer which can be shared by others".'

13. This Sporting Life: More than a Game

Sumo, a national sport – baseball, a national craze – golf, a national obsession –pachinko, a national pastime

Salevaa Atisanoe, a Samoan American from Hawaii who wrestles in Japan under the name of Konishiki, is the heaviest sumo wrestler on record and only the second foreigner in the two-thousand-year history of the sport to win a tournament. Just twenty-five years old when he won that championship in November 1989, he weighed around 36 stones and looked in need of urgent medical treatment. When he visited London two years later to take part in the first sumo tournament held outside Japan – it was part of a huge British festival of Japanese culture – the Kensington hotel rooms in which he and his fellow wrestlers stayed were reinforced to ensure that the outsize occupant of, say, room 316 did not accidentally drop in to join the unsuspecting occupant of room 216 in the middle of the night. Soap bars the size of Judith Krantz paperbacks were made so as to fit more snugly into the outsize grip of the Japanese hotel guests. Bath towels as large as double bedsheets were ordered to meet their drying needs. Always mindful of their passengers' comfort, airline officials had already urged the fighters to eat as little as possible in the day or so preceding the twelve-hour flight from Tokyo to London so as to minimize the need for them to negotiate the aeroplane's compact lavatory cubicles.

Foreigners who have lived in Japan for a while and got used to the sight of these incredible hulks rubbing their bellies against each other in a small sumo ring have to remind themselves, every now and then, that it is not normal for young men to force-feed themselves to a point where only a furniture removal truck or another sumo wrestler can knock them off their balance. Inside the sumo ring, these flabby giants wear nothing but an elaborate loin cloth. Really, many would benefit from a Playtex trainer bra.

Sumo wrestlers do train rigorously, and there are muscles under the fat. They run and jump and manage to swim surprisingly sleekly, like huge walruses barrelling through the deep end. But the bizarreness of Japan's national sport has been lost on the Japanese, and even expatriates in Japan soon get hooked to the television screen when a tournament is playing and begin to enjoy bouts that after five minutes of ceremonial stamping can pass in the blink of an eye as one wrestler forces the other to the floor or out of the ring. The £100 ringside seats are as difficult to get hold of as an invitation to Mustique, and twice as exclusive. The sport has also gained a fanatical following in England ever since Channel 4 started broadcasting sumo bouts on television and exploited that curious British appetite for spectator sports like darts and indoor bowls. The capacity crowds that turned up to watch Konishiki and his colleagues at London's Royal Albert Hall during the Japan Festival were as well versed in the nuances of the different throws and performances as were the Japanese in the audience. And those in the better seats had happily shelled out £60 for their tickets. So far, though, only one Briton has been tempted to try his luck and waistline at the real thing.

'Because I love it,' said Nathan Strange when I asked him why a not specially chunky eighteen-year-old from Herne Bay chooses to become Britain's first sumo wrestler and perhaps the only man of Kent to wear his hair in a greased topknot for purely professional reasons. Probably the only less likely character appearing in the 1990 grand sumo tournament, where Strange made his Tokyo debut, was Marcello Salomon Imach, a twenty-two-year-old Argentinian who had just become the first-ever Jewish wrestler. 'It's like the army,' was how Strange describes life in a sumo stable. 'It's very disciplined and obviously there are some difficulties living with sixteen other people in one big tatami-matted room. But I really like Tokyo and I love sumo.' The only problem was that Strange was finding it difficult to keep his weight above 16 stones, leaving him still very able to get his suits from the local clothes shops rather than turning to the local tentmaker. Worse, he had actually lost weight since arriving in Tokyo the previous summer to join a sumo stable, largely because apprentices do so much fagging for the elders in their stable that they heave and sweat most of their fat away. Sumo tournaments are full of pomp and antique costumes and sake-swilling, but for the stable juniors it is a tough and far from glamorous life.

'You do everything from cooking to cleaning the loos,' says Strange. 'If you're bottom rank you clean the toilets, including the giant-size toilet we've just had installed. I'm on the second rank, so I'm spared toilet duty now. We wake up at 6 and start training at 6.30. Training is a lot harder than I thought it would be. Cooking begins at 9 a.m.'

In spite of a diet of heavy stews made of fish, chicken, soyabean curd and vegetables, mountains of bulk-building rice, and gallons of beer and sake, Strange's weight actually shrank from 19 st 5 lb to 16 st 8 lb after his first six months of stable life, due to the physical demands of his apprentice's duties. These range from chopping onions and acting as a punchbag during training to swabbing a senior's backside after a visit to the loo: apparently they cannot reach themselves. It is a feudal, often brutal existence. And it is not as if there is any immediate prospect of making a killing. An apprentice's board is met by his stable, his wages are basically pocket money.

But there is money at the top. Chiyonofuji, known as 'The Wolf', was one of the most successful wrestlers in the history of the sport and was sumo's darling until he decided to retire in 1991 at the age of thirty-five, quite a senior citizen in the wrestling world. Many wrestlers have passed their peak by the age of thirty, but Chiyonofuji was still winning tournaments right up to his retirement. He was particularly adored by women spectators because he was the only top wrestler who looked vaguely muscular, although all the fighters seem to stir something in women's hearts: the tubbiest of sumo heavyweights is usually seen in private with a pretty wife or a girlfriend, often a model, who looks so petite she could very easily be mistaken for his lunch.

Chiyonofuji's skill and his popularity have made him a jolly rich man. Japanese do not like discussing money, particularly not if they are members of the Sumo Association: they are a cloistered and conservative all-male crowd who will not let a woman near the sacred clay sumo ring because it would then be defiled and would need to be rebuilt. But according to one estimate Chiyonofuji pocketed more than 800 million yen from salary, bonuses, prize money, and showbiz appearance fees in the decade after reaching the rank of Grand Champion in 1981. At a good tournament he can pick up 20 million yen from generous and elated fans in the crowd, that is in addition to the monthly salary he gets from his stable, tournament allowances, prize and bonus money of close to 10 million yen during a successful tournament, a 1 million yen honorarium if he turns up at a party to sign autographs and 3 million yen for a ceremonial sumo performance in a Shinto temple. *Shukan Shincho*, the magazine which calculated these figures, also reckons his retirement was worth a 70 million yen golden handshake from the Sumo Association, a special merit award of 100 million yen from the same association and the proceeds from his valedictory bout, probably another 100 million yen. And the good news for Nathan Strange is that Chiyonofuji made it to the top even though he weighed in at a skimpy 19 stones.

Sumo offers an interesting showcase for Japan. It is ancient, very spectacular to look at and peculiarly Japanese. It's big business, but it is still recognizable as a sport, even to those who might not appreciate all its rules and etiquette. Baseball used to be a sport when it first arrived in Japan in 1872, brought over by an American professor called Horace Wilson. But something happened to it as it crossed the Pacific. You might have guessed something unusual was afoot when the first Japanese pitchers and strikers took to the field dressed in traditional wooden sandals. The game has since become even more Japanized, in the same way that McDonald's hamburgers were Japanized a century later when the firm was forced to break its strict yessir-they're-the-same-all-over-the-world tradition and produce a hamburger spiced with soya sauce to keep picky Japanese customers happy. Visitors to Japan with little time to spare but still keen to go home with a feel for the Japanese way of life could do worse than spend an evening at a Tokyo baseball game. All human life is there, as Henry James might say.

Baseball is widely popular in Japan. Hours of television and page after page of newspapers and magazines are devoted to covering baseball games and baseball-team practice sessions, to armchair analysis of baseball matches and to school baseball. A third of the population is baseball crazy. Baseball is so popular that young boys with young memories assume that Japan invented the game along with inventing the other modern marvels of the world. Americans in Tokyo are often asked if they play baseball back home. Yet while the Japanese may not have invented baseball, they have certainly reinvented it in their own image, investing it with the code of martial arts, the spirit of the samurai and the dawn-to-midnight work ethic of the corporation salaryman. The major league American players who have been brought in on fat salaries to add some muscle to Japanese baseball teams like to joke that the umpire's rallying cry at the beginning of a Japanese game should be changed from the traditional 'Play ball' to 'Work ball'. It did not take very much first-hand experience for Reggie Smith, a former player with the Los Angeles Dodgers, to realize that the Japanese played a novel version of his country's national game. After just one season with the Yomiuri Giants in Tokyo, he told Robert Whiting, the American author of two sharply illuminating books on the Japanese way of baseball: 'This isn't baseball. It only looks like it.'

Whiting is particularly fond of the educational wisdom of a man called Suishu Tobita, a player, manager and essayist who earned a reputation as the guru of Japanese baseball in the 1920s and kept it until his death in 1965. Tobita's idea of training was other people's idea of a penal colony. He is particularly famous for his view that, 'If the players do not try so hard as to vomit blood in practice, then they cannot hope to win games. One must suffer to be good.' Whiting tells us that Tobita liked to compare baseball to Bushido, the way of the samurai warrior, and stressed that only morally correct individuals could excel, which will come as a surprise to quite a few sportsmen and team managers in the West. Japanese baseball players are so well practised that they are often exhausted by the time they come to take the field for an important game. They play almost constantly through the year. They train – often well into the night, sometimes all through the night – whenever they are not playing. Even on the morning of a game, team coaches think nothing of making their prize fielders bend down over and over again to scoop up 1,000 imaginary ground balls and then sprint back and forth across the outfield to keep them on their toes. When they have barely any strength left, they go into the dugout to take on the competition: luckily, the opposition has also trained itself into exhaustion, so the two sides are balanced.

It is a philosophy mirrored in every school playing-field across the country, where you can see thousands of children, dressed in expensive tennis whites or immaculate baseball outfits, serving imaginary tennis balls and striking phantom baseballs, for hours on end, until they can mime perfectly the textbook rhythm of the movement: it is only when a real ball is introduced that the schoolboy athletes encounter a spot of trouble. Again Tobita has the answer:

The purpose of training is not health, but the forging of the soul, and a strong soul is only born from strong practice. Beautiful plays are not the result of technique but the result of good deeds. For all these are made possible by strong spiritual power. Student baseball must be the baseball of self-discipline, of trying to attain the truth, just as in Zen Buddhism. In many cases it must be a baseball of pain and a baseball of savage treatment. Only with the constant cultivation of tears, sweat and bleeding can a player secure his position.

Tobita transmitted this sense of devil-may-care fun to his disciples. One such disciple, a manager called Shuichi Ishimoto, became famous for blurring the familiar distinction between training camp and an abattoir by forcing his players to sharpen their concentration by walking barefoot along the cutting edge of a samurai longsword. According to one contemporary press report dug up by Whiting, Ishimoto put the Osaka Tigers team through such a draconian spring training drill when he was their manager in 1936 that 'half the players were lying on the ground with blood flowing out of their mouths'. Of course, the boys love every minute of it. One of Japan's early baseball heroes was Kotaro Moriyama, a young pitcher who struck such awe into batters that even his victims used to say, 'To be hit by Moriyama's fastball is an honour exceeded only by being crushed to death under the wheels of the imperial carriage.'

The Japanese have turned baseball into a game of guts and endurance, of uncomplaining devotion to one's coach and to one's team-mates, a sport that in a perfect world would probably be played by robots, a game in which star players and show-offs who highlight deficiencies in their team-mates are frowned upon, a competition that should ideally end in a draw (in Japan baseball games *can* end in a tie) so that neither side loses face, and a pastime which, at least to many American spectators, has had most of the fun squeezed right out of it.

Whiting's most recent book is titled *You Gotta Have Wa*, '*wa*' referring to the Confucian idea of social harmony and team identity. As in every aspect of Japanese life from politics to the office, to the classroom, to sport, *wa* counts. So does *gaman*, the tolerance required to endure hardships stoically, whether it is obeying your coach's order to whiz like a crazy shuttlecock across the ballpark during pre-match training even though you are ready to drop from exhaustion, or whether it is coping with shattering military defeat: when Hirohito announced to his defeated and demoralized people in August 1945 that 'the war situation has developed not necessarily to our advantage', exceeding even the Japanese taste for discreet understatement, he told his subjects they must 'endure the unendurable'. Being Japanese, they would have expected nothing less. Enduring is what being Japanese is about. This may be what Tobita meant when he called baseball 'more than just a game. It has eternal value. Through it, one learns the beautiful and noble spirit of Japan.' *Wa* is why American players brought over by Japanese managers to put some zip into their teams are expected to wallop the ball hard enough to make sure their side doesn't lose, but not so hard that they make the other batters on their side look like ping-pong players. They get paid very well (the best expatriates make over $1 million a year, the rest maybe five or ten times as much as their Japanese team-mates, even though most are regarded as past their prime in America) to keep their mouths shut, to obey team rules about length of hair and no moustaches, not to argue with the umpire, and not to show their frustration about the risk-free way Japanese managers like to play the game. Basically, they are being paid not to disrupt the team's harmony, to forget they are American, to act a little Japanese. It is a tall order. Most of the foreigners manage to comply, even though Americans still dominate the roll call of big hitters in Japan.

When these American transplants do lose their self-restraint it is usually when they are getting close to breaking the record of fifty-five home runs in a single season created by Sadaharu Oh. Oh practised his hand–eye coordination at home by swinging a sword at a strip of paper hanging from his living-room ceiling. He is one of the few home-grown legends of Japanese baseball, right up there with Babe Ruth. Oh played for the Yomiuri Giants, another legend in that it has long ranked as the favourite team of almost every person in Japan, even non-baseball fans. Every Giants game is televised and grabs a 20 per cent share of the TV audience nationwide. Patriotism almost demands that if you cannot attend the stadium in person, you at least watch on the box. Because they prefer to move with the crowd, the Japanese stay loyal to the Giants even when the team goes through several seasons of dismal performances. (If you are travelling through Japan with someone who has never visited the country before, and if you happen to be running low on cash, a reliable way of making some fast money is to wager your companion that the hotel concierge, or the driver of the next cab you hire, supports the Giants. The funny thing is that not only will your friend be bowled over by your predictive powers, so will the concierge and the cab-driver.) Anyway, it would upset the *wa* of Japanese baseball if someone were to crack Oh's record, particularly if that someone was an American, so the tacit tradition has been to make sure that no foreigner gets the chance. In 1985 Randy Bass, an American playing for Japan's Hanshin Tigers, came within one home run of Oh's record in the final game of the season against the Giants when he suddenly found that none of the Giants' pitchers would throw him a hittable ball. It was purely coincidental that the Giants' manager at the time was Oh. Bothered and bewildered, Bass packed his bags and returned to America to play the following season.

Yet another way in which Japanese baseball apes life is that it is all done for business. In America, a team will be owned by a rich tycoon or a group of investors, but in Japan they are owned by corporations who put the tax losses on their advertising and marketing budgets. The Yomiuri Giants has a useful symbiotic relationship with its owner, one of the world's biggest media empires and publisher of the *Yomiuri* newspaper, which sells more than nine million copies a day. The newspaper plugs the team and the team's nightly televised game plugs the newspaper. Then take Orix Corporation. It was struggling to make itself recognized as Japan's biggest leasing company. So it bought the Hankyu Braves from the Hankyu retailing and railways group, renamed it the Orix Braves and found itself being advertised for free every night on prime-time television. It became so well known that it started attracting job applications from pukka graduates who would not previously have given the leasing industry a second thought. Similarly, the principal job of the Nippon Ham Fighters is not to break the barriers of sport but to advertise the meat-packing company that owns them. The Yakult Swallows are named after the soft-drinks company that finances them and the Daiei Hawks promote the flourishing Daiei retail chain every time they take the field. And because the players are basically company employees, famous sports stars can be routinely drafted in to do commercials for the firm, in much the same way that the company's boss might call in his secretary to take a letter. And there is always the boost that a company baseball team brings to the company's morale and sense of identity, its corporate *wa*.

In 1992, the Japanese video-games maker, Nintendo, launched a $100 million bid to buy the Seattle Mariners, an American major league baseball team. Americans were distraught. They saw another American icon falling to the Japanese, just the way that Hollywood film studios and the Rockefeller Center had done. Washington officials were anxious that the purchase could bring already worsening US–Japan relations to a new pitch and to the attention of a new American audience which might not recognize Japanese cash on a balance sheet but would have something salty to say on the bleachers about a Japanese owner in the dugout. But it was still the idea of another corporate takeover that bothered Americans' pride. They hadn't even begun to wonder what it might mean for the way the game is played.

If the way they play baseball highlights how the Japanese bring their peculiar social and spiritual sensibilities to bear on an alien sport, their obsession with golf shows just how undaunted they will remain in the face of a challenge, however fierce the odds stacked against them. Only the Japanese or Lewis Carroll would even think of injecting golf fever into the bloodstream of a people who barely have enough room to live, let alone have any land to spare for eighteen-hole golf-courses. Only the Japanese would actually do it. Once again, the Japanese love golf partly because of the appeal of the game, partly because playing golf is a very common way of entertaining business clients and keeping in touch with work colleagues, and partly because every other Japanese they know loves golf, too.

Japan already has more than 1,700 golf-courses. Another 350 or so are under construction and more than 900 are in various stages of their planning applications. They have become a blight on the landscape and the tons of pesticides and chemical fertilizers needed to keep the courses in shape are threatening bird life and polluting the country's rivers. And there are still not enough courses to please everyone. As many as fifteen million Japanese – more than one in ten of the population – claim to be golfers, even though the closest most of them get to swinging a club is visiting their local driving range. These are honeycombs of cubicles in which golfers thrash practice balls to nowhere. They are built inside a vast wire or net cage, often on an office roof. Many are open all night to cater to the crowds who go to practise, practise, practise even though many will grow wings and fly before they get on to a real golf-course. Everywhere you look, on train station platforms, in bus queues, at pedestrian crossings, you can see Japanese businessmen earnestly rehearsing their swings with imaginary irons, sinking putts on imaginary greens. If they make it on to the golf-course once a year, they will be deliriously happy and die contented.

Fewer than 10 per cent of Japanese courses are public. The rest are private and pricey. At the swankiest of these members-only clubs, the memberships change hands at prices that would buy you a fair chunk of Surrey or Florida. One of the specialized brokers who make a market in these things could sell you a membership of Tokyo's finest, the Koganei Country Club, for around 400 million yen, something approaching £2 million. For that you get the chance to tee off with past and present prime ministers and a clutch of business tycoons. Only *nouveaux riches* belong to just one top club, the élite belong to several.

Even a so-so club in a so-so suburb, two or three hours' drive out of Tokyo, might cost thirty million yen to join. Even for those willing to slum it on a cut-price municipal course, where you might get away with green fees of 20,000–30,000 yen, playing golf is not simply a matter of waking up on a sunny morning, calling up Yoshi to see if he fancies a round of golf, and then motoring off into the countryside. These are some of the rules for getting to play on one of the municipal courses near Tokyo: those who want to play at weekends 'are to send in a postcard during the first week of the month which falls two months before their projected date of play. The actual users are to be determined by lottery on the twentieth of each month.' Look on the bright side: weekday players need only book one month ahead. You can understand why, even in typhoon rains, there are still determined foursomes hacking their way across Japan's golf-courses, even if they have to wear fishing waders to cope with the downpour. It may be the only game they get this year.

The crush on Japanese courses has become even more severe since young women decided that playing golf is fashionable. Even better, high green fees and expensive outfits make it a prestigious pastime for young office girls. These women still usually live at home and have few expenses. They splash out on clothes, trips to Hawaii and anything that suddenly takes their fancy. Golf is their latest plaything, although keeping within a hundred strokes of par is less important than being seen in the right designer outfit, preferably with a handful of pastel-coloured golf balls that don't clash with their owner's windcheater. Like debutantes during the season, it is regarded as rather embarrassing to be seen in the same outfit twice. Entrepreneurs are always looking to exploit Japan's love affair with golf, whether it's organizing golfing weekends in Scotland (even including the round-trip air fare it is still almost as cheap as paying visitor's fees at some Tokyo clubs) or making solid-gold or diamond-encrusted golf clubs. One spin-off of the female golfing craze is a string of new magazines that cater only to the new breed of women golfers. They advise less about birdies than what make-up to wear on the green.

Sometimes the pressure for space on which to build new golf-courses leads developers into unexpected confrontations with nature. Golfers unable to afford the membership fees of fancy places like Koganei were looking forward to the opening of a new municipal golf-course in Tokyo Bay until they learned that they might get a bigger bang out of the game than they were used to. The course was built on reclaimed land, made up of layers of raw garbage and sand dumped in the bay in the 1960s; once the course had been built, the Tokyo government found that methane gas was bubbling up from the thirty-year-old layers of rotting garbage beneath the new greens and they worried that the seeping methane might cause a gas explosion if it met a cigarette butt. Rather than risk turning the par 72 course into a makeshift film set for *Apocalypse Now*, an unprecedented smoking ban was imposed temporarily on the course. Four-metre-high towers were plunged into the soil at seventy different places on the greens and fairways to encourage the gas to escape. But the garbage was still producing 30,000 cubic metres of methane gas a day. Club officials felt it would be awkward if golfers started exploding in the bunker. So they decided to keep the 'No Smoking' signs.

Even after reclaiming acres of Tokyo Bay, Japan is running out of land for new courses to amuse the nation's golfers. A Japanese company called Fujita Corporation thinks it has solved the problem by designing a compact golf-course which it has mysteriously named 'Best Intelligent Golf 3-System'. The course has only three greens. Each has three fairways, arranged so that the green is the apex of a triangle. There are two long holes, five middle holes and two short holes for a par 36 nine holes. One imagines that the greens would get fairly cosy. But at least you can smoke while you wait for your turn to putt.

Smoking is the least of what you can do if you settle down for a session in a pachinko parlour, Japan's fantastically popular version of pinball arcades. The fun of pachinko eludes most foreigners, but many Japanese are addicts. Anything from one third to half the population is at it. There are 16,000 gaudy pachinko halls across the country, containing about four million machines. They are more common than supermarkets and attract an even wider range of customers. The pachinko business turns over more each year than Japan earns from exporting cars, televisions and video cassette recorders combined. Maybe even more than that, because the people who run pachinko parlours are on the shady side and rank among the country's top tax evaders. And it's all so simple. A player buys a handful of shiny steel balls, feeds them into a tray at the bottom of an upright pinball-cum-bagatelle machine and watches them shoot up to the top of the board and jiggle their way down. That's it. You used to have to shoot the balls up yourself, with a little metal lever at the bottom of the machine. But now the balls are often propelled upwards automatically. That ensures that players use up their balls quickly and then buy more. It also leaves your hands free to do other things. In a pachinko parlour you can eat, smoke, drink, knit, watch television, read the newspapers, even pick your toes, nobody cares. Everyone else is too busy playing pachinko themselves and the deafening rat-a-tat din of the ricocheting balls and the blaring military march music that screams all day long from all the loudspeakers makes conversation possible only for those skilled at sign language. The idea is to win more balls to trade in for prizes, things like rice and toys and cigarettes and chocolate. This is a discreet fiction to evade gambling controls: prizes can usually be traded in illicitly round the corner for cash at an anonymous side door. It is this facility that has given rise to the professional pachinko player. There are around five million of them by one estimate.

You would find it hard to come across a Japanese who has not been inside a pachinko parlour. What is the attraction? In his book *Empire of Signs*, Roland Barthes, the French semiologist, saw pachinko parlours as 'a hive or a factory – the players seem to be working on an assembly line. The imperious meaning of the scene is that of a deliberate, absorbing labour.' Very Japanese.

14. Where to Now? A Journey without Maps

The next few steps – the economic machine – the political future – the world's newest superpower? – war and peace – what does Japan think? – the Japanese influence in Britain: a template for the world?

Like a conjurer's assistant who is sawn in half and run through with sabres only to emerge unscathed and beaming, Japan has a knack of absorbing the most juddering shocks to its system with hardly a scratch or a murmur. Japan's economy seems to survive and thrive in the face of all setbacks; political scandals come and go without loosening the Liberal Democrats' postwar grip on power; Japan's society freely mingles kimonos with computers, maintaining an insularity that has withstood decades of so-called 'Westernization'; politically it is firmly in the Western camp, though its ways remain a mystery to some of its closest allies.

As the 1990s began, Japan seemed to be preparing to enter the twenty-first century with everything in its favour; a strong economy reflected in a booming stock market, and a determination to change its international diplomatic voice to a lion's roar from the schoolgirl's squeak that has hitherto tended to characterize its contribution to world political debate. Then, just as Japan was brushing off its lapels, ready to make its grand entrance, everything blew up in its face. The Tokyo stock market, which had seemed invincible after surviving the 1987 world stock-market crash with barely a hiccough, collapsed dramatically. The Gulf War in 1991 left Japan tongue-tied and Tokyo's Western allies exasperated by Japan's inability to react quickly to a crisis and its refusal to put its shoulder to the diplomatic wheel along with its political partners. Relations with America, already fraying because of Washington's large and unshakeable trade deficit with Tokyo and because of hostility towards Japanese takeovers of American icons like the Columbia film studios in Hollywood and New York's Rockefeller Center, began to unravel furiously. Racist taunts hurled at Americans by Japanese and at Japanese by Americans did little to help. The convulsions of Eastern Europe left Japan wondering where it fitted into the post-Cold War order: Japan was the only major power still frosty towards the Soviet Union, because of a forty-five-year-old dispute over ownership of a few small islands in the Kurlles, which had prevented the two countries from signing a peace treaty ending the Second World War. Then, all of a sudden, there was no more Soviet Union to be frosty towards, and Japan's hostility towards its northern neighbour seemed even more out of place than it had before.

Probably none of these sent as many shivers of panic and self-pity through Japan as the collapse of the Tokyo stock market, the main measure, for many Japanese, of their country's economic virility. It was a jolt that shocked Japanese even more than it did the many foreigners who had convinced themselves that Japan had found a way to defy the laws of gravity and economics. A stock-market collapse is a headache for any country, but it is a nightmare for a nation that has put all its efforts for half a century into becoming economically successful. After spiralling higher and higher for a dozen years in a row, during which their value grew eightfold, Tokyo share prices started shrivelling at the start of 1990. Within three months they had lost about one quarter of their worth, more than the value of all the shares traded on the London stock market. Within two years, Tokyo stock prices stood 50 per cent below the peak they had reached at the start of the decade. Talk of a complete collapse in the country's financial system began to swell, egged on by the lack of share trading, soggier land prices, the poor performance of some of Japan's big corporations and a train of corruption scandals linking the political and business worlds.

Having been the world's biggest stock market, Tokyo once again fell into second place, behind New York. That descent brought with it a peculiarly Japanese shame. It is a pet pastime in Japan to calculate just how much of America you could buy if you sold the grounds of Tokyo's Imperial Palace at market rates: the whole of California, actually. But Tokyo's stock market fall highlighted the fragility of the arithmetic. Zooming Japanese land prices fed the boom in share-buying through the 1980s. Higher share prices then created sufficient profits and collateral for more land speculation. Money was cheap, so was oil. Inflation was low and the economy was booming. Suddenly everything went into reverse and it seemed that maybe the emperor never really had any clothes on after all. If the Japanese economy were ever to burst, instead of just deflating a little, the bang would pop eardrums from New York to London. But at the end of it all, California would still be there, rich in natural resources. And Japan?

A ballooning bank balance and a stock-market portfolio that clicks up in value faster than a taxi meter do a lot to deaden the drawbacks of a lifestyle that is pinched by Western standards. But if these can no longer be relied on, Japan may have to rethink its priorities. Many Japanese suddenly feel poor and swindled. They have begun to wonder, rather too melodramatically for a country that is still hugely rich by anyone's standards, whether the sun is setting on their golden age before they have had a chance to wallow fully in their country's famed riches.

Like a wealthy but overworked tycoon who rejuggles his priorities after a heart attack at fifty, many people are asking what all these decades of punishing grind have been for if the wealth they have amassed can evaporate so mysteriously, so quickly.

The Japanese can get terribly maudlin about painful spasms in their economy, which takes up a lot more of the average Japanese person's thinking time than it does of Britons' or Americans': business pages in newspapers are devoured not just for information on the economy's or a company's health, but on how well Japan is faring against its international competitors. Business books are bestsellers in a way that John Le Carré and Frederick Forsyth could only dream about. The mood of breast-beating despair that accompanied the Tokyo stock market's fall was typified in an article in *Nikkei Business*, a sober fortnightly magazine read in the corridors of power. Under the headline 'Japan's Economy is at 4 p.m.', it gloomily warned that 'the economy is in the twilight and dusk is at hand', it gave notice that the party was over and it said Japan's famous life-sustaining trade surplus would disappear within a few years. *Aera*, a serious-minded weekly, headlined a cover story 'The Number One Economy was a Myth' and told its readers that the world had lost faith in Japan. The head of the research department at the Long-term Credit Bank of Japan, Hiroshi Takeuchi, predicted gravely, 'Japan will be the first Number One creditor nation to lose its pole position before its standard of living reaches the Number One slot.'

Such comments set many Japanese thinking about their society, a place where even small landowners can be millionaires, but in which many Tokyo families live in apartments the size of a largish British drawing-room; where the average mortgage is so large that borrowers can now arrange for repayments to be spread over three generations, giving their grandchildren an unusual inheritance; where Sunday in the park is more crowded than the rush hour on the London Underground; where, except for the richest company directors, a game of golf is a once-a-year treat; where a bizarrely multi-layered distribution system ensures that even Japanese goods are pricier in Tokyo than they are in London or Boston; where some homes have high-tech lavatories that can analyse your urine while millions are still not connected to mains sewers. Then there are the long commutes to work, long working hours and pressures on office workers not to take their two weeks of annual leave, which combine to make free time scarce and family life difficult. Not surprisingly seven out of ten Japanese do not feel affluent. In many ways, it is Japan's customers abroad, Americans who can buy cheap, reliable motorcycles, Parisians who can buy chic stereos, who have benefited most from the Japanese economic miracle.

It is not the first time that Japanese have wondered whether they have judged their priorities correctly. 'It is questionable whether or not Japan's economic growth is reflected in the quality of Japanese life,' Haruo Maekawa, a former governor of the Bank of Japan, said back in 1987, when he was commissioned to report on ways to improve the imbalance. 'Housing standards are low, the cost of living high and working hours long.' There are more Louis Vuitton bags on women's shoulders since then. But for many, things have not improved all that much. Now some older people wonder if it is too late, whether they have missed the boat, whether it is time to get down to serious work. Their children, brought up with Rolexes rather than rationing, wonder whether all this just provides more evidence of the foolishness of working, working, working and leaving no time for fun.

The re-evaluation of priorities has spread to Japan's role in the world, too. Once happy to stay rich and out of sight, Japan is eager to add its voice to international decision-making. It resents accusations that its diplomacy and its decisions on foreign aid – Japan, helped by the strength of the yen, now ranks alongside America as the world's biggest aid donor – are geared only to its own financial needs. Tokyo traditionally has funnelled 70 per cent of its aid to its own backyard in Asia, prompting complaints that it acts quickest and most generously when its own interests are at stake. Nudged by Washington, it has promised to broaden its vision. In what direction, it is still not always sure. The government's drive to impress Washington has not been helped by the preference of many Japanese to mind their own business and to let others mind theirs. A survey carried out by the *Mainichi* newspaper found that one in two Japanese is against giving more aid to poor countries and thinks the money would be better spent helping those Japanese who are in financial difficulties. The survey prompted the embarrassed government to launch a campaign to explain to the public why Japan had a duty to help the emerging democracies of Eastern Europe and other poor, faraway nations that most Japanese rarely think about.

By shouldering more of the financial burdens of being a superpower, Japan felt it had earned the right to flex its political muscles abroad. It served notice to its allies that it was no longer prepared just to write cheques and smile genially in the group photographs at summits of world leaders. It had views that it wanted to air. It wanted to be taken seriously. The intellectual heart of Japan's new diplomatic assault was mapped out by Takakazu Kuriyama, one of the Foreign Ministry's top policy-makers before he became Japan's ambassador to Washington in 1992. He pointed out that the time had come for Japan to behave like a major power when charting its foreign policy. But at the same time, he was well aware that Japan had to maintain an 'unassuming posture', to allay the fears of Asian neighbours who still recall what happened the last time Japan flexed its muscles abroad. Kuriyama argued that the era when the United States could by itself support the international political and economic orders is long past and the key to world peace and prosperity today rests in the cooperative structure of Japan, the United States and Western Europe . . . Japan, an important member of the industrial democracies, can no longer conduct a passive foreign policy, regarding the international order as given. Today, Japan must actively participate in the international efforts to create a new international order, in order to ensure its own security and prosperity. It is in this context that Japan's foreign policy must develop, as soon as possible, from that of a minor power to the foreign policy of a major power.

But the world can be cruel sometimes, even to superpowers. No sooner had Kuriyama put his pen down after writing this new policy outline, than Iraq crossed the border into Kuwait. It was an opportunity for Japan to show its colours. So how stood Japan?

President George Bush immediately positioned America at the head of an allied coalition force, pledged to repel Iraq back behind its own borders, either by jaw-jaw or war-war. America looked to its friends for help, money and men. Japan was tested and found faceless. Tokyo had just been demanding a bigger say in how the industrialized democracies deal with international problems which affect them all, but it stumbled at the very first hurdle. Japan's low diplomatic profile throughout the Gulf crisis made many Japanese aware that they still lack the will to take centre stage. Japanese ministers and even newspaper leader writers seemed to have little more to say than that Iraq ought to respect the United Nations' resolutions demanding its withdrawal from Kuwait, that war is a nasty thing and must be avoided. When the then prime minister Toshiki Kaifu cancelled a trip through Asia he had planned to take in January 1991 in order to 'stay in Tokyo to pursue efforts towards a peaceful solution to the Gulf crisis', his crueller critics asked, why bother?

Minoru Hirano, a columnist for the *Yomiuri* newspaper, wrote bluntly:

Japan maintains a happy-go-lucky attitude to mid-east policy, even as the Gulf crisis enters its most critical phase . . . On 26 December Prime Minister Toshiki Kaifu sent a letter to Iraq's president, Saddam Hussein, asking for a peaceful resolution to the Gulf crisis. On 1 January, Kaifu, in a telephone conversation with President George Bush, asked Bush to exhaust all avenues of negotiation. This was the extent of Japan's diplomatic efforts to avert war. Unlike the European Community, this country did not explore any new ideas for a diplomatic solution. More regrettably, Japan, at a crucial moment, has shown its insularity.

But most Japanese newspapers themselves seemed to be in a detached dither, too. From Tokyo, media coverage of developments in the Gulf had the same feel as following the progress of a World Cup football tournament: interesting, but not of immediate impact or relevance to a non-playing country. In a remark that captured the distant mood, Akio Morita, chairman of the Sony electronics empire, told a reporter in Tokyo: 'Our Japanese economy is quite good enough to absorb some influence [from a war] by increasing our domestic demand. So I'm not pessimistic, as Japan can stand on its own two feet.' Japan was back to viewing everything through its economic prism. Money still seems to be Japan's most manageable currency. The one diplomatic initiative Japan made was when Kaifu offered economic aid to Saddam if he opted for a peaceful solution in the Gulf. An earlier attempt to get the Japanese parliament to sanction the dispatch of a token number of soldiers to the Gulf, in non-combat roles only, foundered when parliament, the press, the public and many in Kaifu's own party rebelled. Even Japan's promise to send a medical team to the Middle East fizzled: the government could not find enough volunteers and the handful that it did find went and swiftly returned when it became too dangerous. That left Japan playing the type-cast role from which it has been struggling to break free: the man with the fat cheque-book. Even there, the money Japan pledged towards the cost of the multinational forces – after much foot-dragging – was regarded as modest by some Washington politicians. They felt that if Japanese were not going to sweat and die in the desert, they should at least be generous with their cash.

With the confrontation in the Gulf, Japan showed that it was not about to start setting its own international agenda, showed once again how it tended to react rather than act, coughing up more cash only when personally pressed by President Bush. It was Tokyo's usual response to international affairs, doing what seems least likely to damage further its fraught relationship with America. Japan's behaviour prompted Thomas Foley, then speaker of the US House of Representatives, to remark cynically that 'The Gulf crisis has been widely interpreted in Japan as a bilateral problem [between America and Japan]. What would the Japanese government think about the Gulf if it were divorced from its relationship with the United States? Nothing?'

Foley's comment pinpointed Japan's basic diplomatic dilemma. Its postwar alliance with America has kept it safe from military predators and, thus, free to get on with building the world's second biggest economy. America also provides a big market for Japan's exports. But it is not a particularly happy marriage. Japan is not yet in the mood to file for divorce. But some of its more nationalistic politicians are. Will this new generation put Japan's mouth where its money is?

The new breed of Japanese who feel that it is time for Japan to redraft its relationship with America is spearheaded by Shintaro Ishihara, a maverick novelist-turned-politician who urges Japan to snap out of its 'postwar stepchild mentality' and become more assertive. It is a nationalistic battle-cry that is far punchier than anything Kuriyama would dare to voice, and blunter than many Japanese would admit to in conversation with Americans, but it probably arouses greater sympathy up and down Japan than Kuriyama's outlook. Ishihara's call for a fundamental reordering of the world into one that gives Japan a political voice that matches its economic clout carries weight not so much because he is brash and a little boastful, but because he could well be a future ruler of Japan. He was a close runner-up for the prime minister's job in 1989, he is brimming with ambition and, at barely sixty years of age, still a young chick in terms of Japanese politics.

Americans began noticing Ishihara in 1989, when they read *The Japan That Can Say No*, a chart-topping bestseller he co-wrote with Sony's chairman, Morita. What made American readers howl especially loudly was Ishihara's provocative statement in the book that since America's nuclear missiles could not fire straight without Japanese semiconductors, Japan could drastically change the balance of world power by selling advanced microchips to Moscow. It is not the sort of thing Americans expect to hear from a close ally. In an interview with *Time* magazine shortly after publication of his book, Ishihara said the moment had come for Japan to move away from this 'slave mentality' and that Japan had to repel any attempt by the US to prevent it from becoming more self-assertive. Japan, he predicted, would become one of the major players building a new world history.

Ishihara's critics in America call his style of bravado 'America-bashing' – just the sort of bile that Japanese say they routinely receive from Americans. Ishihara says America resents Japan because Americans are racist, and that it was this racism that made them drop the atom bomb on Japan but spare Germany. This is a sentiment that is widely shared among the Japanese, who feel that they were somehow drawn innocently into the last war against their will. So acute is this sense of persecution that the Japanese have even corralled the Jews to support their thesis of victimization. The Japanese feel that they and the Jews were the two people to suffer most unfairly from the Second World War. They do not otherwise share much kindred spirit with Jews. Remember those preposterous books detailing how almost everything from pollution and the 1992 Barcelona Olympics to the creation of the European Community are dangerous Jewish conspiracies – often, though not always, directed specifically against Japan's best interests – which are bestsellers in Japanese bookshops, feeding Japan's well-nourished persecution complex. Ishihara exploits this feeling among many Japanese, that they are a peace-loving and hard-working people, keen to mind their own business, but who keep getting picked on by racists throughout their history. The term they have coined for this irrational and unfair nuisance is 'Japan-bashing', a term no longer used just to describe the many instances of racism directed at Japanese: it has also become Japan's most powerful diplomatic bargaining tool. Trade negotiators who criticize Japan's refusal to sanction imports of, say, cheap foreign rice are branded Japan-bashers who do not understand rice's semi-religious status in Japanese society. It is a convenient way of turning many debates with trading partners or political critics away from the issue at hand to a debate on racism, in the hope that the trading partner or political critic will feel ashamed enough to retreat in silence.

Ask Asians, Hispanics, Indians or blacks living in the US whether whites are racially prejudiced or not, Ishihara snapped at the interviewer from *Time*. He feels they would just laugh at the question and would all answer yes. Now along comes a non-white race, the Japanese, which is catching up with the Americans and taking over the lead in advanced technology. Ishihara says he understands it's humiliating, but the time has come for Americans to give up foolish pride and racial prejudice.

The Americans say the Japanese have become arrogant, but in Ishihara's opinion, the racially prejudiced Americans are much more arrogant.

Ishihara's audience is swelling in Japan because his bluntness coincides with a new mood in the country that blends a self-assurance drawn from its postwar economic success with an impatience at the constant carping from an America that, many Japanese feel, blames Japan for its own laziness and profligacy. Ishihara's views are not shared only by extremist cranks. In 1992, shortly after becoming prime minister, Kiichi Miyazawa got into diplomatic hot water by openly blaming America's economic ills on the laziness of Americans. Nor was it the first time he had betrayed his contempt for America. In an interview he gave to the weekly magazine *Aera* in 1990, Miyazawa explained: 'Japan is an old society that's been going for two thousand years – very different from some country [that is, America] that's spent a mere two hundred years galloping around wide open plains in covered wagons.' This same tenor of confidence-cum-arrogance dominated an evening at the Japan Society in New York, held at about the same time as Miyazawa shared his views on the Wild West. Adding some spice to the usual dull conclusion that Japan and America could well be on a collision course, Kazuo Nukazawa, the managing director of Keidanren, the powerful Japan Federation of Economic Organizations, betrayed just how little he thought of American management techniques and America's sad dependence on Japan. He said, 'Japan will continue to invest until they learn the US economy is incurably ill. How will they know when that is? It's something of a tautology, because America will be incurably ill when Japanese stop investing there.'

When Ishihara penned a second book on the same theme, he proved just how strong Japanese readers' appetites are for his hold-your-head-up bravado. *The Japan That Can Say No*, his first nationalistic salvo across the Pacific, took six months to clear 300,000 copies. When his sequel, *Nevertheless, Japan Can Still Say No*, arrived in bookshops in 1990, it sold over 300,000 and topped the bestseller lists within a week of publication. Once again Ishihara saw signs of Western racism, the West's decay and Japanese superiority almost everywhere. Japan was civilized when Europe was still bedevilled by yahoos; America cannot come to terms with its decline; without Japanese technology and Japanese cash the Channel Tunnel between England and France would not meet in the middle; Eastern Europe also needs technology and money, and Japan has the most of both. Even at a Tokyo performance of the musical *Jesus Christ Superstar*, he decides that the Westerners sitting near him, looking at a Japanese actor playing the role of Jesus, see one more painful sign of Japan's dominance. He suspects them of thinking, Oh dear, Christ was coloured, but since he was from the Middle East, it is probably more suitable for a Japanese to play the part than for a Westerner like ourselves. Ishihara imagines that the Western playgoers were forced to confront their unease about worshipping a coloured man.

In a chapter in which he describes America as class-ridden and blames this on America's racism, Ishihara accuses Americans of flattering themselves that the world revolves around them and reckons that they find it hard to accept that people with different-coloured skin can cap their success. Racism, says Ishihara, is deep-rooted in Western minds and Americans who accuse Japan of being unfair are really just saying 'follow us humbly'. But he adds that Japan is not obliged to obey America.

Ishihara's tongue-lashing is significant because he says out loud what many Japanese say privately in the office or in bars and restaurants after work but are often hesitant to say to Westerners' faces. The message appeals particularly to young Japanese, who have never known Japan to be anything but rich and technologically advanced and who feel no reason to hide their contempt for an America that lags in technical innovations, where street crime is high, poverty widespread, illiteracy common, and where race-inspired riots can set cities ablaze for days, as they did in Los Angeles in 1992. It is rather fantastical to think, as some anxious foreigners do, that this headstrong confidence will once again give birth to militarism in Japan: young Japanese aren't interested in getting their clothes dirty or risking their lives in battle, and they are well aware how rich and powerful you can become while peace reigns. But it could make international decision-making trickier at a time when more and more problems, ranging from the future of Russia and Eastern Europe to the continuing indebtedness of Third World countries, call for coordinated responses from the world's leading nations.

In his book *The Enigma of Japanese Power*, the Dutch political scientist Karel van Wolferen notes:

It is inconceivable that a state with a responsible government sensitive to long-term national interests could have allowed the Japan–US relationship to deteriorate to the extent it has. Banking too heavily on US indulgence, Tokyo has badly mishandled its most important relationship – the one on which the entire edifice of its foreign relations is built. Preoccupied with their special pleading in Washington, the administrators failed to notice, or at least failed to communicate effectively to fellow administrators, the fact that Japanese actions, or inaction, were frittering away most of the considerable and genuine affection that the United States had come to have for Japan.

Just how threadbare relations have become between the world's two most powerful economies became clear when a report, sponsored by America's Central Intelligence Agency, leaked out to the public in the summer of 1991, just a few months after the ceasefire in the Gulf War. The report described the Japanese as 'creatures of an ageless, amoral, manipulative and controlling culture', a racist and non-democratic people intent on 'world economic dominance', who believe they are superior to others. With the Communist threat dying, the 'yellow peril' has re-emerged. The leaking of the report gained impact because it coincided with publication of a controversial book by two American academics, George Friedman and Meredith Lebard, called *The Coming War with Japan*. The book's theme, that economic rivalry and a battle for world markets will nudge Japan and America to war, may still be wildly fanciful, but somehow it no longer seems wildly unthinkable, or at least unbroachable. And then, just to add a little spice to the pot, along came the fiftieth anniversary of Pearl Harbor.

Just how little Washington feels it can trust Tokyo was betrayed when a leading American general declared that American troops would stay in Japan to make sure that Japan did not take up arms once more. Major-General Henry C. Stackpole III, commander of Marine Corps Bases in Japan and a highly decorated Vietnam veteran, told a *Washington Post* reporter who went to visit him at his base in Okinawa, 'No one wants a rearmed, resurgent Japan. So we are a cap in the bottle, if you will.'

America distrusts Japan. Much of Asia fears her or resents past cruelties. She makes Europe twitch, though for commercial rather than military or historical reasons. Does Japan have no real friends, does it wield no influence abroad?

Even in those countries where it may be friendless, Tokyo's influence is often still huge. It affects our lives in ways most of us have barely thought of. America may be Japan's most important partner, both politically and commercially, but the country with which Japan has the least prickly ties is probably Britain. London is almost alone in Europe in welcoming, even inviting, Japanese investment and Japanese factories. Will the relationship stay sweet, or will Britain grow resentful, too, once it realizes how many fingers Japan has in British pies? Britain provides an instructive example of Japan's influence on the world, even in those countries where its influence is barely acknowledged as obvious or intrusive, and certainly not as irksome enough for the locals to get upset or angry about. What has happened in Britain is either already being mirrored in other countries, or will be replicated as Japan's reach spreads.

But measuring that influence is not always easy. It is not often you find London secretaries dressed in those sternly pleated Issey Miyake frocks that make women look like human-sized hand accordions, and there are still relatively few Japanese restaurants in England, especially when compared to America. So to many British people, Japan's contribution to the texture of their everyday life can be totted up in a list of car factories and computer-chip plants, and an inventory of their living-room hi-fi and video equipment. We may all be karaoke singers now, but there is still no sushi at Sainsbury's. But eating fresh fish straight off the fishmonger's slab isn't everything. Japanese money, design, technology and industrial culture are changing the complexion of Britain far beyond the factory gates. Not just in the gadgets Britons buy, but in ways that are not necessarily stamped 'Hitachi' or 'Made in Japan' on the bottom.

Several British university dons, some of whose views are often solicited on Japan, now depend on Japanese boardrooms for their salaries. Quite a few British musicians, like the London Symphony Orchestra and the London Sinfonietta, do too. Those that do not woo Japanese benefactors still depend on touring Japan, where concert seat prices start at £200 a pair, to subsidize the performances that they deliver in London or Liverpool. And we're not just talking about St Martin-in-the-Fields. Top British rock bands now become rich when they become big in Japan. In London, the Victoria and Albert Museum and the British Museum both relied on wads of yen to finance new displays of their Far Eastern collections. Britain's National Poetry Library is now called the Saison Poetry Library to honour its Japanese sponsor. The world's two top art auctioneers have for years found that rich Japanese bidding for Renoirs helped to pay for the cocktail cabinets in their posh West End galleries; now that the Japanese no longer shoot their arms up like eager schoolboys every time an Impressionist comes under the hammer, both Sotheby's and Christie's feel the pinch.

British architects look to Japan for new technologies. But even more prized is the freedom to put up starkly modernist buildings in the heart of Tokyo, a city which has so little planning control that most streets look like cramped urban theme parks. Tokyo has become the only major capital rich enough and unfettered enough to allow British architects free rein on the drawing-board. European architects are fashionable in Japan. Sir Norman Foster has finished an office building in Tokyo for a Japanese publishing tycoon and is hoping to build a 1,000 metre high steel cone of offices and housing, a sort of huge, high-tech wimple, in Tokyo Bay just as soon as cash is available. Richard Rogers keeps busy in Japan, too. Philippe Starck, the unconventional French designer, puts up buildings in central Tokyo that would not just make the architecturally conservative Prince of Wales faint. They would send him into a coma. This freedom to experiment with space, money and new materials in Japan gives British architects ideas and experience that they can milk for the projects they work on in Britain, Germany or America.

There is more. Japanese money is hidden under the most unlikely British mattresses. As Ishihara pointed out, Japanese banks are among the biggest lenders to the 'Anglo-French' Channel Tunnel. Japanese investors have helped to make successes of many British government share privatizations, propping up the price of the stock that British people own. When you play a round of golf at Turnberry or stay at an Intercontinental hotel or buy a few cases of some of France's ritzier clarets, you give your custom to Tokyo. We have already seen that if you watch a movie made by Columbia Pictures or Universal Studios you are in debt to Hollywood via Tokyo, since both have been taken over by Japanese firms. Those two shrines of British tailoring, Aquascutum (Margaret Thatcher's favourite) and Daks Simpson, are both now owned by Japanese companies, partly because the Japanese were some of the biggest spenders in both stores. Simpson has a sushi bar, as well as a private Japanese tea-room where all the Mr and Mrs Sakamotos who have bought enough trenchcoats to survive the journey on Noah's Ark are discreetly entertained.

Japanese visitors spend so much money in Britain – maybe £400 million a year – that wooing them has become a frantic priority for British tourism officials. They are urging British shops to stock petite Japanese sizes and telling hotels to 'avoid putting Japanese visitors in rooms with the number four, as this is considered unlucky'. Seaside landladies are told to provide twin beds 'even for honeymooners', green tea bags and sachets of *miso* soup in the room. There is no official lobby yet for landladies to offer *shiatsu* pressure-point massage, which is probably the sensible place to draw the line. Hotel employees are told not to expect tips from Japanese, who are not used to this custom. Hotels and shops are listening and adapting.

In business, the impact is greatest of all. British companies, thrashed or threatened by the management and industrial-relations practices imported into Britain by Japanese-owned factories that have sprouted in their backyards, are often adopting the same practices in a struggle to keep up. 'The competitive gap has been very obvious to economists for years,' says Barry Wilkinson of Cardiff University's Business School. Dr Wilkinson specializes in what he calls the Japanization of British industry. He reckons Japanese manufacturers in Britain are setting the precedent and providing the model for future industrial relations. 'Companies are waking up to it now that the competitor is on the doorstep. I think it's going to spread much wider, very quickly. It's very difficult to find a British manager who doesn't know everything about basic Japanese management techniques.' These range from an obsession with quality and introducing more flexible working practices so that everyone is capable of doing more than one task, to stepping up peer pressure by displaying lists of absentees or of workers who made mistakes on the production line. Panicked car-making rivals are scrambling to impose the same disciplines on their workforces.

And Japanese factories have a social slipstream. In south Derbyshire, schools have added Japanese to the curriculum. It was part of a dowry offered to Toyota executives when they came to Britain scouting for suitable sites for the car plant they opened in 1992. The ripples, invisible to the eye, spread much further. A Toyota executive once criticized Americans who moaned about the arrival of Toyota factories in the US. He argued that instead of whining, Americans should thank Toyota for raising American educational standards: young Americans were so keen to get a job with Toyota that they were working harder at school to improve their exam results.

Japanese arrogance or matter-of-fact honesty? Ask Edwina Currie, the Conservative MP in whose constituency Toyota's first British factory was built. She says that even before the factory opened, local students were aware that they would need to study harder to land work with the tolerate-no-slacking-on-the-job Japanese. Currie, who helped to lure Toyota to south Derbyshire, says the impact of the Japan effect is entirely wondrous, not just because the £700 million car factory created several thousand jobs, or because the factory's local pub now sells sake or because Toyota's arrival boosted the number of planning applications to build new golf-courses in the region.

'The main effect is that people now expect to have good employment packages, pensions, a good working environment, on-site recreational facilities. The standards imposed by Japanese companies on their employees push through to the schools and colleges very quickly. I've seen a big jump in the number of children staying on at school. There is a recognition that there is a difference between going down the pits and making cars, and that they have to make the best of their school years. Some other employers get anxious about it. Rolls-Royce, the biggest employer around here, has had to raise the pay rates of apprentices to ensure a steady supply.'

Some Japanese influence, such as Sony Walkmans and Nikon cameras, has come into Britain through the customs sheds. Some of it, like the small-is-beautiful spirit of nouvelle cuisine and the minimalism of some modernist British architecture, filtered back in the brains of British cooks and architects who have visited Japan and joined Western artists like Van Gogh and Frank Lloyd Wright in drawing inspiration from kimonos and Kyoto cherry blossom. Today, a big chunk of Japan's cultural influence comes from the pages of a cheque-book, with Britain begging for more. What is in it for both sides? Quite a lot.

A case study: Sumitomo Trust and Banking, one of Japan's heavyweights, seems to have studied the school ties of several British cabinet ministers before stumping up £1 million to sponsor Japanese studies at Eton. Its researchers clearly decided that much is still decided on the playing-fields of Eton. 'Eton has educated many of your country's leaders and many of those future leaders will very likely play an important role in financial services and foreign affairs and maybe in the arts,' Sumitomo's Yoshinori Hitoki told me. Hitoki, manager of the bank's strategic planning division in Tokyo, which made the decision to end Eton's search for a wealthy sponsor, said it was not quite like a cold-blooded profit-and-loss account, but everyone was aware of the potential benefits of such deals. It is all refreshingly candid. 'After receiving a request from Eton for an endowment, we studied its merits and the possible impact of that endowment, that is, what benefits we could enjoy, and we decided to make a donation to Eton,' Hitoki said. 'One benefit is the improvement of Anglo-Japanese relations. Also, if we contribute part of our profits to the improvement of educational institutions we could expect that our company's public image will improve. We could raise the awareness of Sumitomo Trust among the British people and that would help us to attract the top-quality staff we need to operate well in the UK. We would like to think we can expect that kind of effect from this donation. But also, if we make donations to established institutions like Eton, then the graduates of those institutions could treat us favourably in very many things that might happen in the future. Graduates of any school have a favourable view of their school and if Sumitomo Trust is associated with that school they will have a favourable view of Sumitomo Trust. For example, one of the graduates of Eton College is now the Governor of the Bank of England.'

Two Oxford colleges, Keble and Pembroke, have fellowships sponsored by Japanese companies. Oxford University was also chosen as the home for the Nissan Institute for Japanese Studies. The London School of Economics has a £2 million endowment for its snappily named Suntory Toyota International Centre for Economics and Related Disciplines. On a chilly spring day in April 1991, Shoichi Okinaga, a Japanese millionaire, was made an honorary fellow at Wadham College, Oxford, and at St Edmund's College, Cambridge, the same day. Why him? Well, he had donated £4.5 million to Wadham and another £1.5 million to St Edmund's. With his spare change Dr Okinaga, president of the Teikyo University Group and the biggest shareholder in Mitsubishi Bank, built a £7 million campus in Durham.

This is still fairly small-scale compared with the money that

Japanese corporations have put into plumping up professors' chairs at America's posher universities. The result is that in America some voices are now asking whether Japan, which seems to have a new trade tiff with Washington once a week, is indirectly nurturing silence from academics who might otherwise argue against high-profile Japanese takeovers of American firms and Manhattan skyscrapers, or against trade barriers that Japan may impose on imports. Critics dub this sympathetic crooning chorus the Chrysanthemum Club. Could this same thing happen in Britain? Dr Kaoru Sugihara, who heads the Japan Research Centre at London University's School of Oriental and African Studies, SOAS, reckons the danger is great. 'It hasn't come yet, but it will if you don't do anything. That is why I have been pressing for the British to fund Japanese studies in Britain. Part of the reason that Japanese money has come to Britain so quickly is that the British are reluctant to put money into Japanese studies.'

Dr Sugihara says the Japanese are just looking for international prestige, a chance to become the Rockefellers and Gettys of the twenty-first century. They would probably be as happy sponsoring the arts and financing new buildings as education. SOAS, which has been involved with Japanese studies for three quarters of a century and which breeds Japan hands for the British Foreign Office, has twenty-three full-time Japan-related academic posts, all paid for by British money. Elsewhere in Britain Japanese studies are more dependent on the kindness of Japanese strangers. 'You could end up,' says Dr Sugihara, 'with professors in British universities who feel unable to speak out against, or criticize Japan. I don't mean that the Japanese funding source would steer the professors, but there would be self-censorship. Unless you have some independent funding, there will be no room for an independent mind.'

Remarks like that nag at the mind. The British may be

hospitable hosts, but every now and then they do ask themselves if they are offering the Japanese too cosy a welcome. When Fujitsu, Japan's biggest computer maker, took over ICL, the flagship of Britain's computer industry, there was much hand-wringing over whether the Japanese should be allowed to control what many in Britain regarded as a strategic asset. It was one of the few occasions where the British have thought twice about the yen in their pockets, and wondered whether they should be worrying or whooping about the Japanese accent in their lives. It was, after all, Tokyo's technological edge that gave Shintaro Ishihara his best chance to taunt the West, when he boasted about the unreliability of American nuclear weapons without Japanese microchips. It was a blunt example of the sort of remark that does little to improve Japan's relations with other countries. And it is at just such moments that America's Chrysanthemum Club can prove soothingly useful. Will Britain, and other countries, soon get one too? 'The race is not always to the swift, nor the battle to the strong,' said Damon Runyon, 'but that's the way to bet.'

Index

abortion, 45, 46
advertising, 4, 5, 13, 15, 110–15, 240; Ishioka, 50–54; Regain, 31
Aera magazine, 249, 257
Agata, Soji, 135
ageing of population, 47
Aichi, 221
aid, foreign, 197, 250–51
air conditioning, 17, 26–7, 70
air travel, 86, 99–101, 175, 230
Akahori, Masao, 212
Akihito, Emperor, 55, 177, 180, 183–4, 186–9
Amano, Ikuo, 229
Amaterasu Omikami (goddess), 39, 177
American Express, 33
Amnesty International, 212
amusement arcades, 131
animals, pet, 55, 63–5
announcements, public, 134
anthem, national, 229
Aoki, Amehiko, 76
Aoki, Ihei, 171
aphrodisiacs, 89
architecture, 12, 262, 265
Arikawa, Dr Kiyoyasu, 25
army: Imperial, 14, 54, 150, 227–8; postwar, 14, 32, 200
art, pictorial: Japanese, 16, 151, 265; Western, 11, 62, 72, 75–6, 207, 262, 265
arts: funding of foreign, 15, 83, 261; traditional Japanese, 10, 12; *see also individual arts*
Asahara, Shoko, 178–9

Asahi Shimbun, 88, 116, 121, 185–6, 187, 195
Asanuma, Inejiro, 185
Asia, 14, 93, 146, 250, 251; *see also* China; Korea
Asian Wall Street Journal, 123
Atake, Rentaro, 157, 158
Atisanoe, Salevaa, 230
Aum Supreme Truth Sect, 178–9

banking, 131, 208
Barthes, Roland, 245
baseball, 78, 117, 234–40
Bass, Randy, 239
beef, 130, 153, 198
Benedict, Ruth, 167–8
birth rate, 45–7
bomb, atom, 255
books: business, 14, 29, 249; comic, 117; Ishihara's, 255, 257–8; *see also* literature
bowing, 16, 22, 91, 105
brand names, 4
Branson, Richard, 110
bribery, 10, 108, 151, 157, 185, 248; *see also* Lockheed; Recruit
Britain, 260–68; business, 263–4; English style, 2, 7, 64; Japan Festival, 16, 230, 231; Japanese funding of culture and education, 83, 261–2, 265–6, 266–7; lobby journalists, 119; television, 231; tourism, 164, 263; Toyota, 264–5

Buddhism, 151, 154, 175–6
Burakumin, 153–4, 155, 159
bureaucracy, 17–19, 126, 197, 198
Bush, George (US President), 252, 254
business: Britain, 263–4; cross-shareholdings, 115, 172–3; entertainment, 32–3, 98, 240; and politics, 115, 190, 197, 198, 200–201; secrecy, 78, 204; *yakuza* and, 203, 206–7; *see also* work

cards: business, 16, 135, 213; pre-paid, 131, 132
cars, 92–3, 261
censorship, 13, 14, 15, 116, 227–8
Channel Tunnel, 258, 262
chemical warfare, 228
Chiba zoo, 139
China, 14, 148, 149, 151, 159, 227–8
Chivas Regal whisky, 163
Chiyonofuji (sumo wrestler), 233–4
chopsticks, 138
Christianity, 176, 189
Christmas, 44, 69, 165
Cimino, Michael, 124
cinema, 13, 15, 50, 111, 124; *see also* Hollywood
Club Mediterranée, 85
Coburn, James, 111–12
Columbia film studios, 122–6, 247, 263

Index

Columbus company, 22
comic books (*manga*), 117
commuting, 1–2, 8, 23, 25,
    86–90, 250
company affiliations, 33–4
company loyalty, 21, 25, 33–4,
    78–9, 82
computers, 70–75
concubines, 39–40, 41, 195–6,
    198
conformity, 2, 10, 22–3, 128,
    224–5, 237, 238; in
    education, 150, 191, 219–20,
    225–7; *see also* consensus
confrontation, avoidance of, 9
Confucianism, 43, 237
congestion, 2, 86–7, 92, 99–
    100, 101–2, 127, 249–50
Conjugal Day, 47, 48
consensus, 100, 116, 167; in
    press, 88, 116, 118–20
constitution, 14, 175, 177, 184,
    189
consumers, 130–31, 132, 136
contraception, 45–6
conversation, Japanese, 8–9,
    17–19
cosmetics, 52, 63
crime, 2, 102–3, 109, 131,
    202–14; *see also* yakuza
Currie, Edwina, 264–5
customs, clearance, 17–19

Daiei Hawks baseball team,
    239–40
Daijosai (Shinto rite), 177
Daimaru department store,
    166
Dan, Yoshio, 158
Davis, Miles, 50
Dean, James, 113
death: children's, from
    punishment, 221, 222, 223;
    from overwork, 13, 24–6;
    see also suicide

Delon, Alain, 112
Dentsu advertising agency,
    31–2, 114–15
Dime magazine, 23
Disneyland, Tokyo, 23
distribution system, 130, 250
divorce, 48
dogs, 63–5, 127
dolls, talking, 34–7
drama, 16, 50, 83, 108–10,
    169–70
drinking, 2, 23, 33–4, 36, 47,
    89, 98; brand names, 4, 137;
    tonics, 30–32, 88–9
drug trafficking, 204, 205,
    207–8
Dubro, Alex, 210
Duskin company, 21–2

earthquakes, 143–5
East–West magazine, 60
education, 215–29; British,
    264, 265–6, 266–7; bullying,
    224–5; competition, 177,
    216–17, 219; conformity,
    150, 191, 219–20, 225–7;
    discipline, 220–23; evening
    schools, 14, 215, 216; exam-
    orientation, 6, 215–16; and
    family life, 216, 218–19;
    history censored, 227–8; of
    imperial family, 189;
    language teaching, 6–7;
    nationalism and, 227–9;
    pre-nursery, 219; reform
    schools, 223, 224; sports,
    236; truancy, 224; women's,
    13, 46, 218–19; *see also*
    universities
elections, 82, 132, 178, 179,
    192
emperor, 180–89; divinity,
    183, 184, 229; *see also*
    Akihito; Hirohito
employment, 20–37;

background and prospects,
    150, 154, 217; company
    prestige, 21; corporate
    etiquette, 22; death from
    overwork, 13, 24–6; Hell
    training, 27–9; holidays, 2,
    22–3, 26, 47, 128, 250;
    hours, 2, 13, 26, 30, 128,
    129, 250; induction rituals,
    20–22; industrial relations,
    91, 263, 264; in-house
    training, 218; labour
    shortage, 21, 26, 42; and
    marriage, 21, 54;
    productivity measures, 26–
    9; resignation, 167, 174–5;
    returnees from abroad, 150;
    secret dreams of male office
    workers, 34–7; stress, 23–6;
    see also business; company
    loyalty; women
    (employment)
endurance, 237; TV
    programme, 105
English language, 1–8, 91,
    224–5
entry formalities, 17–19
environment, 135, 136, 137–
    43, 241, 256
espionage, 174
Eton College, Windsor, 265–6
European Community, 151
Ezoe, Hiromasa, 191, 192–3

face, *see* shame
family: background, and
    marriage, 108–9; deference
    to parents, 75; government
    campaign, 26, 32, 47, 128–
    9; hereditary succession,
    170, 199; home-phobia, 23–
    4, 34; lack of privacy, 67,
    87–8; lack of time for, 23,
    30, 35, 216, 250; mothers'
    role, 13, 35, 167–8

Index

family planning, 45–6
Fanuc robotics company, 25
farmers, 61, 100, 130
fashion, 12–13, 50, 51, 62, 136, 242; Western, 2, 7, 64, 65–6
Foley, Thomas, 254
food, 12, 15, 16, 55, 62, 91; for pets, 64; prices, 130; whalemeat, 140, 141; *see also* beef; melons
Forbes magazine, 78
forces, *see* army
foreign affairs, 198, 246–7, 250–60; aid, 197, 250–51; *see also under* United States
foreigners, 3, 146–60; attitude to Japanese, 226; journalists, 119, 120, 123; mistrust of, 102, 119; residents in Japan, 17–19, 149–50, 159, 160; on television, 4, 106–7, 110–13; as unhygienic, 68, 152; *see also* insularity; superiority
Foster, Sir Norman, 12, 262
Friedman, George, 260
Friends of the Earth, 138
Fuji, Mount, 136–7
Fuji Bank, 112
Fujii, Seiji, 221–2
Fujima, Teruaki, 169
Fujimori, Alberto, 159
Fujisankei media empire, 25
Fujita Corporation, 243
Fujitsu computer company, 268
Fukuoka Mutual Life Insurance, 34
funerals, 164, 176, 192, 210; Hirohito's, 87, 176–7, 181–2; for pet dogs, 65; satellite broadcast, 172–4; Tsutsumi family, 82–3, 84
futons, 15

gaman (tolerance of hardships), 237
gambling, 156, 205
gangsters, 147; *see also yakuza*
geishas, 32, 41, 94, 121–2, 195
Genji, The Tale of, 39
germ warfare, 228
gifts, 12, 77, 161–6, 192, 196, 210
giri (obligation), 168–9
Glass, Phillip, 50
Gogh, Vincent Van, 75, 265
gold, 62–3
Golden Week holiday, 101–2
golf, 30, 32–3, 166, 240–44, 250, 262, 264
Greenpeace, 138, 139
group spirit, 22–3, 224–5, 237, 238
Growing Bud school, Tokyo, 219
Grumann company, 172

Haga, Ken, 107
hair, body, 2, 67, 68–9
Hankyu Braves baseball team, 239
Hanshin Tigers baseball team, 239
Hawaii, 85, 108
health, 23–4, 30–32, 117, 137–8, 162
Hell training, 27–9
hierarchy, social, 21, 153–4
Hirano, Minoru, 253
Hirohito, Emperor, 170, 180–83, 184–5, 185–6, 187–8, 237; funeral, 87, 176–7, 181–2
history, censorship of, 14, 227–8
Hitoki, Yoshinori, 265–6
holidays: company, 2, 22–3, 26, 47, 128, 250; national, 47, 48, 101–2

Hollywood film studios, 15, 122–6, 240, 263
honeymoons, 108
Hosoi, Toshihiko, 222–3
Hot Dog magazine, 69–70
hotels, 89, 155, 230; 'love', 67, 69, 87–8; Tsutsumi, 80, 81, 84–5, 262–3
Hotta, Yasuhiko, 65–6
houses: automation, 70–75; lack of privacy, 67, 87–8, 209; prices, 11, 50, 70, 98, 128, 193, 249; size, 49, 71, 76, 87–8, 127, 151–2
human rights groups, 211–12
Hungary, 226
Hwang, David, 50
hygiene, 67–70, 91, 152; *see also* lavatories; sewage

ice hockey, 79
Ichikawa, Hiroya, 153
ICL, 268
Ienaga, Saburo, 227
Imach, Marcello Salomon, 232
immigrants, 149–50, 159, 160
industrial relations, 91, 263, 264
insularity, 14, 146–9, 151, 197, 198, 246, 253
Inukai, Tomoko, 75
Iran, 109–10
Iraq, 252
Ireland, 93
Ishida, Ryoko, 222–3
Ishihara, Shintaro, 254–8, 262, 268
Ishii, Kenrijo, 212
Ishimoto, Shuichi, 236
Ishioka, Eiko, 50–54
Ishizaka, Tsuneko, 82–3, 84
Isoda, Ichiro, 175
Italy, 5, 55, 196–7
Ito-Yokado Group, 22

ivory trade, 138

James, Clive, 105
Japan Air Lines, 175, 181
Japan-bashing, 140, 143, 159–60, 256
Jesuits, 176
Jews, 151, 176, 232, 256
Jiji news agency, 115
Jump (comic book), 117
justice, 194, 210–12

kabuki, 16, 169–70
Kaifu, Toshiki, 120, 196, 252, 253
Kaiko, Takeshi, 29, 30
Kajiyama, Seiroku, 147
Kamagasaki Day Labourers' Union, 158
Kamakura, 83
Kanagi, 61
Kaplan, David, 210
karoshi, 13, 24–6
Kasahara, Masanori, 171
Kase, Hideaki, 177, 184
Kato, Mr (shipping agent), 17–19
Kawaguchi, Seiichi, 202–3
Kawamoto, Saburo, 67
Kawasaki, 223
KDD company, 172
Keidanren, 153, 174, 257
keiretsu, 33–4
kimonos, 151
Kinugawa spa resort, 64
Kita, Yoji, 142–3
Kobayashi, Kazunari, 82
Kobe, 154, 203, 214
Koganei Country Club, Tokyo, 241
Kohama, Wataru, 140–42
Konishiki (sumo wrestler), 230
Korea: cultural heritage, 151, 176; Japanese occupation,

150, 182, 228; residents in Japan, 149–50, 159, 160
Koshiro Matsumoto IX, 169–70
Kurile Islands, 247
Kuriyama, Takakazu, 251–2
Kurosawa, Akira, 143–4
Kusaka, Kimindo, 151–2
Kyodo news agency, 115
Kyoto, 134, 154, 217
Kyubin, Sagawa, 194

labour shortage, 21, 26, 42
land: prices, 61–?, 91, 248; reclamation, 135, 243
language, 1–8; English, 1–8, 91, 224–5; Japanese, 5, 6–7, 8–9; women's, 17, 40
Lark cigarettes, 4, 110, 111–12
Last Emperor, The (film), 15
laundry, 49
Laurencin, Marie, 76
lavatories, 10, 49, 61, 63, 72–4, 250
Lebard, Meredith, 260
Liberal Democratic Party, 115, 190, 199–200, 200–201, 246
life, quality of, 127–45, 249–50
literacy rate, 7, 216
literature, 29, 39, 83, 167, 262
loan-sharking, 207
Lockheed scandal, 120–21, 171, 193

MacArthur, Gen. Douglas, 38, 183, 184
McDonald's hamburgers, 131, 234
McDonnell Douglas, 172
McEnroe, John, 112
Maekawa, Haruo, 250
magazines, 13, 114, 116–17, 199; women's, 54, 55, 243; *see also individual titles*

Mainichi Shimbun, 88, 116, 251
manga (comic books), 117
manners, social: advice on, 22, 57–8, 69–70, 117; body functions, 9–10, 16, 88, 117; bowing, 16, 22, 91, 105; corporate etiquette, 22; importance of form, 94
Marauchi, Michimasa, 76
marriage: age at, 46, 50; background and, 21, 61, 108–9, 150, 154, 217; between workmates, 54; failure, 48–9, 167–8; introductions, 57–61; mothers-in-law, 167–8; wedding ceremony, 40; working wives, 40, 44, 50
Marriage Man Academy, Osaka, 57–8
martial arts, 235
massage, 14, 63
Matsushita, Konosuke, 173
Matsushita company, 123–6
MCA company, 123–6
medicine, 45–6, 65, 73, 158, 178
Meiji Emperor, 172
melons, musk, 16, 77, 161, 162
mercury pollution, 137–8
methamphetamines ('speed'), 208
Michiko, Princess, 189
militarism, 227, 229, 259
Minakami, Tatsuzo, 173
Minamata mercury pollution, 137–8
Mitsubishi group, 22, 33–4, 67–8
Mitsui company, 173
Mitsukoshi department store, 63, 64
Miyagi, 11

Index

Miyake, Issey, 50, 51, 261
Miyazawa, Kiichi, 194, 257
Mizuno, Masahiro, 173
Monroe, Marilyn, 113
Moore, Roger, 4, 110, 111–12
morality, 175
Morita, Akio, 122, 123–4, 253
Moriyama, Kotaro, 237
Moriyama, Mayumi, 45
Motoshima, Hitoshi, 184–5
Motown Records, 125
Murasaki Shikibu, 39
Murphy, Eddie, 111
museums, 16, 76, 83, 261–2, 207
music, 134, 261

Nagasaki, 184–5
Nakasone, Yasuhiro, 82–3, 148, 191
Nanking, Rape of, 14, 227, 228
Nara, 62
Narita airport, 99–100, 102, 139, 164
nationalism, 134, 184–6, 227–9, 254
Netherlands, 3
New Year, 77, 83, 165, 182
New York Times, 153
New Zealand, 93
Newman, Paul, 110, 112
news agencies, 115
newspapers: advertising, 114; broadsheets, 115–16, 117, 118–20; consensus, 88, 116, 118–20; on foreign relations, 253; sports dailies, 117
Newsweek magazine, 122
NHK broadcasting corporation, 40, 105, 109, 156
night life, 8, 14, 42, 94, 98, 134, 147

Nihon Kezai Shimbun, 116
Nikkan Gendai (sports daily), 117
Nikkei Business magazine, 249
Nikon cameras, 265
Nintendo corporation, 240
Nippon Ham Fighters baseball team, 239
Nippon Telegraph & Telephone, 163
Nishioka, Takeo, 229
Nissan company, 69, 266
Nissho-Iwai company, 172
Nogi, General Maresuke, 172
noise pollution, 133–5
Nukazawa, Kazuo, 257
numbers, unlucky, 161–2, 263

obligation, 23, 162–3, 164–5, 166–70, 172–4
o-chugen (summer gift-giving), 165
Oda, Kaoru, 145
Oh, Sadaharu, 238
Okada Corporation, 36
Okinaga, Shoichi, 266
Olympic Games, 83, 151, 256
Omori, Aki, 44
O'Neal, Tatum, 112
Orix Braves baseball team, 239
Osaka, 57–8, 126, 154, 155–8, 204
Osaka Tigers baseball team, 236
o-seibo (winter gift-giving), 165
Overseas Enterprises Association, 102–3
Oxford University, 189, 266

pachinko, 244–5
Pakistanis, 149
Panasonic company, 63, 125

Paramount Pictures, 126
Parco department stores, 50–51, 52
parties, 57, 59–60, 192
pawnbrokers, 165–6
Pearl Harbor, 260
Perry, Commodore M. G., 4
Peru, 159
Philippines, 61, 214, 228
Picasso, Pablo, 76
Pickens, T. Boone, 198
Platzer, Stephen, 226–7
poetry, 83, 262
police, 32, 35–6, 109, 134, 149, 209–12; and gangsters, 157, 204, 209–10, 212; dolls to resemble, 35–6; and underclass, 154, 155, 156–7, 157–8; women in, 35–6, 44
politics, 180–201; comments on foreigners, 146–9; company loyalty and, 82; consensus, 88, 100; constituency system, 192, 194; cost, 130, 161, 173, 192, 196; Eastern and Western view, 196–9; nepotism, 199; Tsutsumi family, 79, 80, 82–3; women in, 13, 38–9; *see also* elections; Liberal Democratic Party; nationalism; scandals; *and under* business
pollution, 133–5, 137–8, 241–256
pornography, 44, 105–6
press, 115–22; reporters' clubs, 118–20, 121; emperor and, 187, 188; foreign reporters, 119, 120, 123; and scandals, 120–22, 199; women, 44; *see also* magazines; newspapers
prices, 128, 129, 130; *see also under* houses; land
Prindle, Tamae, 29

273

privacy, lack of, 67, 87–8, 209
propaganda, 118, 134
prostitution, 13–14, 147, 205

racism, 146–60, 247, 255, 256, 258
radio broadcasting, 105
Recruit scandal, 121, 171, 190–94
Reebok footwear company, 63
'Regain' (tonic drink), 30–32
religion, 175–9; *see also individual religions*
Renoir, Auguste, 62, 75
reptiles, pet, 55
returnees from abroad, 150, 224–5
Ridley, Nicholas, 146
right wing, *see* nationalism
rights, human, 211–12
road transport, 92–3; *see also* taxis
Rockefeller Center, 240, 247
Rogers, Richard, 262
Rohlen, Professor Thomas, 221, 225–6
Rourke, Micky, 112
rubbish, 135–7

Saba, Shoichi, 174
Sacred Heart College, Tokyo, 189
Saison Group, 83–4, 85, 262
Saito, Ryoei, 75
Sakai, Yukio, 223
Sakaiya, Taichi, 30
Sakamoto, Misoji, 46
Sakamura, Ken, 74
Sakurauchi, Yoshio, 148
samurai drama, 108
sanitation, *see* hygiene; sewage
Sankei Shimbun, 116
sarakin (loan sharks), 207

scandals, public, 10, 108, 151, 185, 189–96, 248; press exposure, 120–22, 199; suicide after, 171–2; *see also* bribery; Lockheed; Recruit; Uno, Sosuke
scents, 26–7
Schrader, Paul, 50, 52
Schwarzenegger, Arnold, 112
Scott, C. P., 118
script, kanji, 151
Seattle Mariners baseball team, 240
Seibu department stores, 84
Seibu Lions baseball team, 78
Seidensticker, Edward, 76–7
seismic activity, 143–5
Sekiya, Dr Toru, 24
Seoul, South Korea, 156
sewage system, 10, 73, 250
sex, 13, 53–4, 117, 209; Sosuke Uno scandal, 39–41, 121–2, 195–6; *see also* concubines; hotels (love); night life; pornography; prostitution
sexual harassment, 41–2, 54
shaken car inspection, 92–3
shame, 167, 175, 197, 207, 248
Shimada, Mitsuhiro, 171–2
Shintoism, 39, 175, 176, 177, 184, 233
Shirai, Yoshio, 108
Shiroyama, Saburo, 29
Shiseido company, 52, 67
shoguns, Tokugawa, 80
shops and shopping: abroad, 101, 164, 263; department stores, 22, 50–51, 62, 63, 83–4, 89, 163; sales tax, 194; station kiosks, 89
Shukan Asahi magazine, 220–21
Shukan Shincho magazine, 233–4
Sinatra, Frank, 110

skiing, 80–81, 85, 134–5, 152–3
Smith, Reggie, 235
Soaplands, 14
social democrats, 200
Socialist Party, Japan, 185, 200
Softnomics Centre, 151–2
Sogo department stores, 62, 64
Somegoro Ichikawa, 169
Sony company, 13, 122–6, 265
souvenirs, 164
spitting, 88
sports, 55, 85, 230–45; Yoshiaki Tsutsumi and, 78–9, 80–81, 82, 83; *see also individual sports*
sports daily newspapers, 117
springs, hot, 13, 63, 64
Stackpole, Maj.-Gen. Henry C., III, 260
Stallone, Sylvester, 110
Starck, Philippe, 12, 262
stock market, 62, 181, 193, 204, 206, 246–9
Strange, Nathan, 231–2
stress, 13, 23–6, 216
students, 35, 68
Sugihara, Dr Kaoru, 267
suicide, 167, 170–72, 181, 207, 216–17, 225
Sumitomo Bank, 34, 175, 265–6
Sumiyoshirengokai gang, 214
sumo wrestling, 16, 45, 109, 230–34
Sunday *Mainichi* magazine, 49, 121–2
Suntory company, 33, 112
superiority, 15, 148, 150–52, 260
superstitions, 44–5, 161–2, 233, 263
surgery, cosmetic, 66

Index

Suzuki, Yukio, 67–8
swimming-pools, 17

Taga, Mikiko, 43
Taiji, southern Japan, 140–43
Takagi, Yasumoto, 175
Takano, Masahiro, 76
Takara toy company, 37
Takeshita, Noboru, 121, 171, 191, 192, 193, 196, 201
Takeuchi, Hiroshi, 249
Tanaka, Kakuei, 171, 193, 120–21
Tawa, Taro, 82
tax, sales, 194
taxis, 9–10, 86, 93–9, 131, 132
Technics company, 125
telephone services, 7–8, 131, 132–3
television, 104–15, 134, 238; advertising, 4, 5, 31, 50, 110 15, 240; in Britain, 231; funeral relayed by, 173–4; obsession with, 77, 104, 177; sets, 63, 125
Tezuka, Chisako, 212
Thatcher, Margaret, 121, 263
tipping, 10, 96, 263
Tobita, Suishu, 235, 236, 237
Togo, Admiral Heihachiro, 229
Tokai Bank, 145
Tokyo: architecture, 12, 262; congestion, 86–7, 132; directions in, 95–7; Disneyland, 23; earthquakes, 143–5; gangsters, 203–5, 213–14; house prices, 80, 98; land prices, 80; sanitation, 10, 73, 135–7; Shinjuku station, 87, 89, 164; universities, 20, 51, 217–18; Zozo-ji temple, 84; see also Narita airport; night life; stock market;

taxis; and individual institutions
tonics, health, 30–32, 88–9
Toshiba Corporation, 174
Toto company, 49, 73, 74
town planning, 12
Toyota company, 111, 264–5
trade; international negotiations, 130–31, 153, 198, 256, 267
tradition, 10, 12, 61, 151
trains, 16, 17, 86–92, 131, 134; Shinkansen, 17, 91–2
transport, 86–103; see also air travel; roads; trains; travel
travel abroad, 55, 58, 68, 100–103, 128, 164, 242; fears of, 68, 75, 102; see also hotels
T-shirts, 3
Tsuji, Takashi (pen-name of Seiji Tsutsumi), 83
Tsutsumi, Misao, 83
Tsutsumi, Seiji, 79, 83–5
Tsutsumi, Yasujiro, 81, 83, 84, 79–80
Tsutsumi, Yoshiaki, 77–85
tunnels, superstitions about, 44–5
Turnberry golf course, UK, 262

Umeda, Yoshimitsu, 212
underclass, 153–60
uniforms, 44, 220, 221
Union of Soviet Socialist Republics, 93, 174, 247
uniqueness, Japanese, 152–3, 184, 198
Unit 731, 228
United Nations, 137, 252
United States of America: baseball, 237–9, 240; Central Intelligence Agency, 259–60; and 1947 constitution, 183, 184, 229; education, 215, 226–7; first

contact with Japan, 4; and Gulf War, 252; Japanese derogation, 146, 148; Japanese takeovers in, 122–6, 240, 247; political relations, 197, 247, 254–60; trade relations, 130–31, 145, 178, 247, 267
Universal film studios, 123–6, 263
universities: foreign, 189, 261, 266, 267; Kyoto, 217; Tokyo, 20, 51, 217–18
Uno, Masao, 151
Uno, Sosuke, 39–41, 121–2, 194–6

video-cassette formats, 124–5
video films, 44, 133, 177
Video Research, 115
Voice magazine, 151–2
volcanoes, 143

wa (social harmony), 237, 239, 240
War, Gulf, 247, 252–4
War, Second World, 208, 228, 229, 255–6, 260; Hirohito and, 182, 183, 184, 237
Watanabe, Hachiro, 37
Watanabe, Michio, 148
wealth, 11, 14, 56–85
weather, 153
Weekly Yomiuri magazine, 61
whaling, 139–43
whisky, 112, 161, 162–3
Whiting, Robert, 235, 237
wildlife, 138–43
Wilkinson, Barry, 263–4
Willoughby, Anthony, 28–9
Wilson, Horace, 234
Wolferen, Karel van, 115, 259
women, 38–55; appearance of Japanese ideal, 37; and birth rate, 45–7; concubines,

Index

women – *contd*
39–40, 41; deference, 39, 40,
43, 51, 54, 106; education,
13, 46, 218–19; Eiko
Ishioka, 50–54;
employment, 13, 39, 40–42,
43, 44, 46, 49–50, 54–5; and
extra-marital affairs, 198,
199; golf craze, 242–3;
independence, growing, 24,
37, 40–44, 54–5, 199;
language, 17, 40; magazines,
54, 55, 243; mothers, 13, 35,
218–19; policewomen, 35–6,
44; in politics, 13, 38–9;
purchasing power, 49–50,

55, 101; superstitions about,
44–5, 233; travel, 55; *see
also* marriage; prostitution
World Wide Fund for Nature,
139
wrestling, 109; *see also* sumo
Wright, Frank Lloyd, 265

Yakult Swallows baseball
team, 239
yakuza gangsters, 154; and
underclass, 154, 156–7, 158;
business intimidation, 203,
206–7; drug trafficking,
207–8; gang warfare, 203,
204, 213–14; and police,

157, 204, 209–10,
212
Yamaguchi-gumi gang, 203–5,
213–14
Yamanashi, 11
Yamanouchi, Mikiko, 49
Yokohama, 64
Yokoyama family, 70–75
Yomiuri Giants baseball team,
117, 235, 238, 239
Yomiuri Shimbun, 44, 88, 115,
213–14, 239
young people, 56–61, 62, 208,
242–3

zoo, Chiba 139